MARVEL

SPIDER-GIRL®

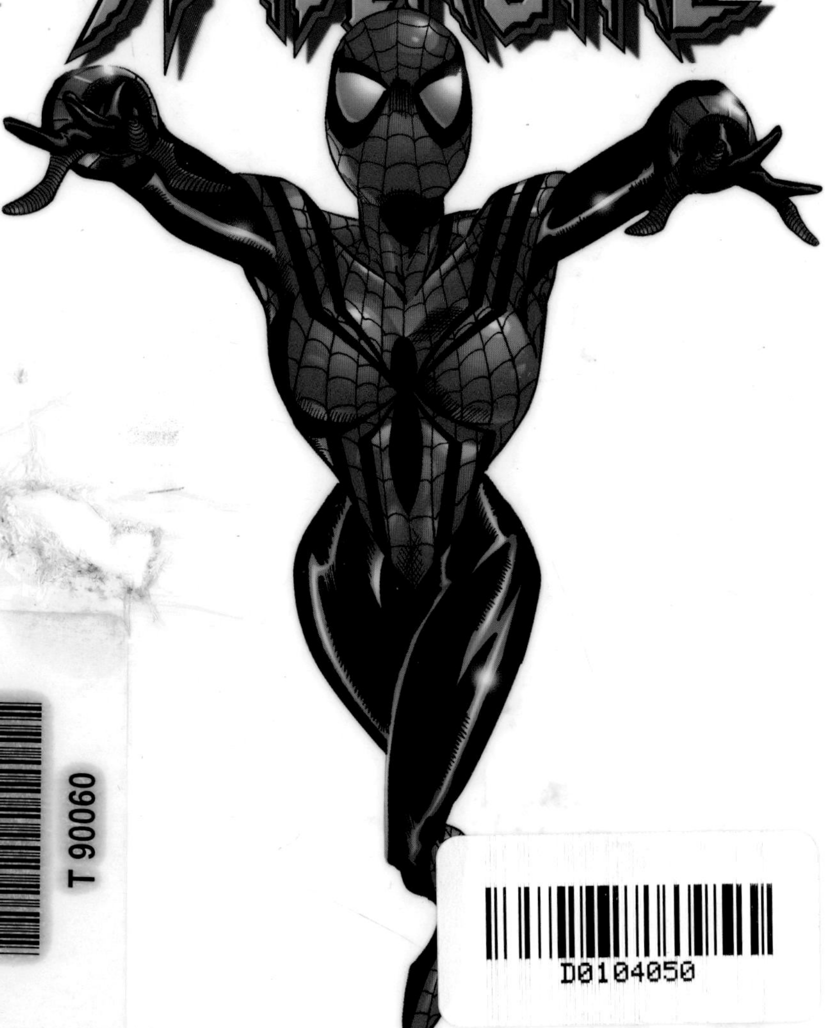

LIKE FATHER, LIKE DAUGHTER

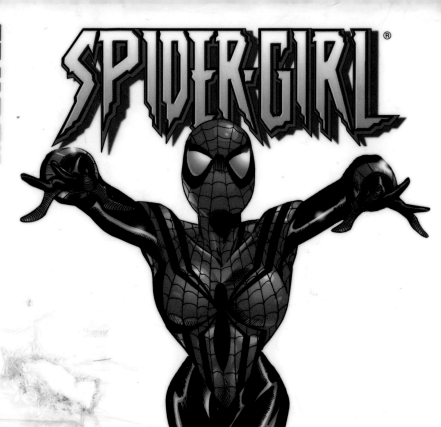

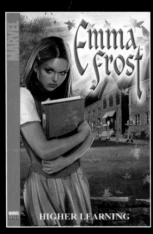

SPIDER-GIRL VOL. 2. Contains material originally published in magazine form as SPIDER-GIRL #6-11. First printing 2004. ISBN# 0-7851-1657-5. Published by MARVEL COMICS, a division of MARVEL ENTERTAINMENT GROUP, INC. OFFICE OF PUBLICATION: 10 East 40th Street, New York, NY 10016. Copyright © 1999 and 2004 Marvel Characters, Inc. All rights reserved. $7.99 per copy in the U.S. and $12.75 in Canada (GST #R127032852); Canadian Agreement #40668537. All characters featured in this issue and the distinctive names and likenesses thereof, and all related indicia are trademarks of Marvel Characters, Inc. No similarity between any of the names, characters, persons, and/or institutions in this magazine with those of any living or dead person or institution is intended, and any such similarity which may exist is purely coincidental. **Printed in Canada.** ALLEN LIPSON, Chief Executive Officer; AVI ARAD, Chief Creative Officer; ALAN FINE, President & CEO of Toy Biz and Marvel Publishing; DAN CARR, Director of Production; ELAINE CALLENDER, Director of Manufacturing; DAVID BOGART, Managing Editor; STAN LEE, Chairman Emeritus. For information regarding advertising in Marvel Comics or on Marvel.com, please contact Joe Maimone, Advertising Director, at jmaimone@marvel.com or 212-576-8534.

10 9 8 7 6 5 4 3 2 1

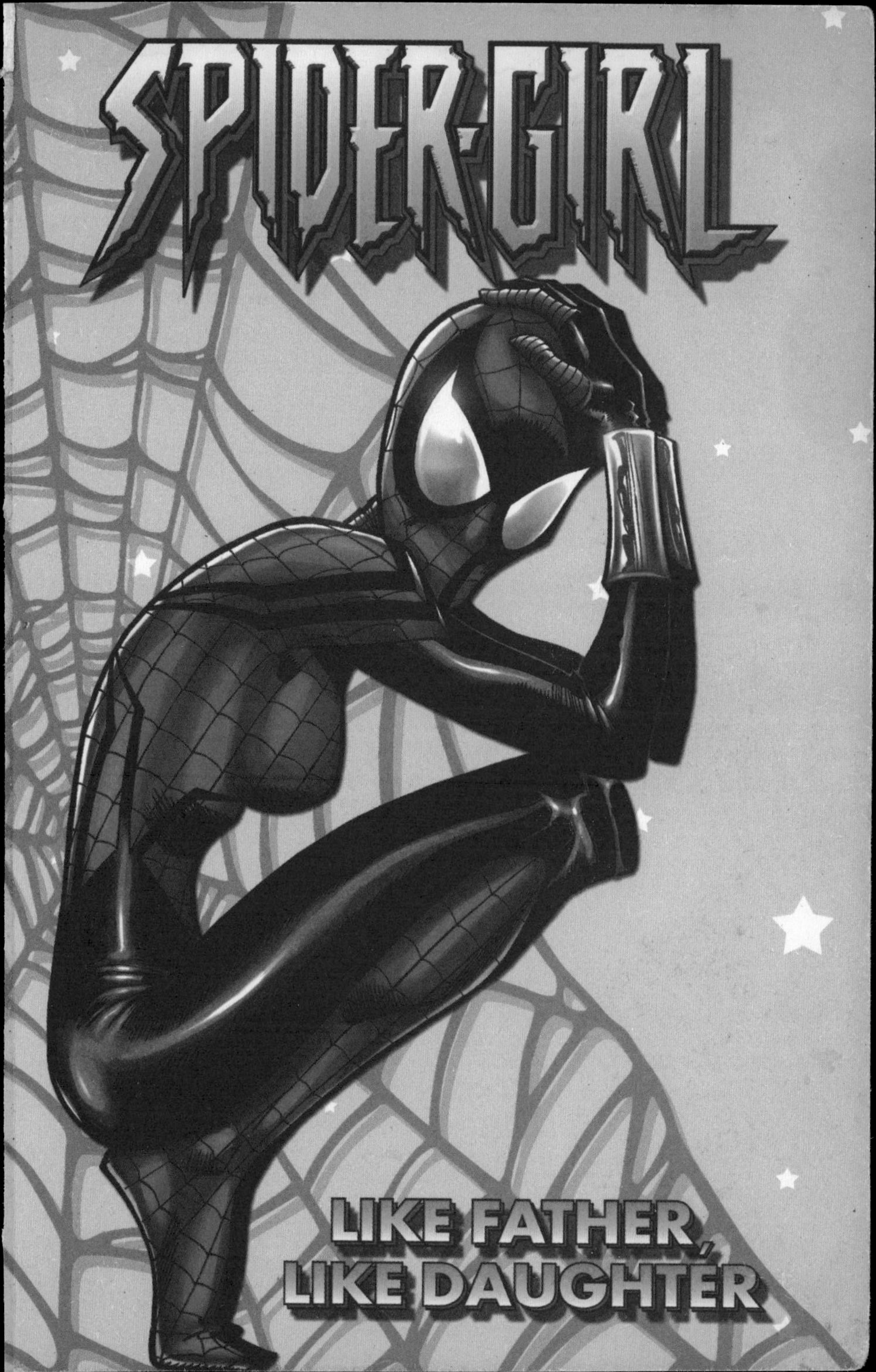
SPIDER-GIRL
LIKE FATHER, LIKE DAUGHTER

writer
TOM DEFALCO

pencils
PAT OLLIFFE

inks
AL WILLIAMSON

colors
CHRISTIE SCHEELE

letters
DAVE SHARPE

cover art
PAT OLLIFFE

collections editor
JEFF YOUNGQUIST

assistant editor
JENNIFER GRÜNWALD

sales manager
DAVID GABRIEL

book designer
CARRIE BEADLE

creative director
TOM MARVELLI

editor in chief
JOE QUESADA

publisher
DAN BUCKLEY

LIKE FATHER, LIKE DAUGHTER

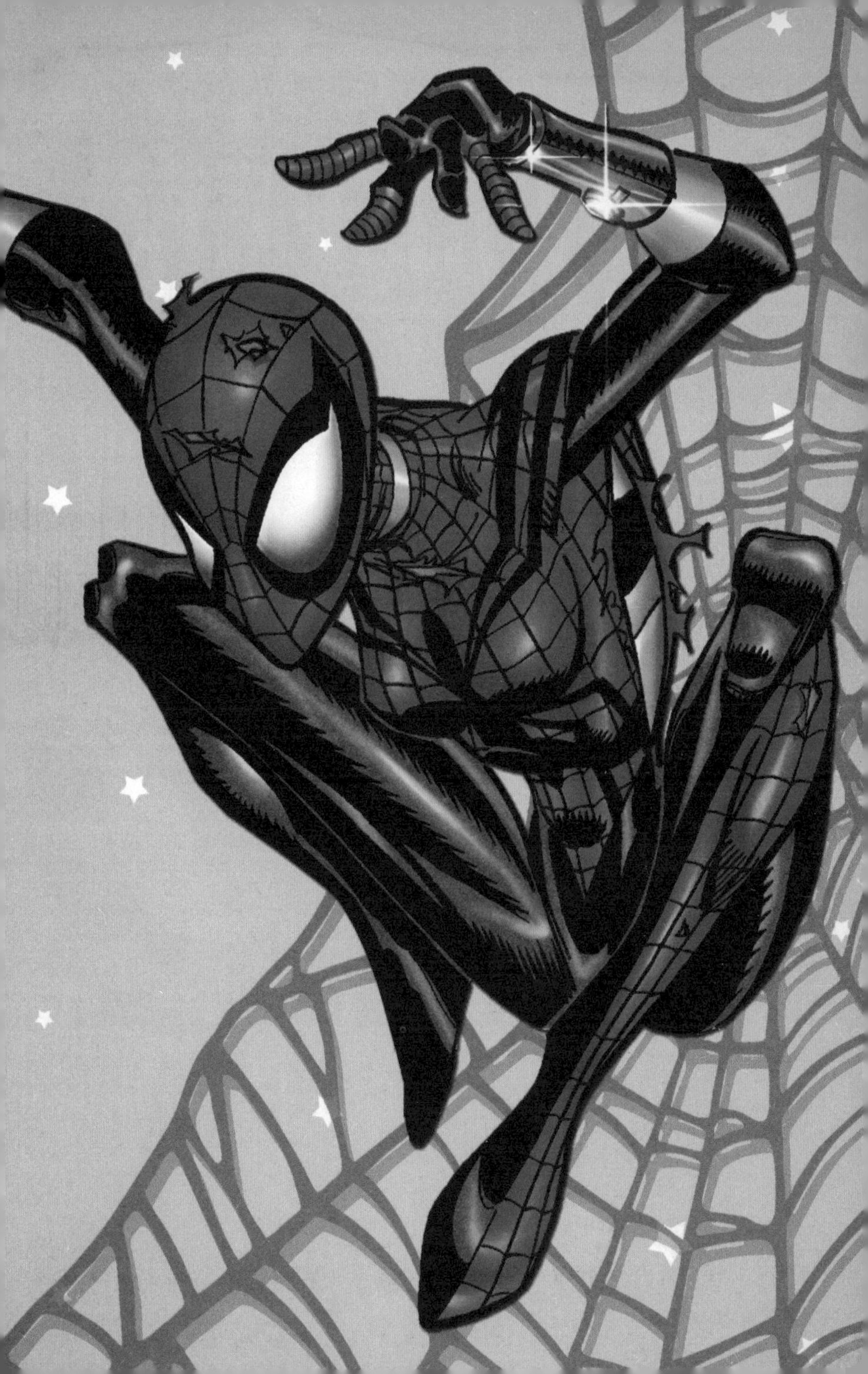

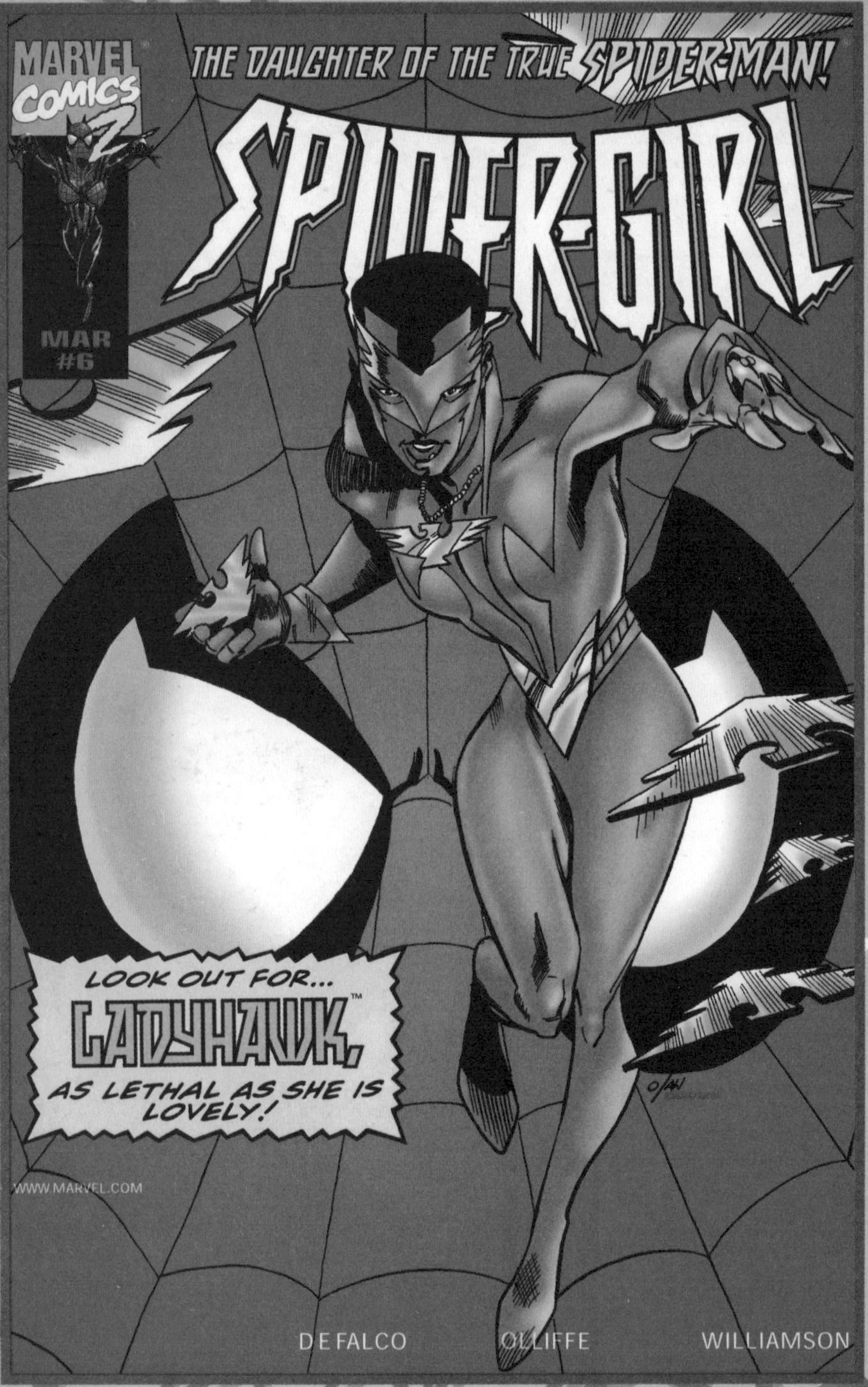
MARVEL COMICS
MAR #6
THE DAUGHTER OF THE TRUE SPIDER-MAN!
SPIDER-GIRL
LOOK OUT FOR...
LADYHAWK,
AS LETHAL AS SHE IS LOVELY!
WWW.MARVEL.COM
DEFALCO
OLLIFFE
WILLIAMSON

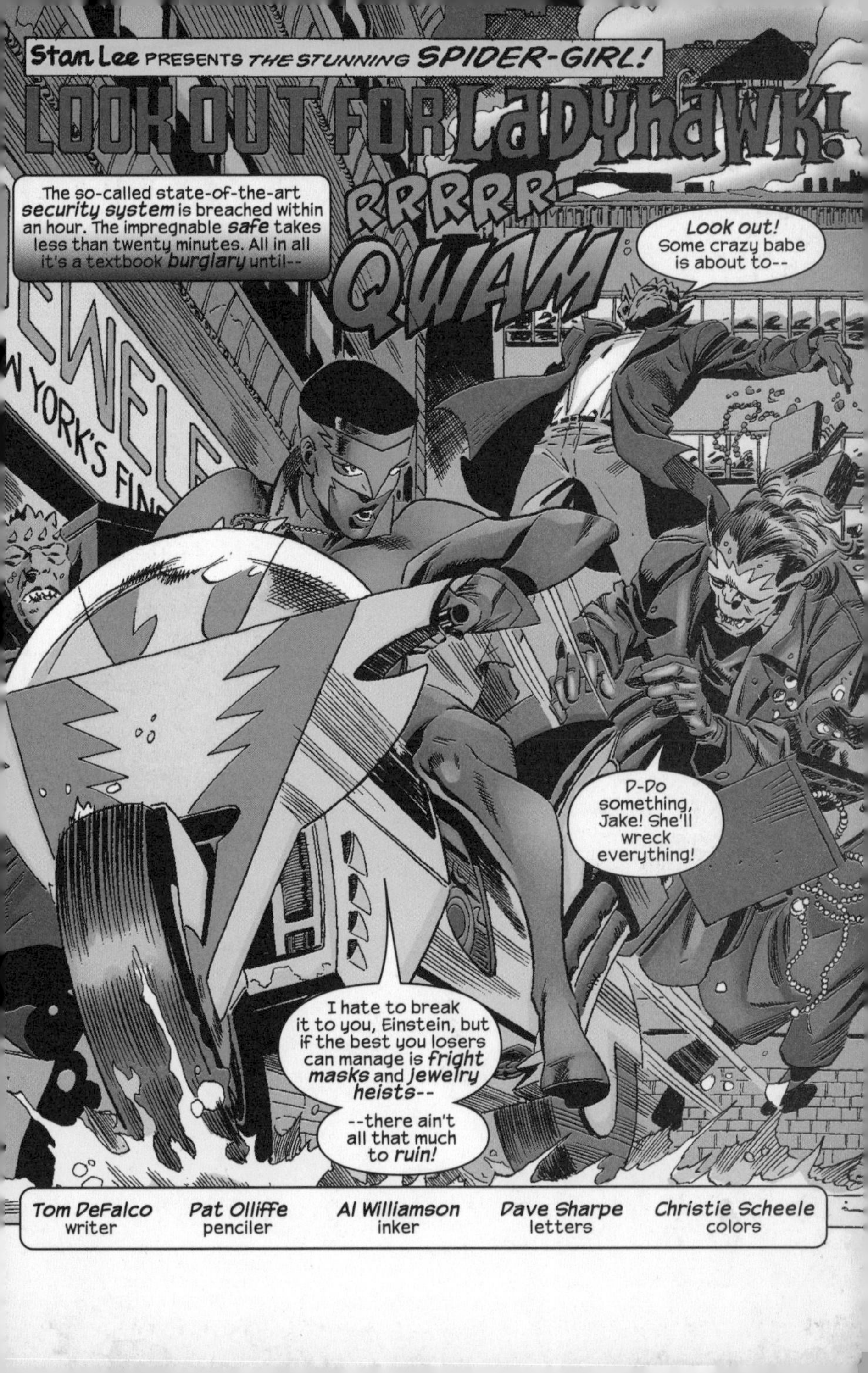

Stan Lee PRESENTS THE STUNNING SPIDER-GIRL!
LOOK OUT FOR LADYHAWK!
The so-called state-of-the-art security system is breached within an hour. The impregnable safe takes less than twenty minutes. All in all it's a textbook burglary until--
RRRRR-
QWAM
Look out! Some crazy babe is about to--
D-Do something, Jake! She'll wreck everything!
I hate to break it to you, Einstein, but if the best you losers can manage is fright masks and jewelry heists--
--there ain't all that much to ruin!
Tom DeFalco writer
Pat Olliffe penciler
Al Williamson inker
Dave Sharpe letters
Christie Scheele colors

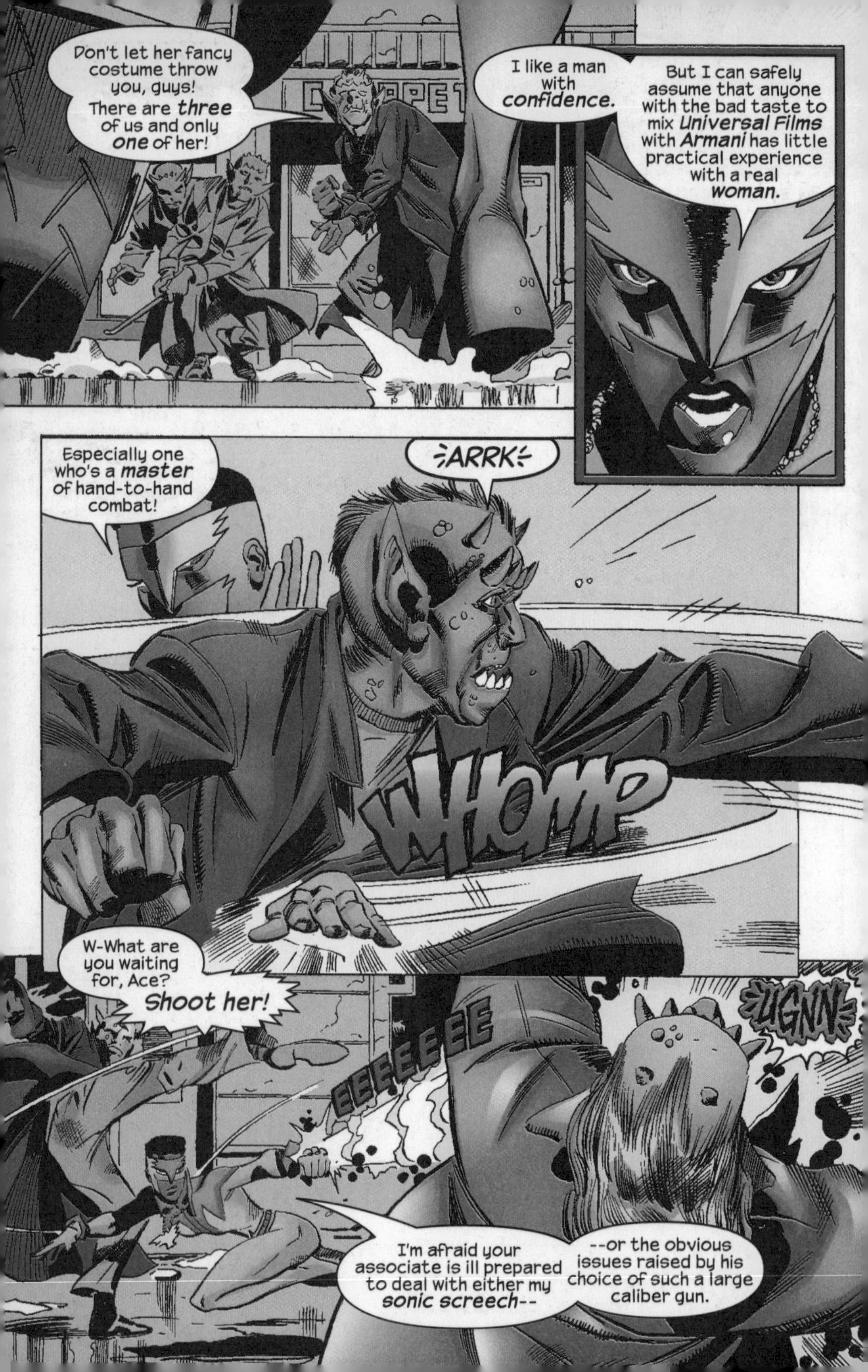
Don't let her fancy costume throw you, guys! There are three of us and only one of her!
I like a man with confidence.
But I can safely assume that anyone with the bad taste to mix Universal Films with Armani has little practical experience with a real woman.
Especially one who's a master of hand-to-hand combat!
ARRK
WHOMP
W-What are you waiting for, Ace? Shoot her!
EEEEEEEEE
UGNN
I'm afraid your associate is ill prepared to deal with either my sonic screech--
--or the obvious issues raised by his choice of such a large caliber gun.

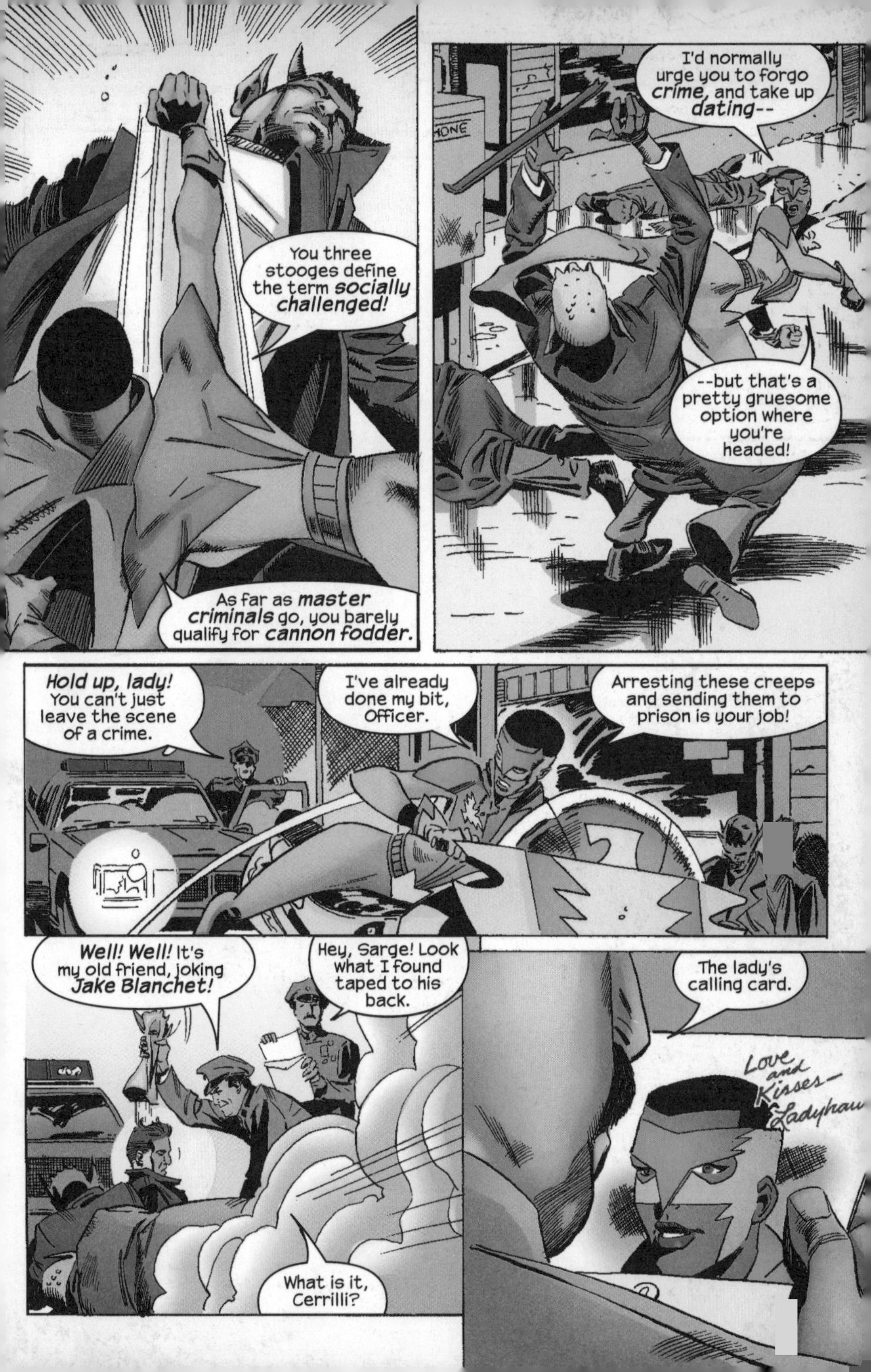
You three stooges define the term *socially challenged!*
As far as *master criminals* go, you barely qualify for *cannon fodder.*
I'd normally urge you to forgo *crime,* and take up *dating--*
--but that's a pretty gruesome option where you're headed!
Hold up, lady! You can't just leave the scene of a crime.
I've already done my bit, Officer.
Arresting these creeps and sending them to prison is your job!
Well! Well! It's my old friend, joking *Jake Blanchet!*
Hey, Sarge! Look what I found taped to his back.
What is it, Cerrilli?
The lady's calling card.
Love and Kisses— Ladyhaw

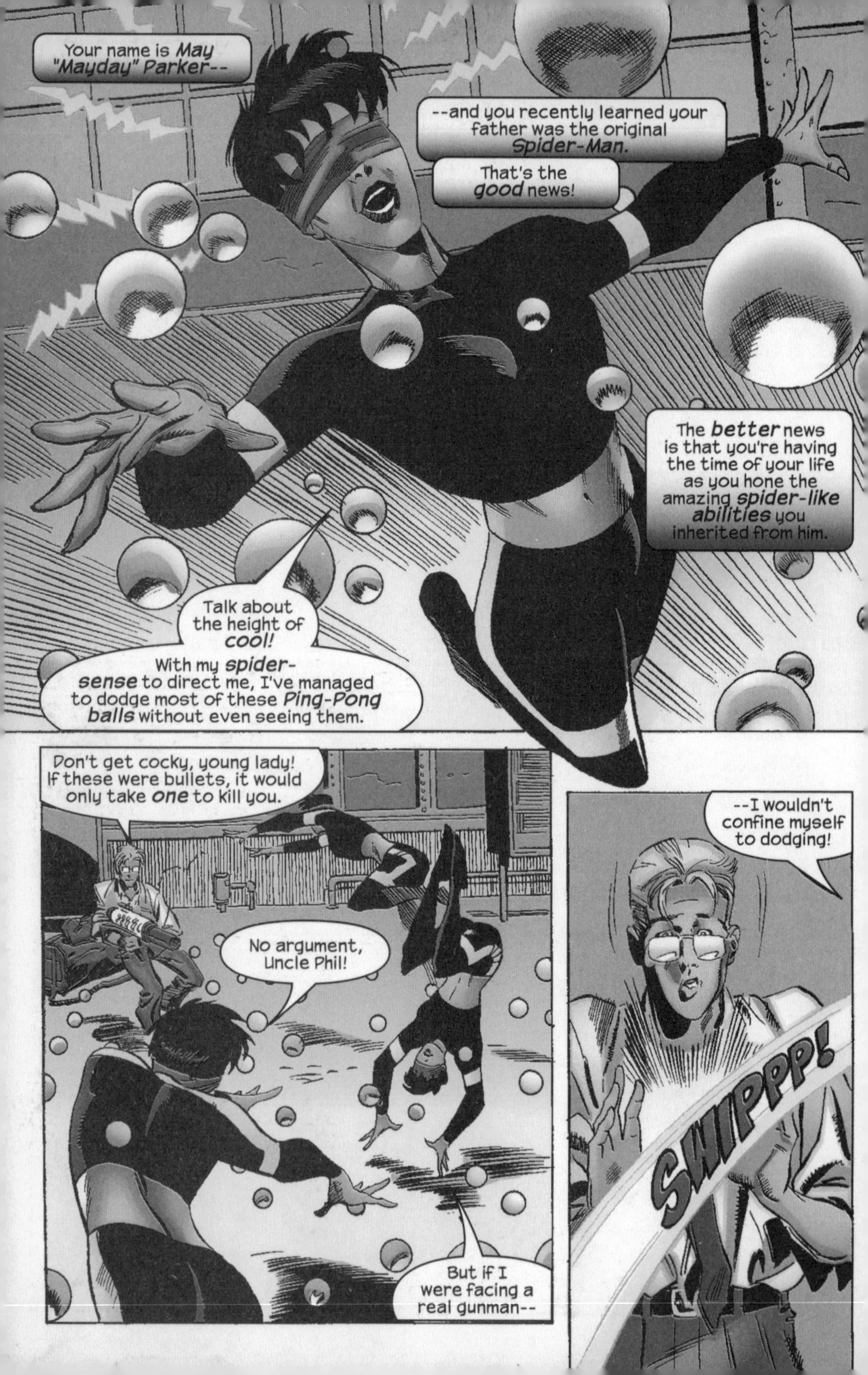
Your name is May "Mayday" Parker--
--and you recently learned your father was the original Spider-Man.
That's the good news!
The better news is that you're having the time of your life as you hone the amazing spider-like abilities you inherited from him.
Talk about the height of cool!
With my spider-sense to direct me, I've managed to dodge most of these Ping-Pong balls without even seeing them.
Don't get cocky, young lady! If these were bullets, it would only take one to kill you.
No argument, Uncle Phil!
But if I were facing a real gunman--
--I wouldn't confine myself to dodging!
SWIPPP!

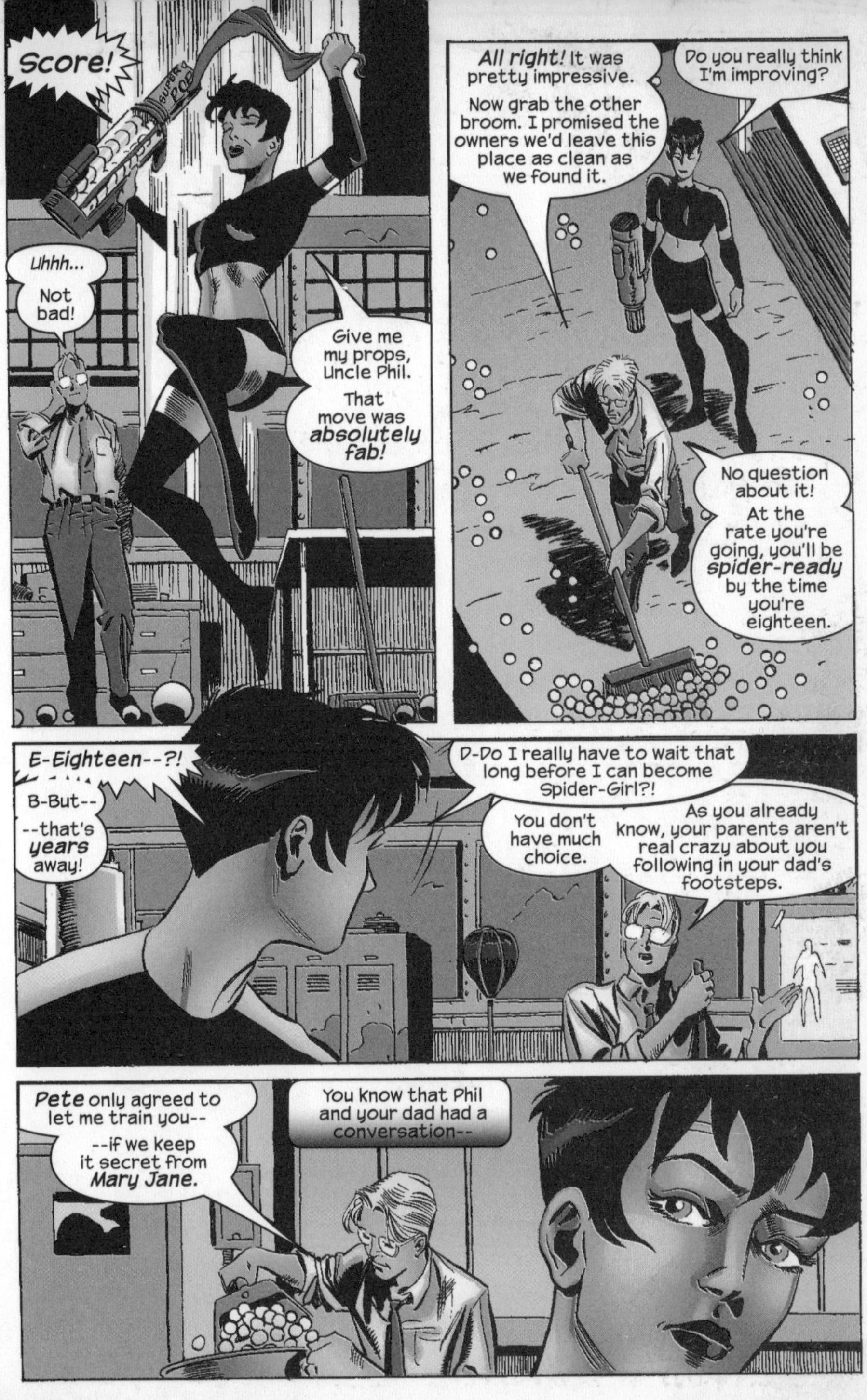
Score!
SUPER POP
Uhhh...
Not bad!
Give me my props, Uncle Phil.
That move was absolutely fab!
All right! It was pretty impressive.
Now grab the other broom. I promised the owners we'd leave this place as clean as we found it.
Do you really think I'm improving?
No question about it!
At the rate you're going, you'll be spider-ready by the time you're eighteen.
E-Eighteen--?!
B-But--
--that's years away!
D-Do I really have to wait that long before I can become Spider-Girl?!
You don't have much choice.
As you already know, your parents aren't real crazy about you following in your dad's footsteps.
Pete only agreed to let me train you--
--if we keep it secret from Mary Jane.
You know that Phil and your dad had a conversation--

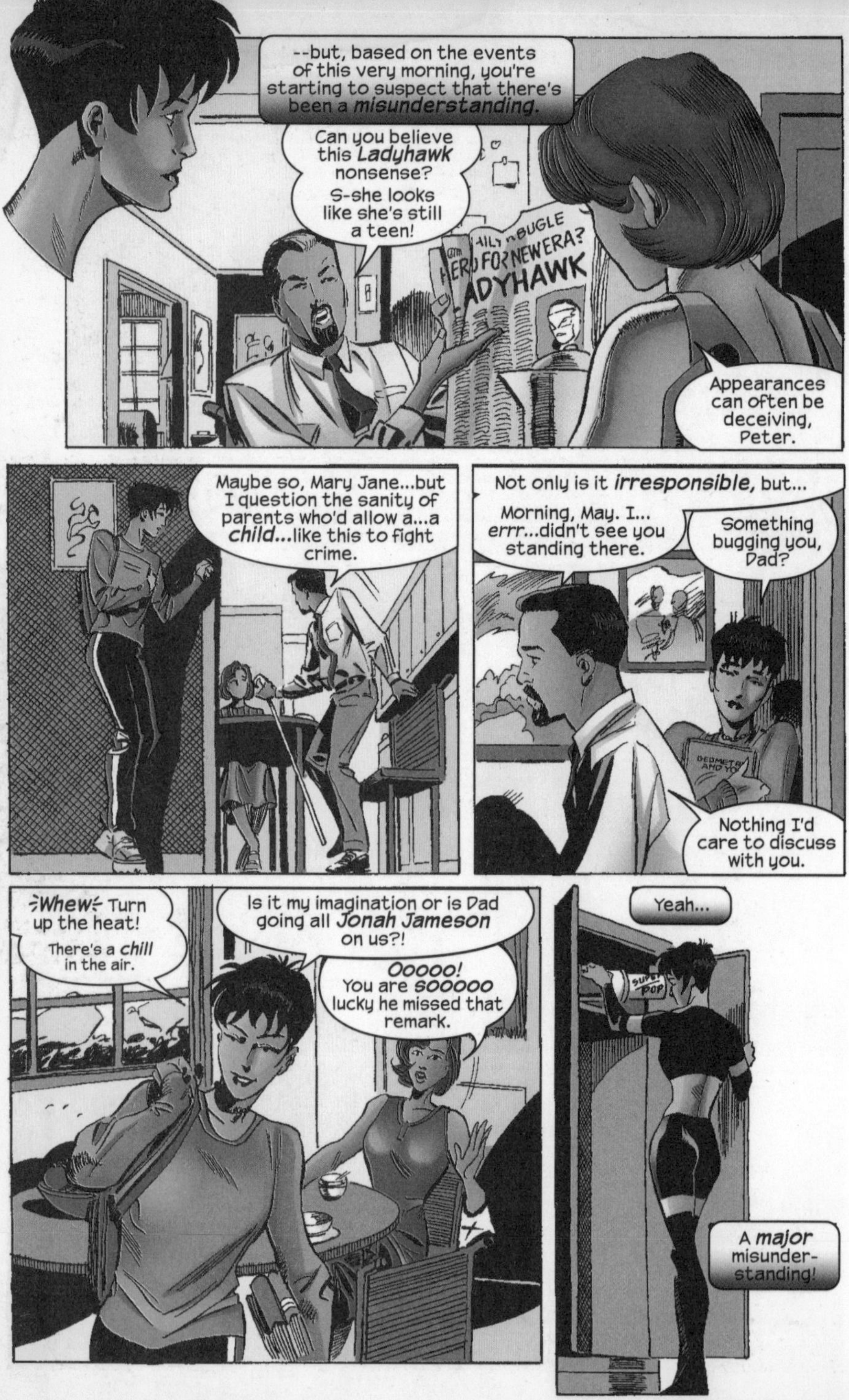
--but, based on the events of this very morning, you're starting to suspect that there's been a misunderstanding.
Can you believe this Ladyhawk nonsense?
S-she looks like she's still a teen!
HERO FOR NEW ERA? LADYHAWK
Appearances can often be deceiving, Peter.
Maybe so, Mary Jane...but I question the sanity of parents who'd allow a...a child...like this to fight crime.
Not only is it irresponsible, but...
Morning, May. I... errr...didn't see you standing there.
Something bugging you, Dad?
GEOMETRY AND YOU
Nothing I'd care to discuss with you.
Whew Turn up the heat!
There's a chill in the air.
Is it my imagination or is Dad going all Jonah Jameson on us?!
Ooooo! You are SOOOOO lucky he missed that remark.
Yeah...
A major misunderstanding!

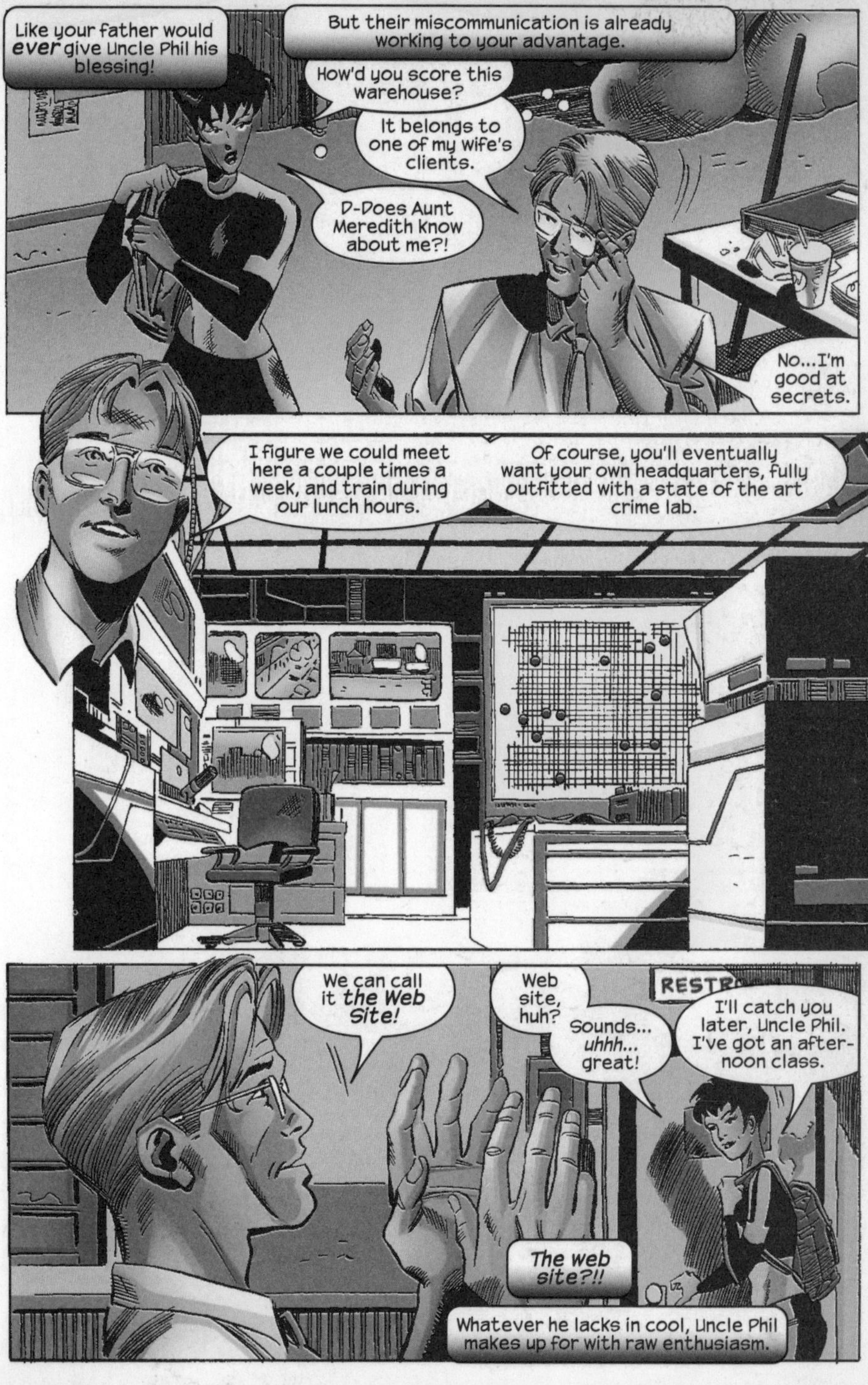
Like your father would *ever* give Uncle Phil his blessing!
But their miscommunication is already working to your advantage.
How'd you score this warehouse?
It belongs to one of my wife's clients.
D-Does Aunt Meredith know about me?!
No...I'm good at secrets.
I figure we could meet here a couple times a week, and train during our lunch hours.
Of course, you'll eventually want your own headquarters, fully outfitted with a state of the art crime lab.
We can call it *the Web Site!*
Web site, huh?
Sounds... *uhhh...* great!
I'll catch you later, Uncle Phil. I've got an after-noon class.
The web site?!!
Whatever he lacks in cool, Uncle Phil makes up for with raw enthusiasm.

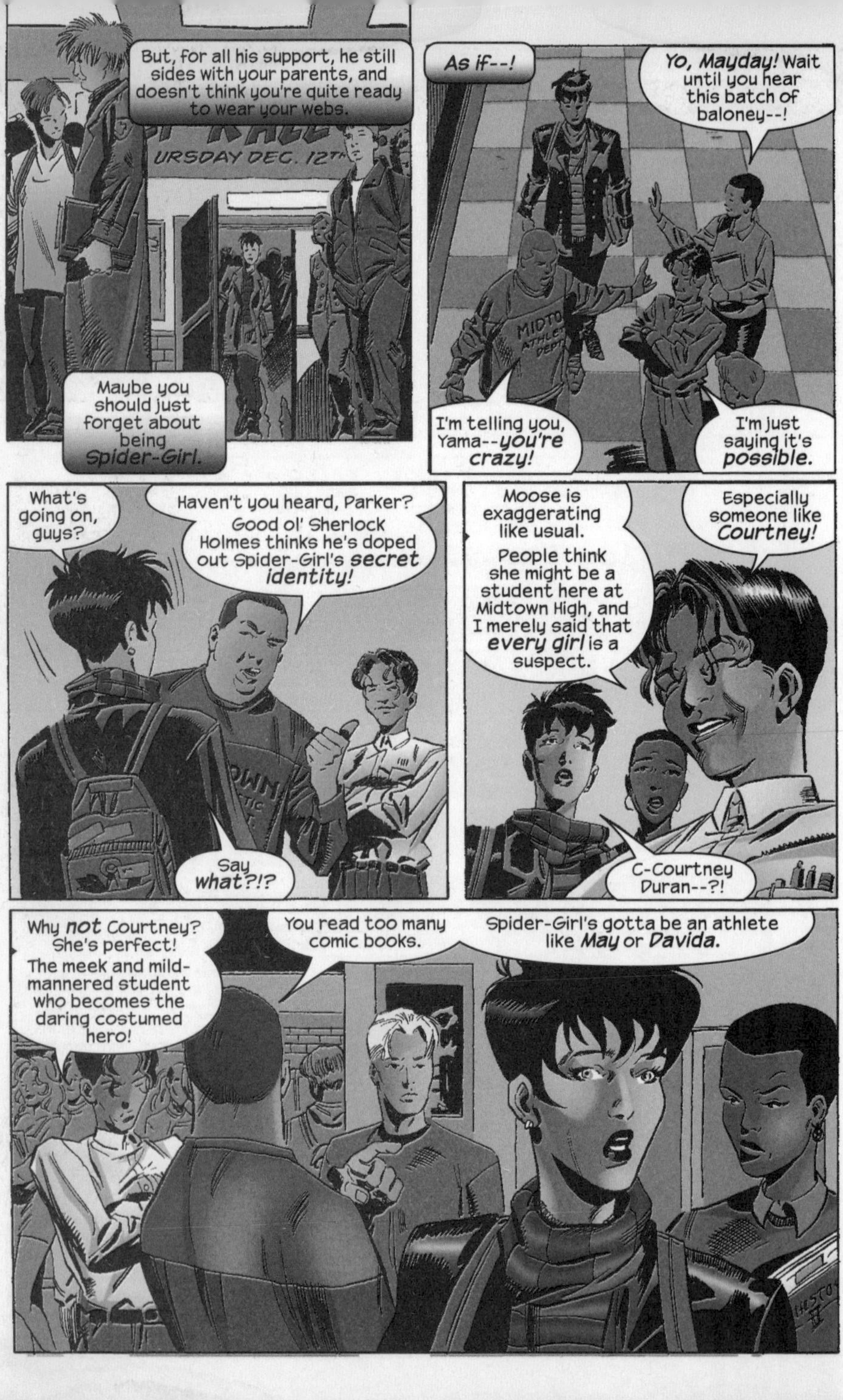
But, for all his support, he still sides with your parents, and doesn't think you're quite ready to wear your webs.
URSDAY DEC. 12TH
Maybe you should just forget about being Spider-Girl.
As if--!
Yo, Mayday! Wait until you hear this batch of baloney--!
MIDTO ATHLET DEPT
I'm telling you, Yama--you're crazy!
I'm just saying it's possible.
What's going on, guys?
Haven't you heard, Parker? Good ol' Sherlock Holmes thinks he's doped out Spider-Girl's secret identity!
Say what?!?
Moose is exaggerating like usual.
People think she might be a student here at Midtown High, and I merely said that every girl is a suspect.
Especially someone like Courtney!
C-Courtney Duran--?!
Why not Courtney? She's perfect!
The meek and mild-mannered student who becomes the daring costumed hero!
You read too many comic books.
Spider-Girl's gotta be an athlete like May or Davida.

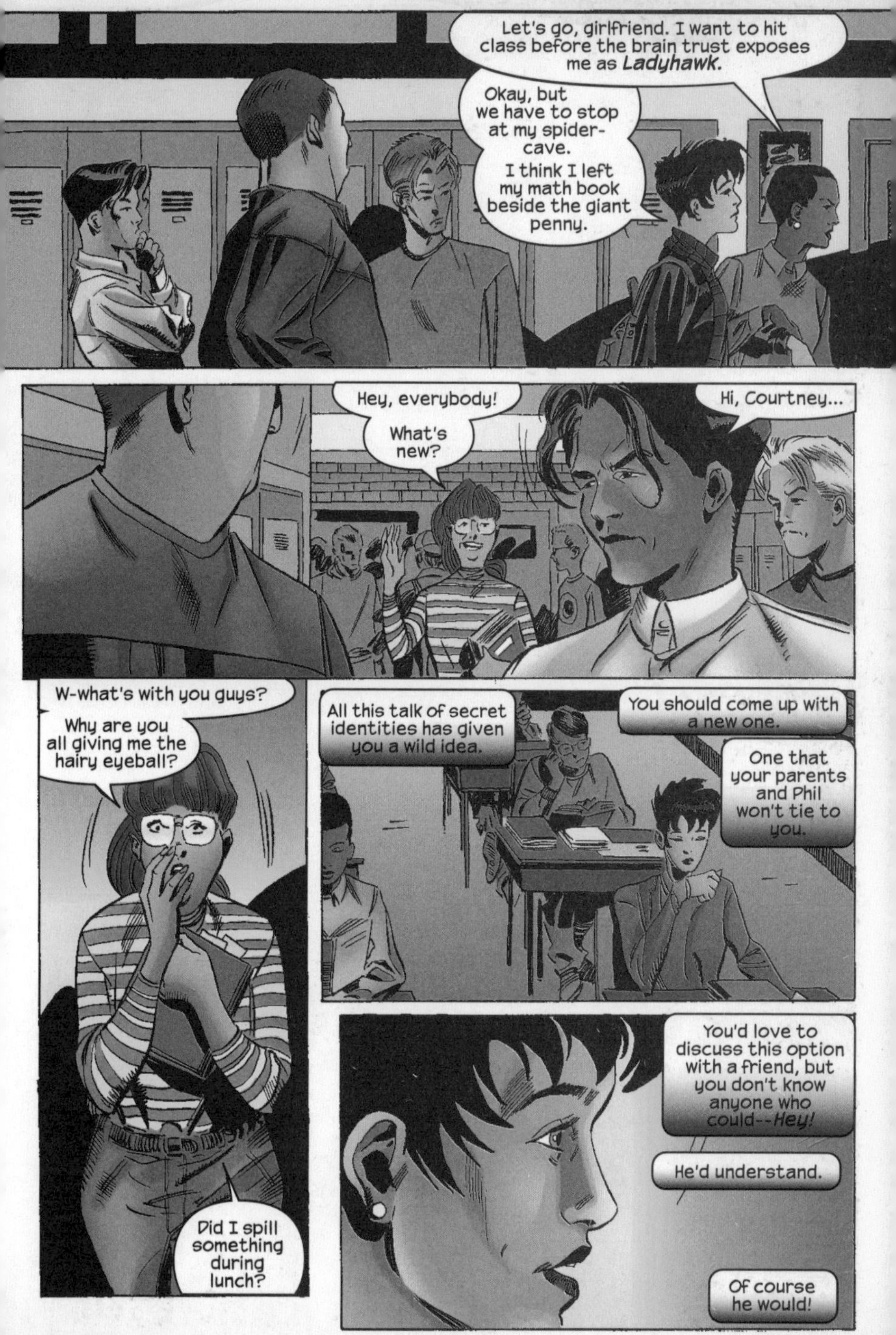
Let's go, girlfriend. I want to hit class before the brain trust exposes me as *Ladyhawk.*
Okay, but we have to stop at my spider-cave.
I think I left my math book beside the giant penny.
Hey, everybody!
What's new?
Hi, Courtney...
W-what's with you guys?
Why are you all giving me the hairy eyeball?
Did I spill something during lunch?
All this talk of secret identities has given you a wild idea.
You should come up with a new one.
One that your parents and Phil won't tie to you.
You'd love to discuss this option with a friend, but you don't know anyone who could--*Hey!*
He'd understand.
Of course he would!

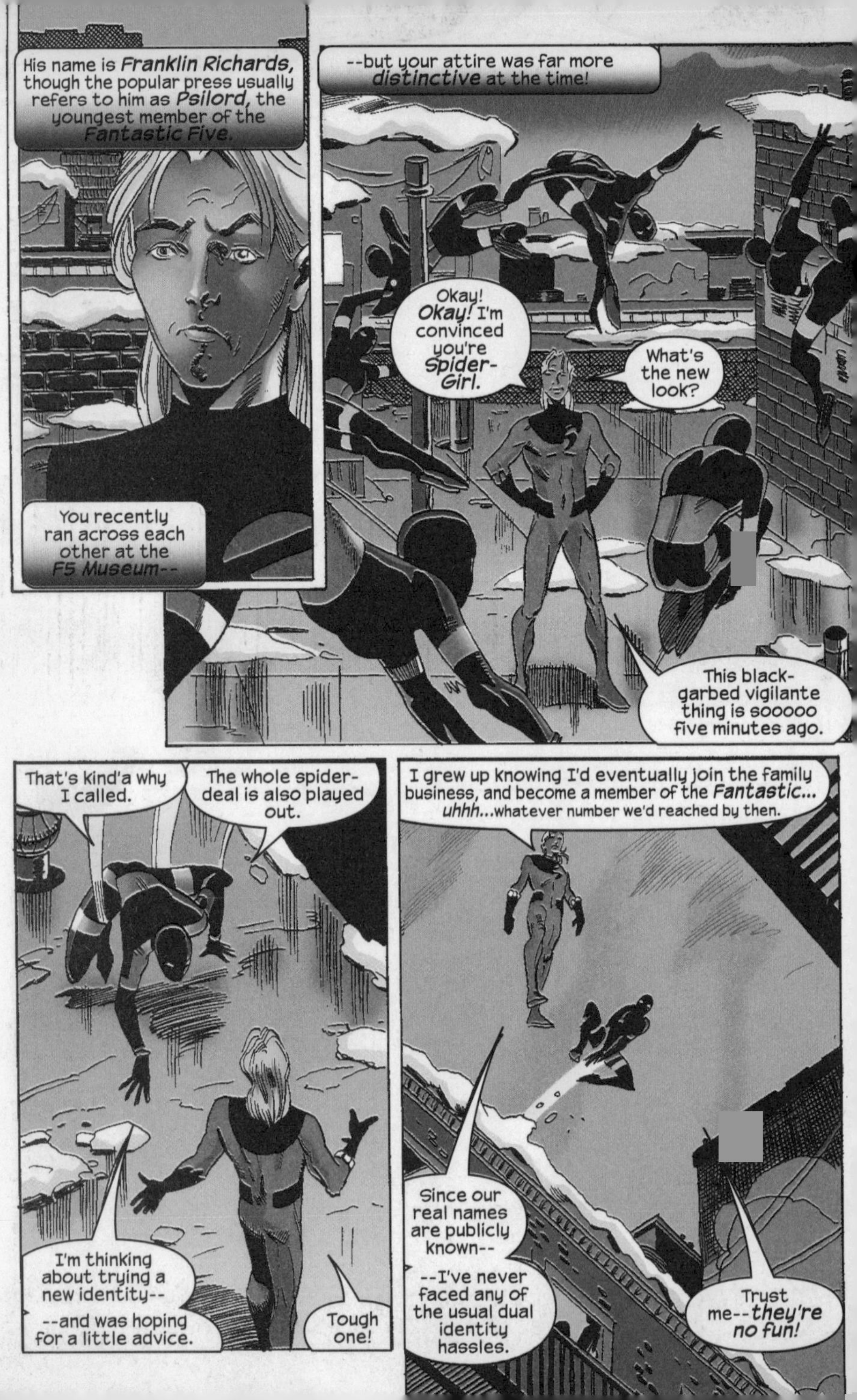
His name is Franklin Richards, though the popular press usually refers to him as Psilord, the youngest member of the Fantastic Five.
You recently ran across each other at the F5 Museum--
--but your attire was far more distinctive at the time!
Okay! Okay! I'm convinced you're Spider-Girl.
What's the new look?
This black-garbed vigilante thing is sooooo five minutes ago.
That's kind'a why I called.
The whole spider-deal is also played out.
I'm thinking about trying a new identity--
--and was hoping for a little advice.
Tough one!
I grew up knowing I'd eventually join the family business, and become a member of the Fantastic... uhhh...whatever number we'd reached by then.
Since our real names are publicly known--
--I've never faced any of the usual dual identity hassles.
Trust me--they're no fun!

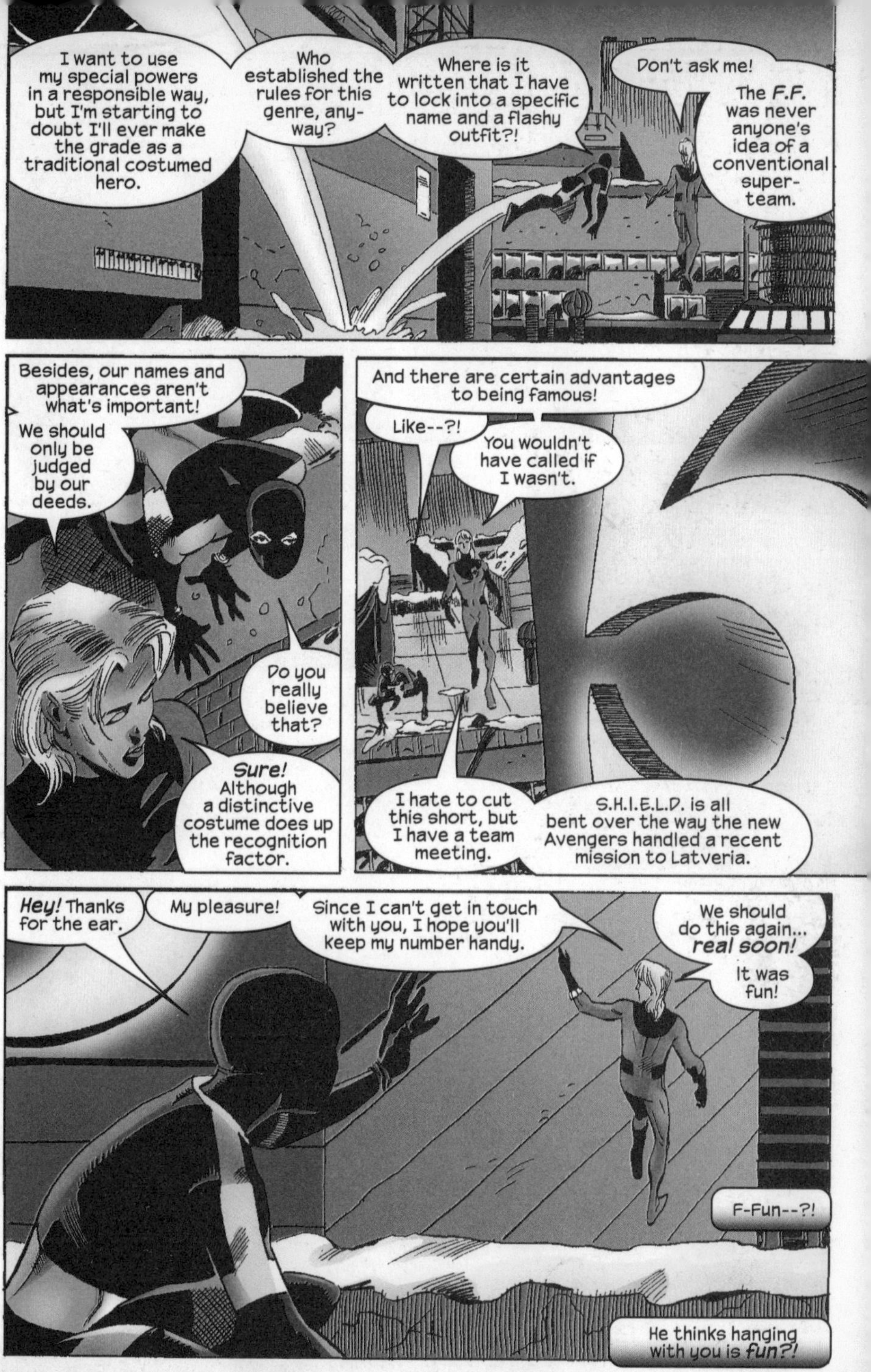
I want to use my special powers in a responsible way, but I'm starting to doubt I'll ever make the grade as a traditional costumed hero.
Who established the rules for this genre, anyway?
Where is it written that I have to lock into a specific name and a flashy outfit?!
Don't ask me!
The F.F. was never anyone's idea of a conventional super-team.
Besides, our names and appearances aren't what's important!
We should only be judged by our deeds.
Do you really believe that?
Sure! Although a distinctive costume does up the recognition factor.
And there are certain advantages to being famous!
Like--?!
You wouldn't have called if I wasn't.
I hate to cut this short, but I have a team meeting.
S.H.I.E.L.D. is all bent over the way the new Avengers handled a recent mission to Latveria.
Hey! Thanks for the ear.
My pleasure!
Since I can't get in touch with you, I hope you'll keep my number handy.
We should do this again... real soon!
It was fun!
F-Fun--?!
He thinks hanging with you is fun?!

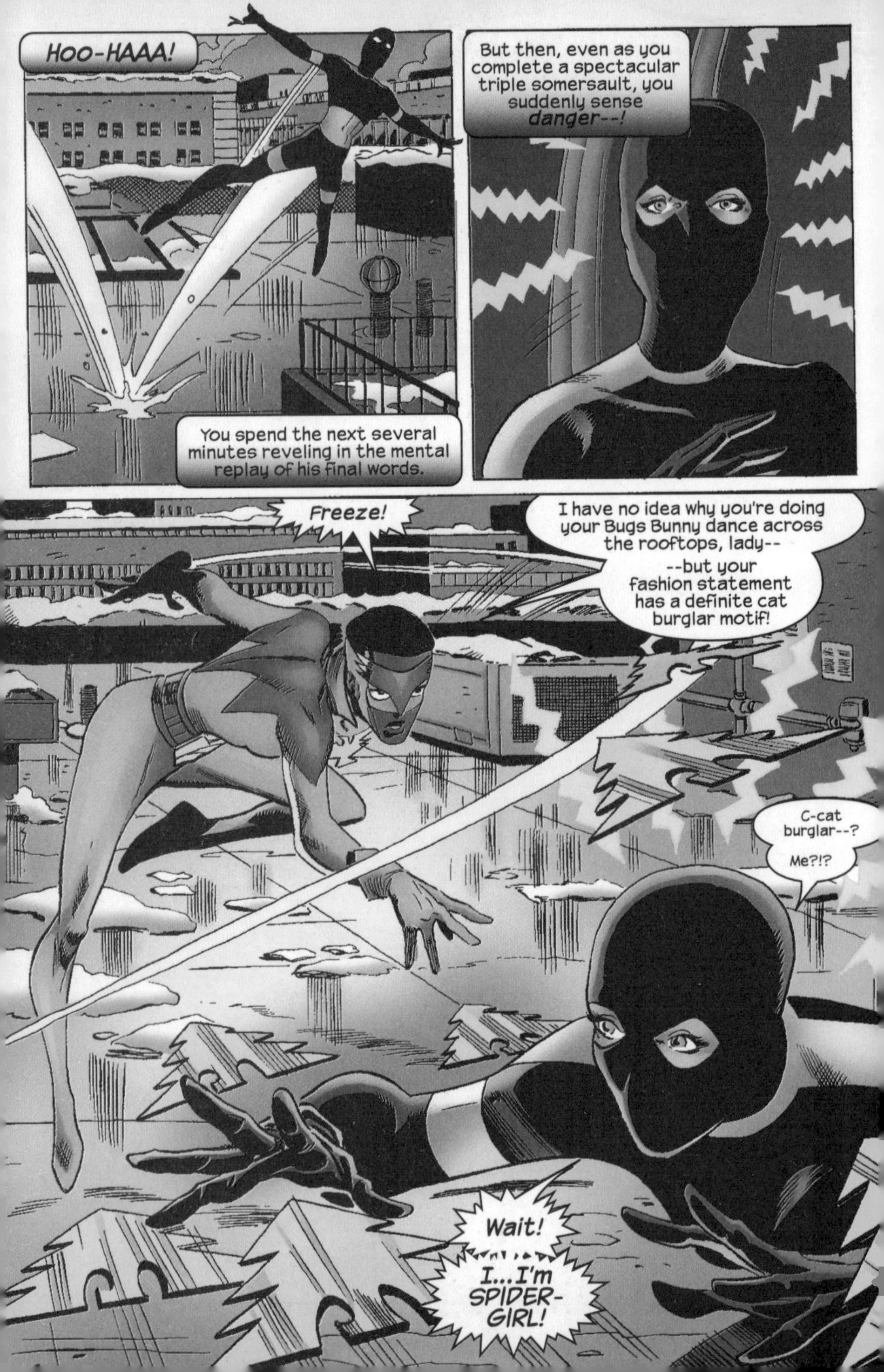
HOO-HAAA!
You spend the next several minutes reveling in the mental replay of his final words.
But then, even as you complete a spectacular triple somersault, you suddenly sense danger--!
Freeze!
I have no idea why you're doing your Bugs Bunny dance across the rooftops, lady--
--but your fashion statement has a definite cat burglar motif!
C-cat burglar--?
Me?!?
Wait!
I...I'm SPIDER-GIRL!

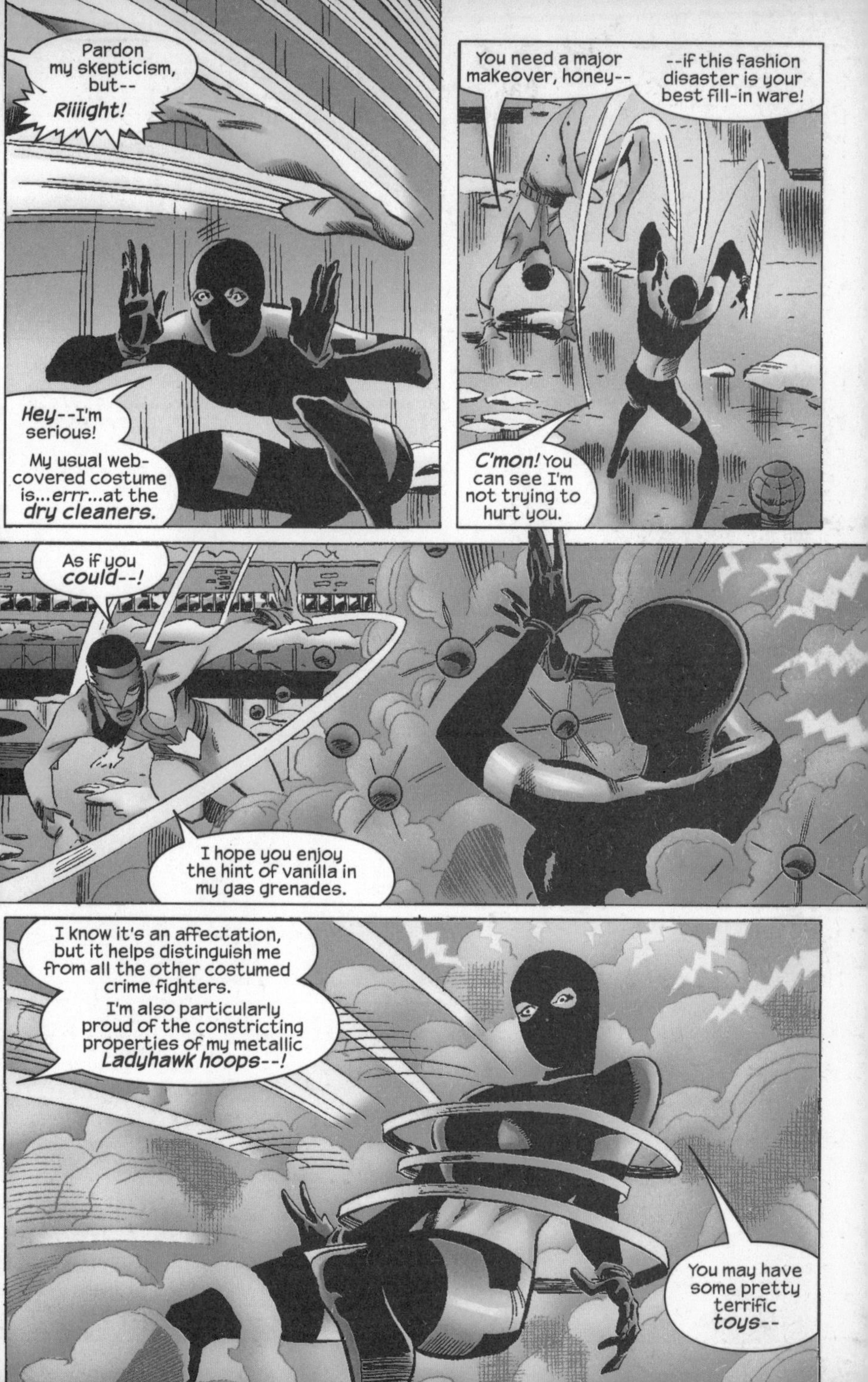
Pardon my skepticism, but--
Riiiight!
Hey--I'm serious!
My usual web-covered costume is...errr...at the dry cleaners.
You need a major makeover, honey--
--if this fashion disaster is your best fill-in ware!
C'mon! You can see I'm not trying to hurt you.
As if you could--!
I hope you enjoy the hint of vanilla in my gas grenades.
I know it's an affectation, but it helps distinguish me from all the other costumed crime fighters.
I'm also particularly proud of the constricting properties of my metallic Ladyhawk hoops--!
You may have some pretty terrific toys--

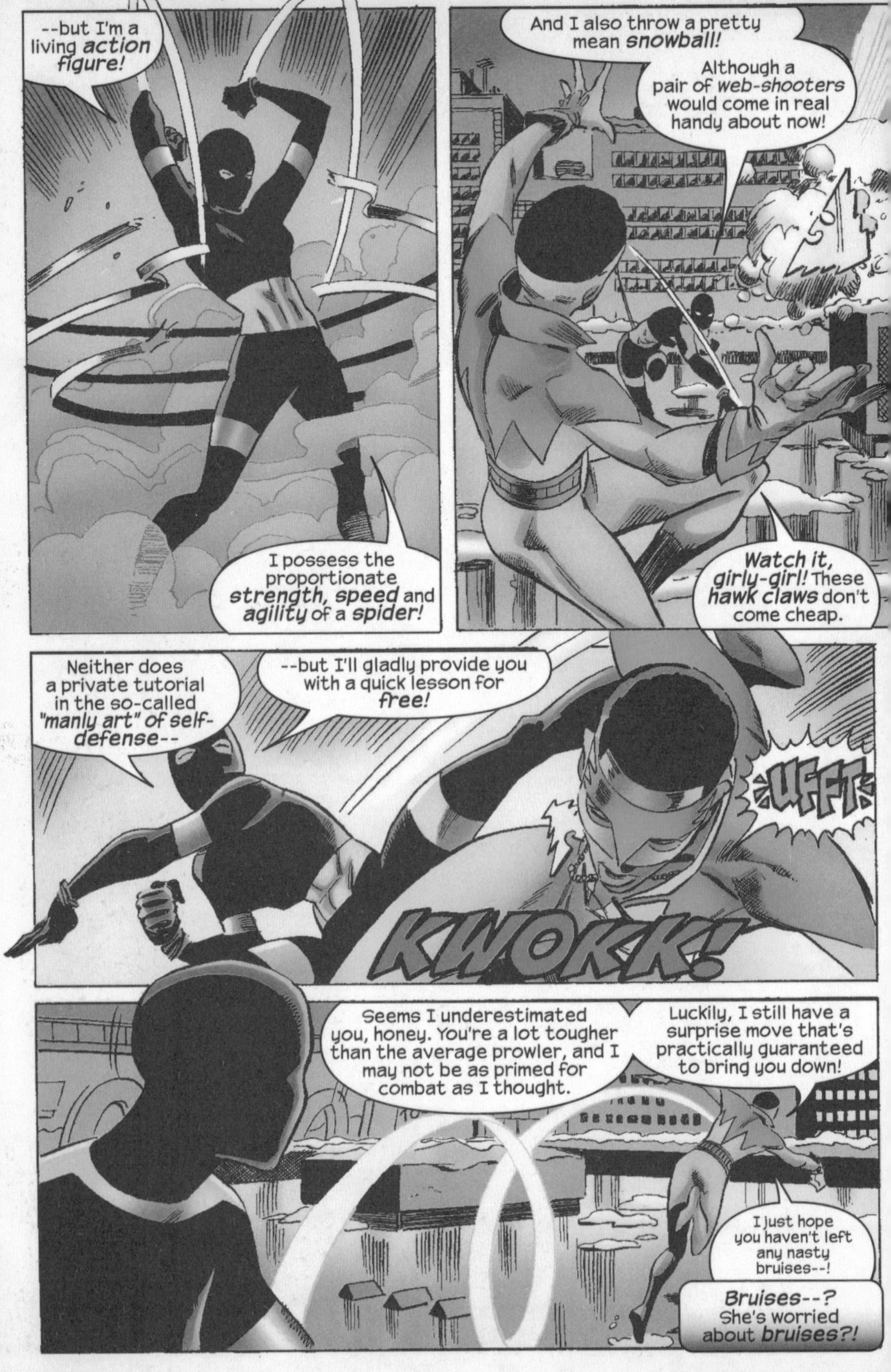
--but I'm a living action figure!
I possess the proportionate strength, speed and agility of a spider!
And I also throw a pretty mean snowball!
Although a pair of web-shooters would come in real handy about now!
Watch it, girly-girl! These hawk claws don't come cheap.
Neither does a private tutorial in the so-called "manly art" of self-defense--
--but I'll gladly provide you with a quick lesson for free!
UFFT
KWOKK!
Seems I underestimated you, honey. You're a lot tougher than the average prowler, and I may not be as primed for combat as I thought.
Luckily, I still have a surprise move that's practically guaranteed to bring you down!
I just hope you haven't left any nasty bruises--!
Bruises--? She's worried about bruises?!

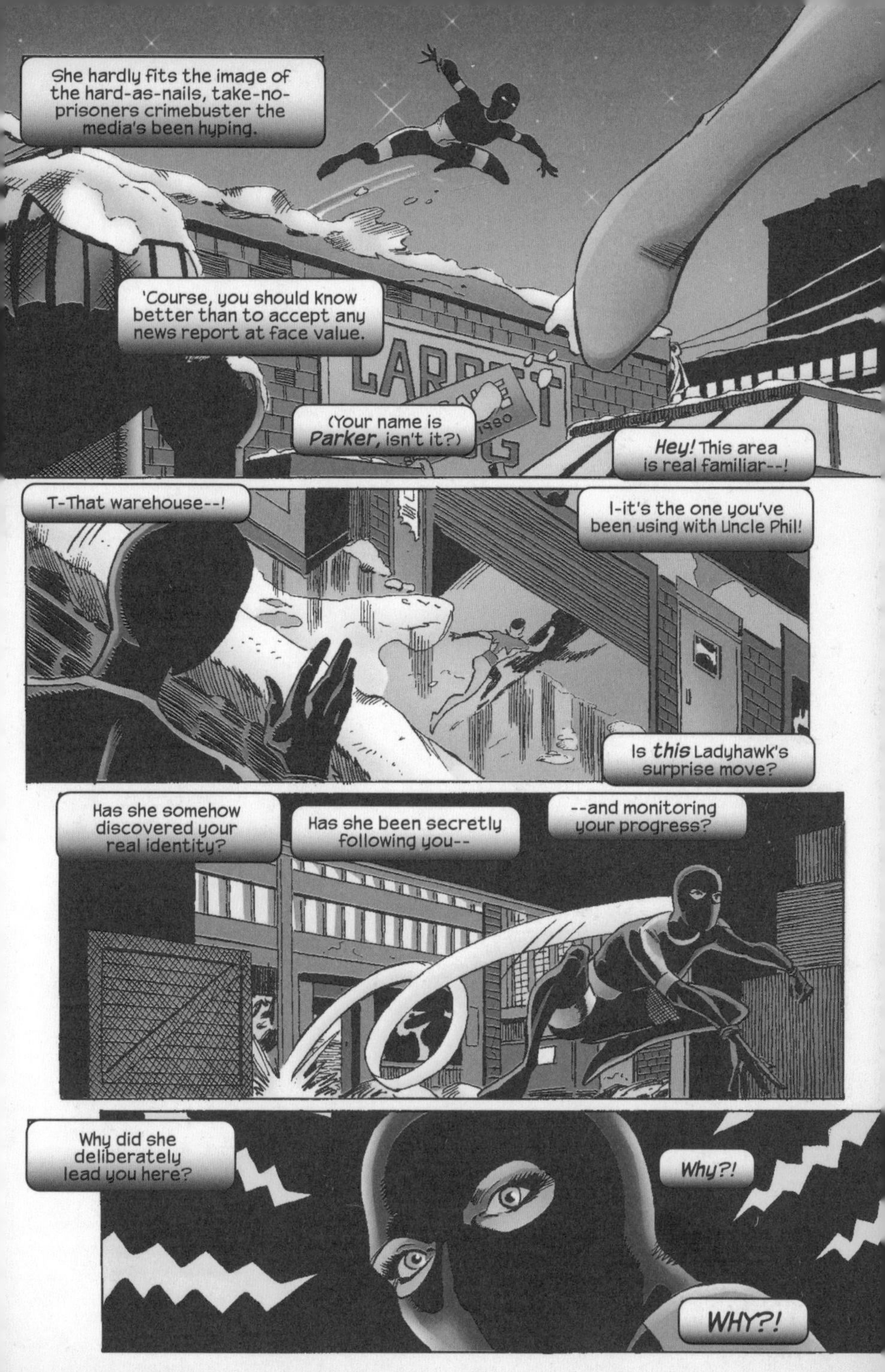

She hardly fits the image of the hard-as-nails, take-no-prisoners crimebuster the media's been hyping.
'Course, you should know better than to accept any news report at face value.
(Your name is *Parker,* isn't it?)
Hey! This area is real familiar--!
T-That warehouse--!
I-it's the one you've been using with Uncle Phil!
Is *this* Ladyhawk's surprise move?
Has she somehow discovered your real identity?
Has she been secretly following you--
--and monitoring your progress?
Why did she deliberately lead you here?
Why?!
WHY?!

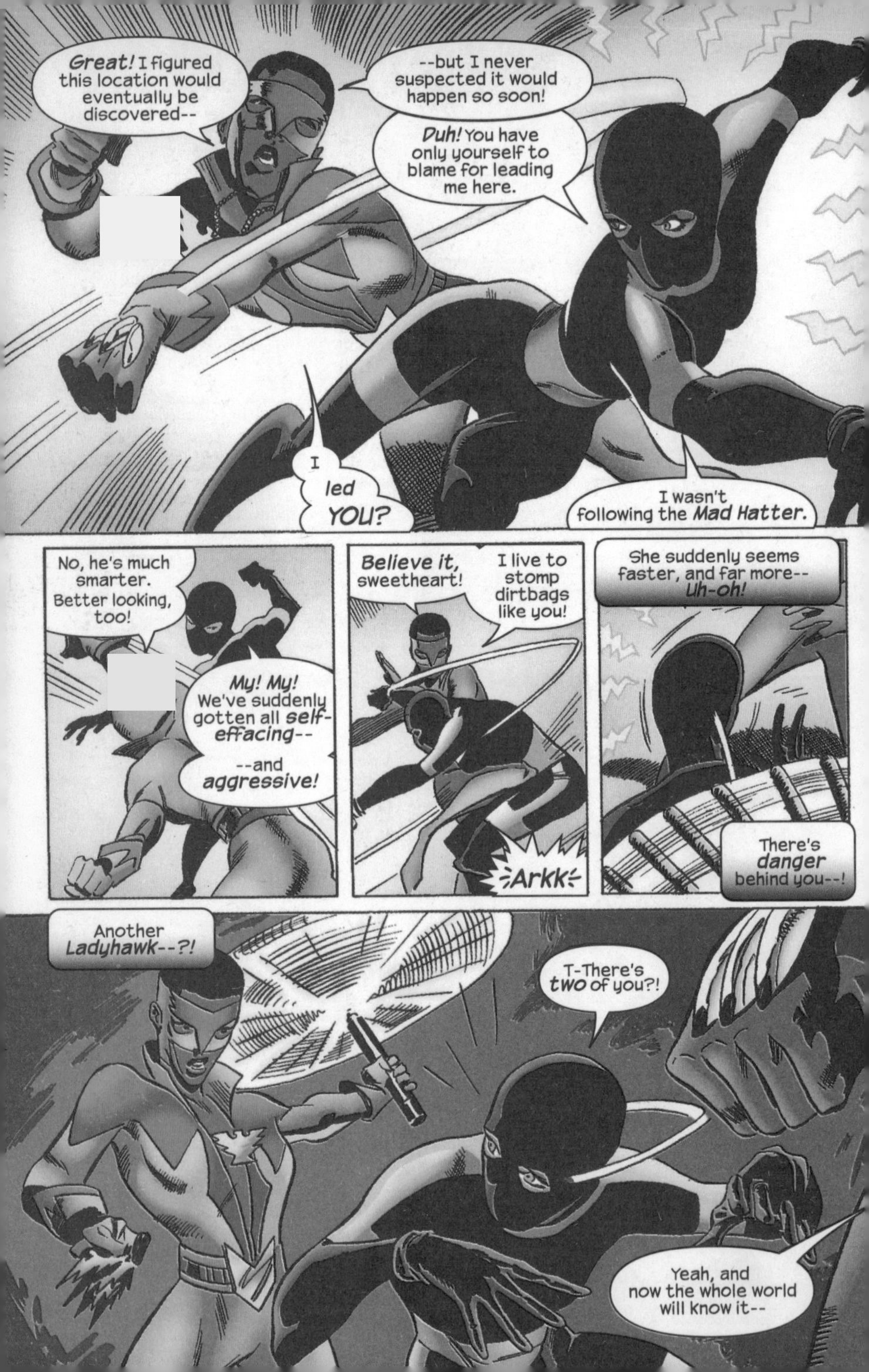
Great! I figured this location would eventually be discovered--
--but I never suspected it would happen so soon!
Duh! You have only yourself to blame for leading me here.
I led YOU?
I wasn't following the Mad Hatter.
No, he's much smarter. Better looking, too!
My! My! We've suddenly gotten all self-effacing--
--and aggressive!
Believe it, sweetheart!
I live to stomp dirtbags like you!
Arkk
She suddenly seems faster, and far more-- Uh-oh!
There's danger behind you--!
Another Ladyhawk--?!
T-There's two of you?!
Yeah, and now the whole world will know it--

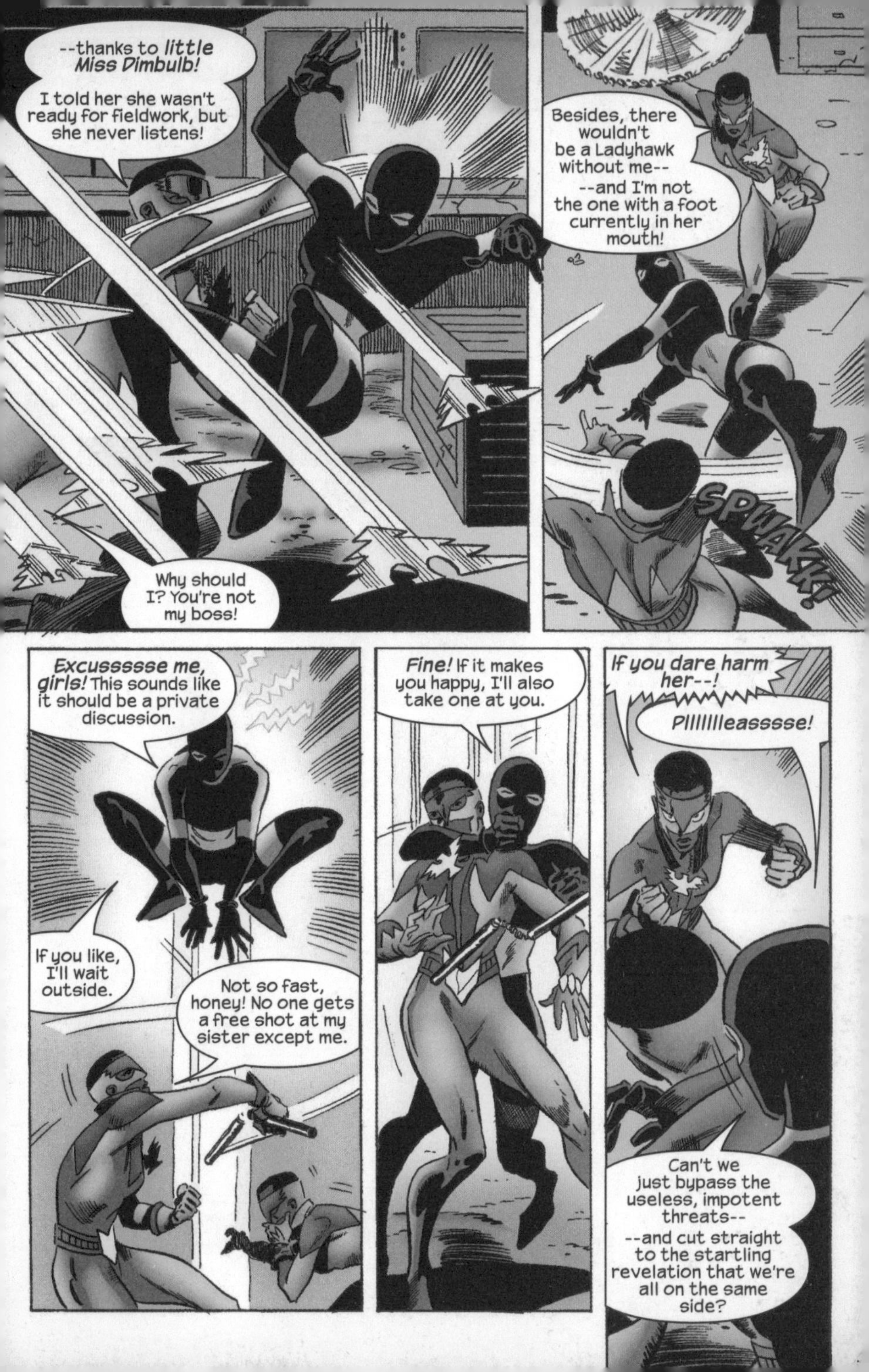
--thanks to *little Miss Dimbulb!*
I told her she wasn't ready for fieldwork, but she never listens!
Why should I? You're not my boss!
Besides, there wouldn't be a Ladyhawk without me--
--and I'm not the one with a foot currently in her mouth!
SPWAKK!
Excussssse me, girls! This sounds like it should be a private discussion.
If you like, I'll wait outside.
Not so fast, honey! No one gets a free shot at my sister except me.
Fine! If it makes you happy, I'll also take one at you.
If you dare harm her--!
Plllllleassssse!
Can't we just bypass the useless, impotent threats--
--and cut straight to the startling revelation that we're all on the same side?

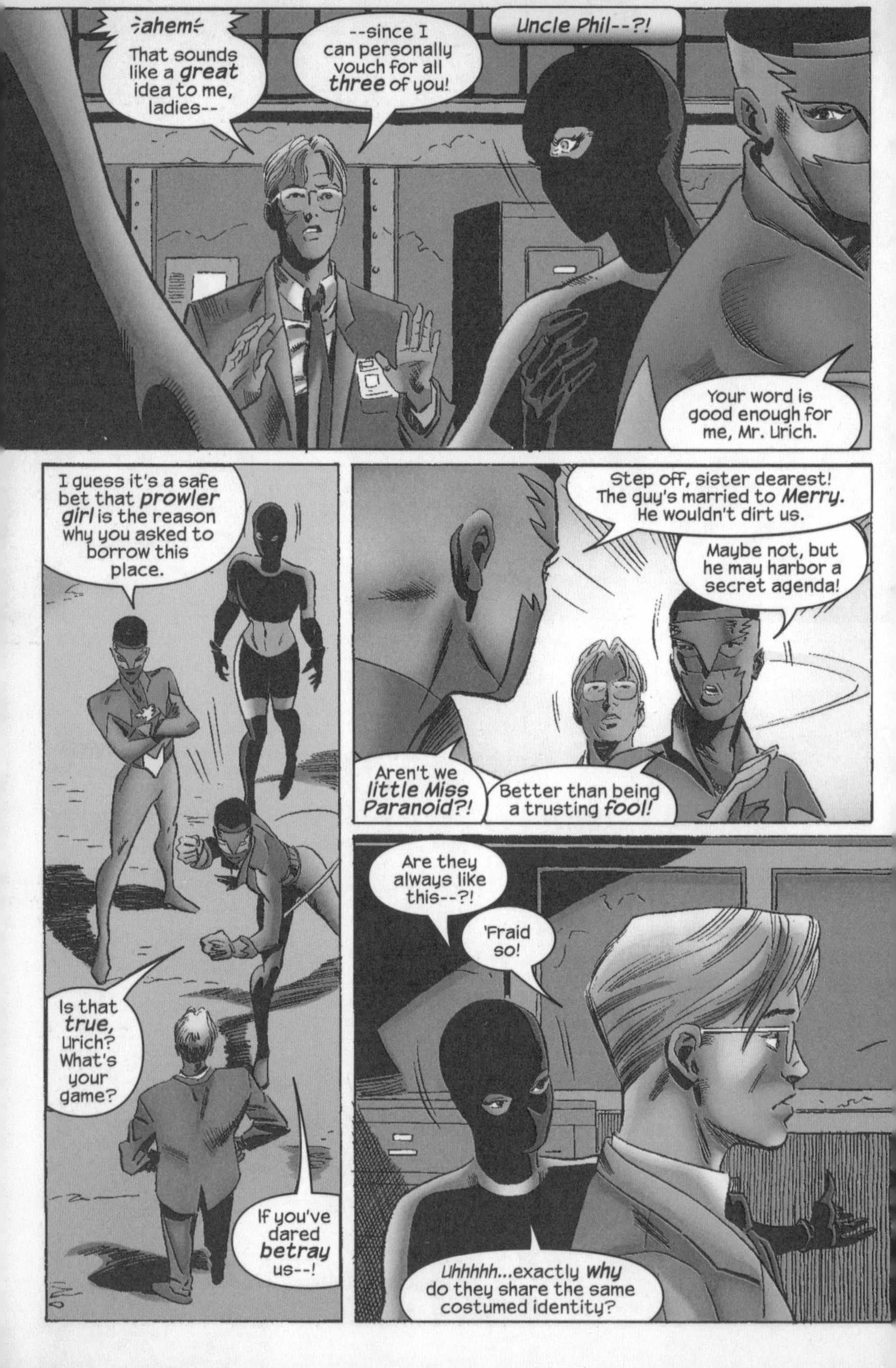

ahem
That sounds like a great idea to me, ladies--
--since I can personally vouch for all three of you!
Uncle Phil--?!
Your word is good enough for me, Mr. Urich.
I guess it's a safe bet that prowler girl is the reason why you asked to borrow this place.
Is that true, Urich? What's your game?
If you've dared betray us--!
Step off, sister dearest! The guy's married to Merry. He wouldn't dirt us.
Maybe not, but he may harbor a secret agenda!
Aren't we little Miss Paranoid?!
Better than being a trusting fool!
Are they always like this--?!
'Fraid so!
Uhhhhh...exactly why do they share the same costumed identity?

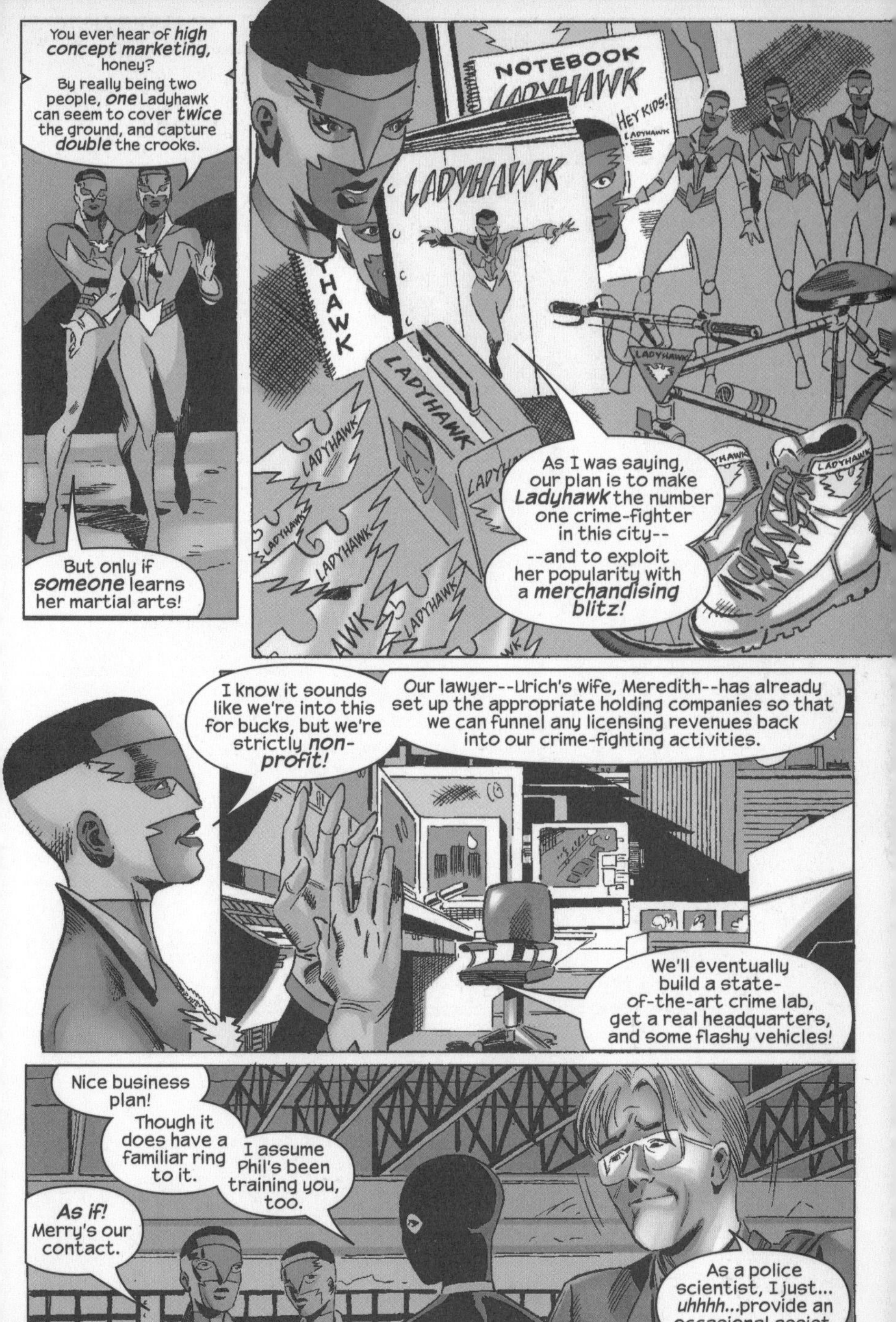
You ever hear of *high concept marketing,* honey?
By really being two people, *one* Ladyhawk can seem to cover *twice* the ground, and capture *double* the crooks.
But only if *someone* learns her martial arts!
NOTEBOOK LADYHAWK
HEY KIDS! LADYHAWK
LADYHAWK
YHAWK
LADYHAWK
As I was saying, our plan is to make *Ladyhawk* the number one crime-fighter in this city--
--and to exploit her popularity with a *merchandising blitz!*
I know it sounds like we're into this for bucks, but we're strictly *non-profit!*
Our lawyer--Urich's wife, Meredith--has already set up the appropriate holding companies so that we can funnel any licensing revenues back into our crime-fighting activities.
We'll eventually build a state-of-the-art crime lab, get a real headquarters, and some flashy vehicles!
Nice business plan!
Though it does have a familiar ring to it.
I assume Phil's been training you, too.
As if! Merry's our contact.
As a police scientist, I just... *uhhhh*...provide an occasional assist.

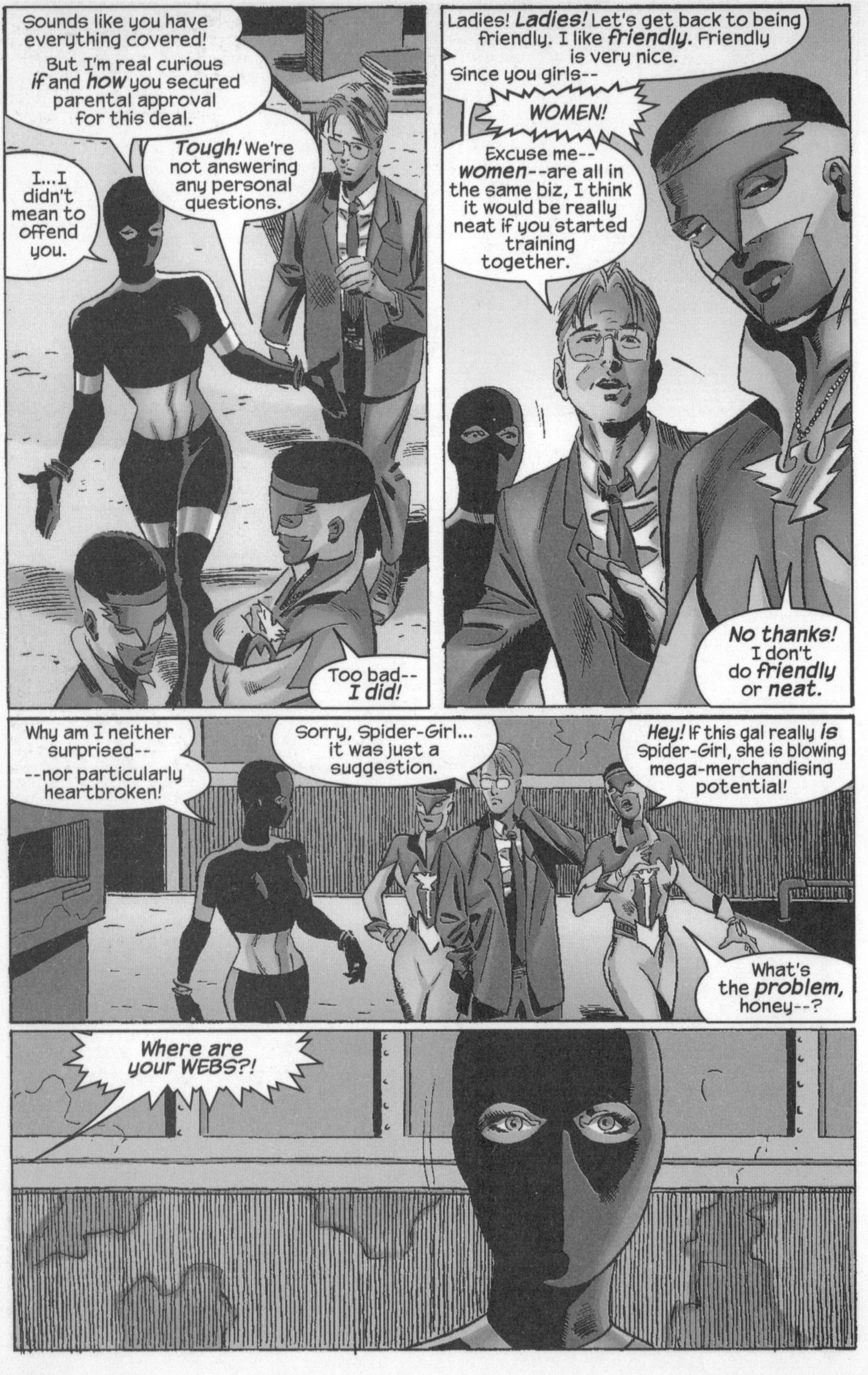
Sounds like you have everything covered!
But I'm real curious *if* and *how* you secured parental approval for this deal.
Tough! We're not answering any personal questions.
I...I didn't mean to offend you.
Too bad-- I did!
Ladies! *Ladies!* Let's get back to being friendly. I like *friendly*. Friendly is very nice.
Since you girls--
WOMEN!
Excuse me-- *women*--are all in the same biz, I think it would be really neat if you started training together.
No thanks! I don't do *friendly* or *neat*.
Why am I neither surprised--
--nor particularly heartbroken!
Sorry, Spider-Girl... it was just a suggestion.
Hey! If this gal really *is* Spider-Girl, she is blowing mega-merchandising potential!
What's the *problem*, honey--?
Where are your WEBS?!

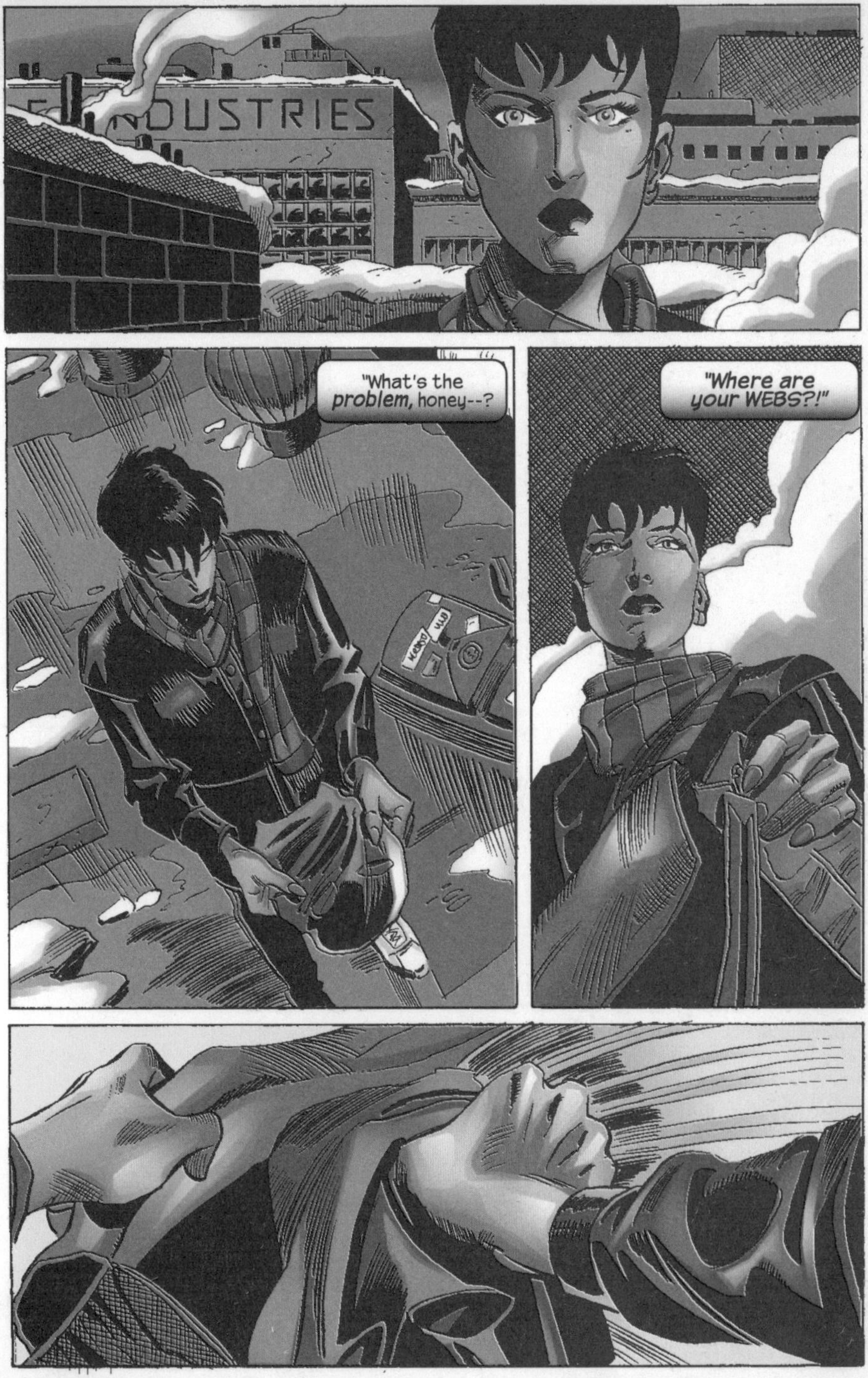

INDUSTRIES
"What's the *problem,* honey--?
"Where are your WEBS?!"

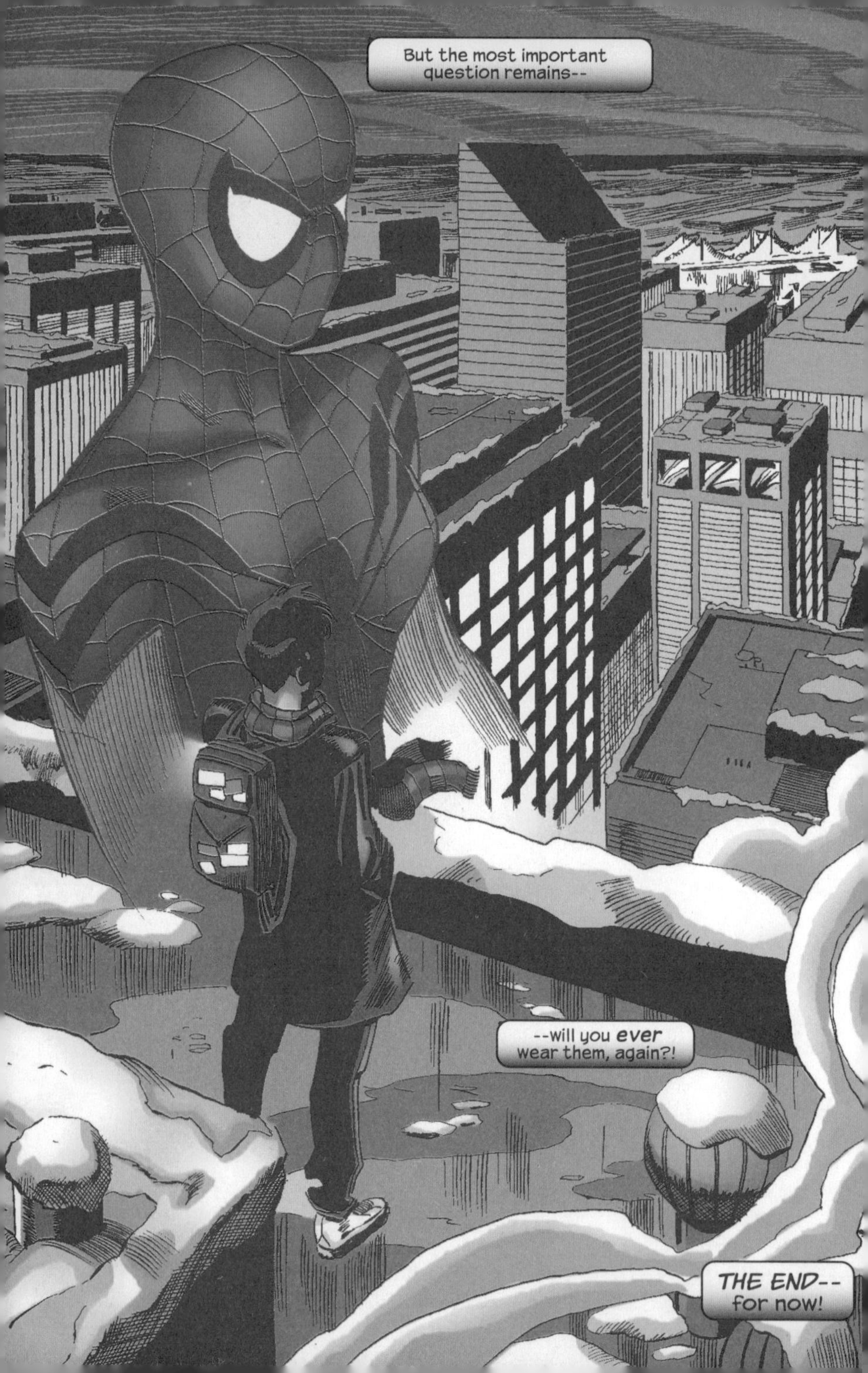
But the most important question remains--
--will you *ever* wear them, again?!
THE END-- for now!

MARVEL COMICS
THE DAUGHTER OF THE TRUE SPIDER-MAN!
SPIDER-GIRL
APR #7
YOU MAY HAVE FOUND A WAY TO DEFEAT DARKDEVIL, YOUNG MISSY--
--BUT YOU'LL NEVER BEAT THE MAN CALLED NOVA!
FOR RENT
"YOUNG MISSY"--!
WHAT A JERK!
WWW.MARVEL.COM
BONUS FEATURE! "THE LAST DAYS OF SPIDER-MAN!"
DEFALCO
OLLIFFE
WILLIAMSON

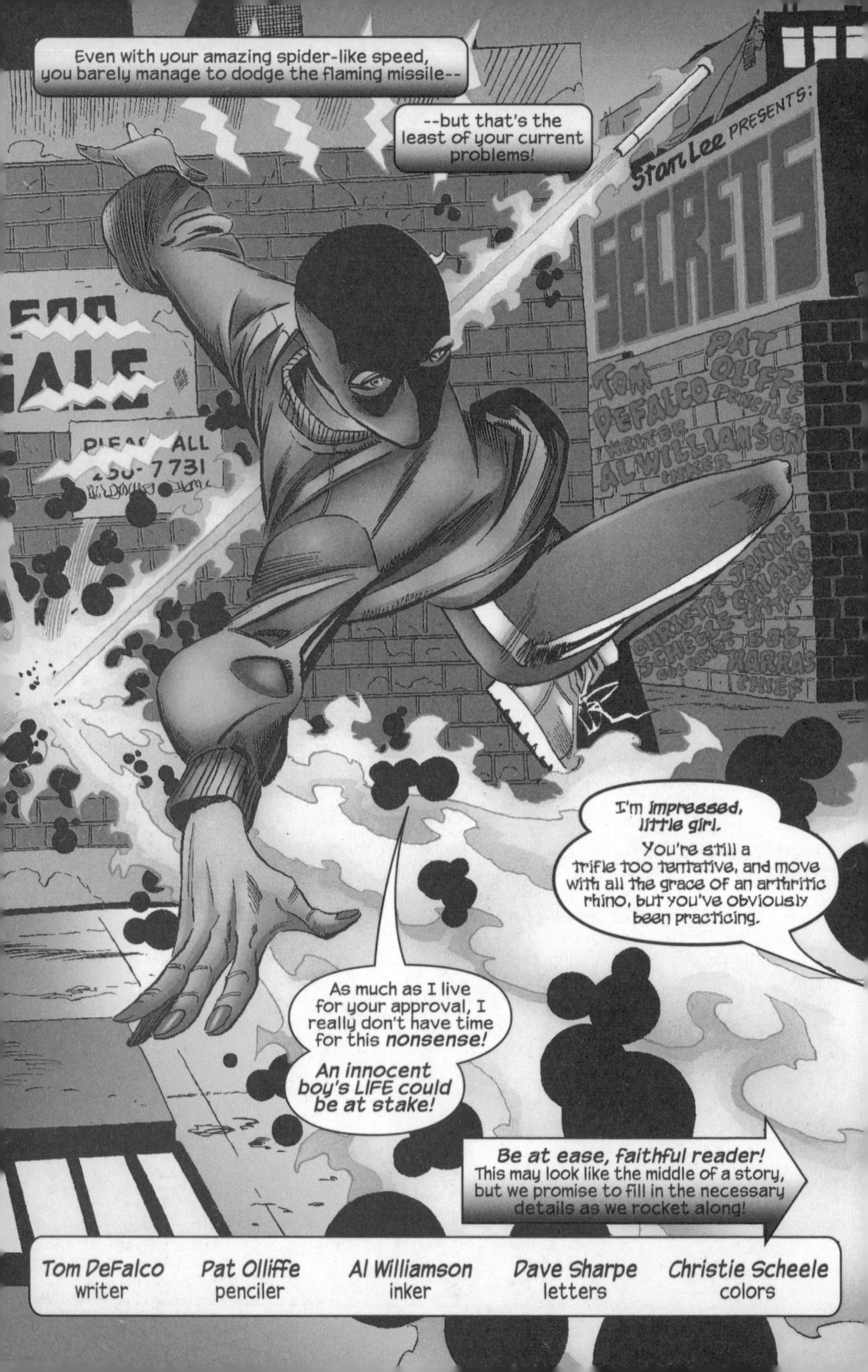
Even with your amazing spider-like speed, you barely manage to dodge the flaming missile--
--but that's the least of your current problems!
Stan Lee PRESENTS:
SECRETS
I'm impressed, little girl.
You're still a trifle too tentative, and move with all the grace of an arthritic rhino, but you've obviously been practicing.
As much as I live for your approval, I really don't have time for this nonsense!
An innocent boy's LIFE could be at stake!
Be at ease, faithful reader! This may look like the middle of a story, but we promise to fill in the necessary details as we rocket along!
Tom DeFalco writer
Pat Olliffe penciler
Al Williamson inker
Dave Sharpe letters
Christie Scheele colors

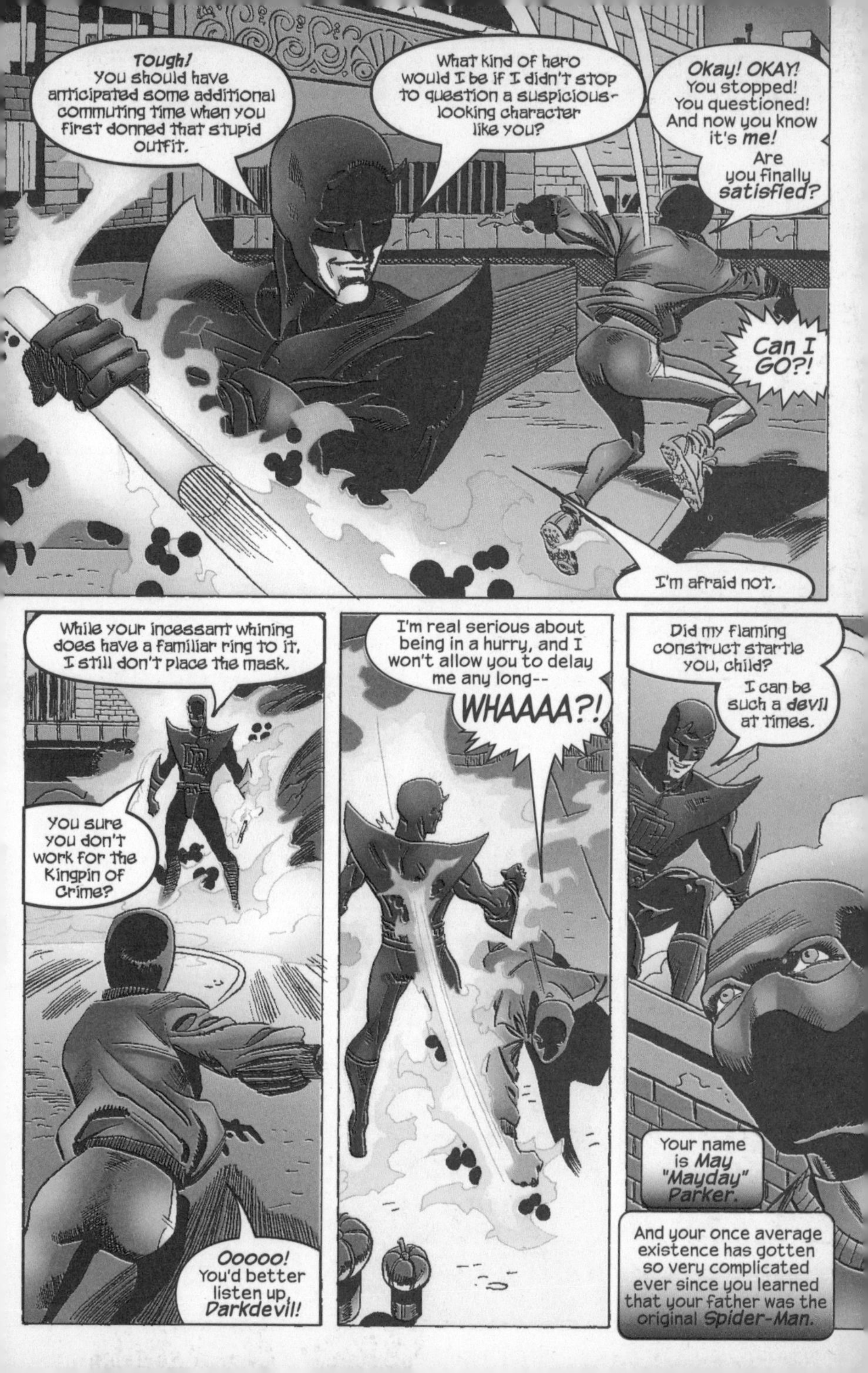

Tough! You should have anticipated some additional commuting time when you first donned that stupid outfit.
What kind of hero would I be if I didn't stop to question a suspicious-looking character like you?
Okay! OKAY! You stopped! You questioned! And now you know it's me!
Are you finally satisfied?
Can I GO?!
I'm afraid not.
While your incessant whining does have a familiar ring to it, I still don't place the mask.
You sure you don't work for the Kingpin of Crime?
Ooooo! You'd better listen up, Darkdevil!
I'm real serious about being in a hurry, and I won't allow you to delay me any long--
WHAAAA?!
Did my flaming construct startle you, child?
I can be such a devil at times.
Your name is May "Mayday" Parker.
And your once average existence has gotten so very complicated ever since you learned that your father was the original Spider-Man.

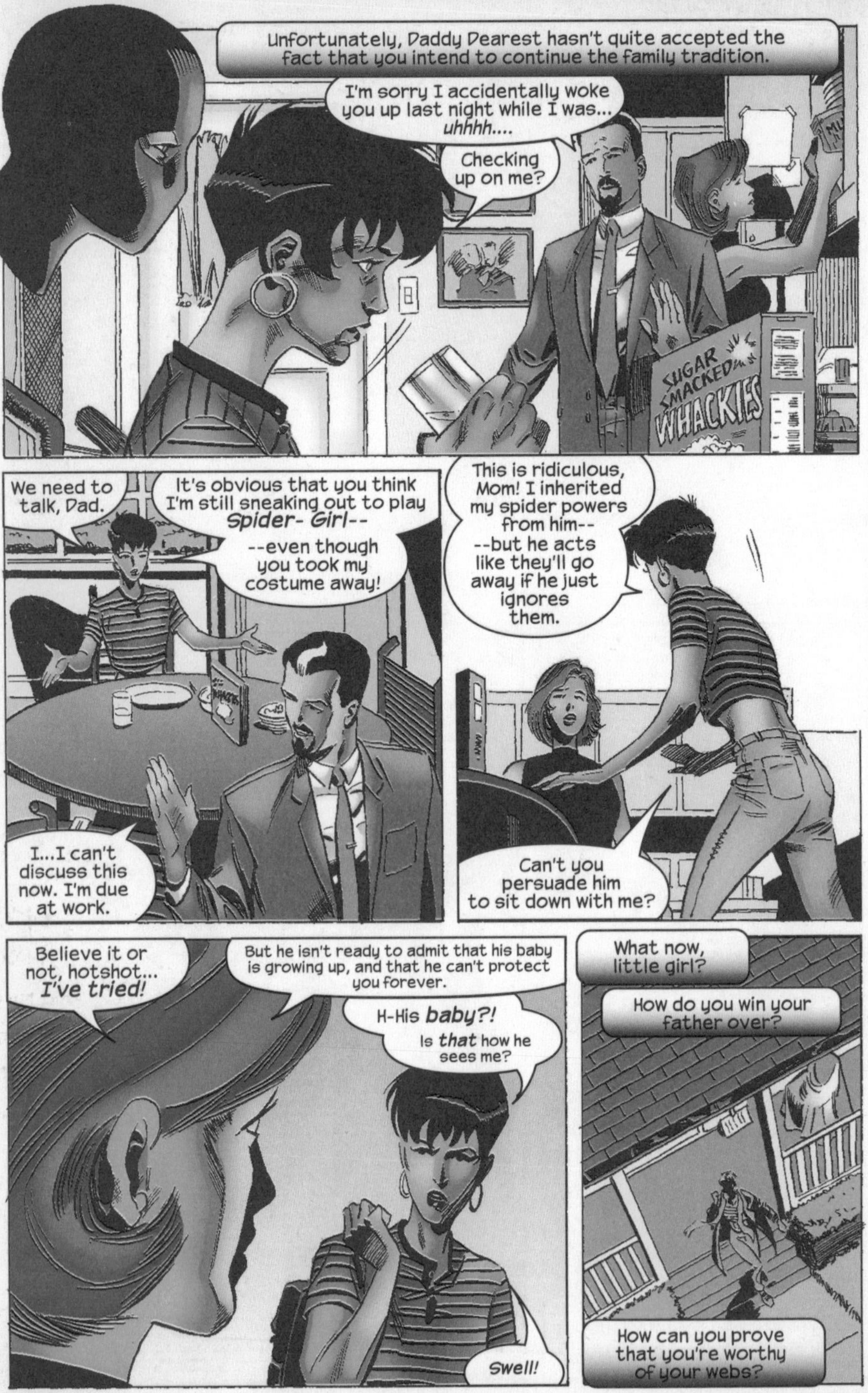
Unfortunately, Daddy Dearest hasn't quite accepted the fact that you intend to continue the family tradition.
I'm sorry I accidentally woke you up last night while I was... uhhhh....
Checking up on me?
SUGAR SMACKED WHACKIES
We need to talk, Dad.
It's obvious that you think I'm still sneaking out to play Spider- Girl--
--even though you took my costume away!
I...I can't discuss this now. I'm due at work.
This is ridiculous, Mom! I inherited my spider powers from him--
--but he acts like they'll go away if he just ignores them.
Can't you persuade him to sit down with me?
Believe it or not, hotshot... I've tried!
But he isn't ready to admit that his baby is growing up, and that he can't protect you forever.
H-His baby?!
Is that how he sees me?
Swell!
What now, little girl?
How do you win your father over?
How can you prove that you're worthy of your webs?

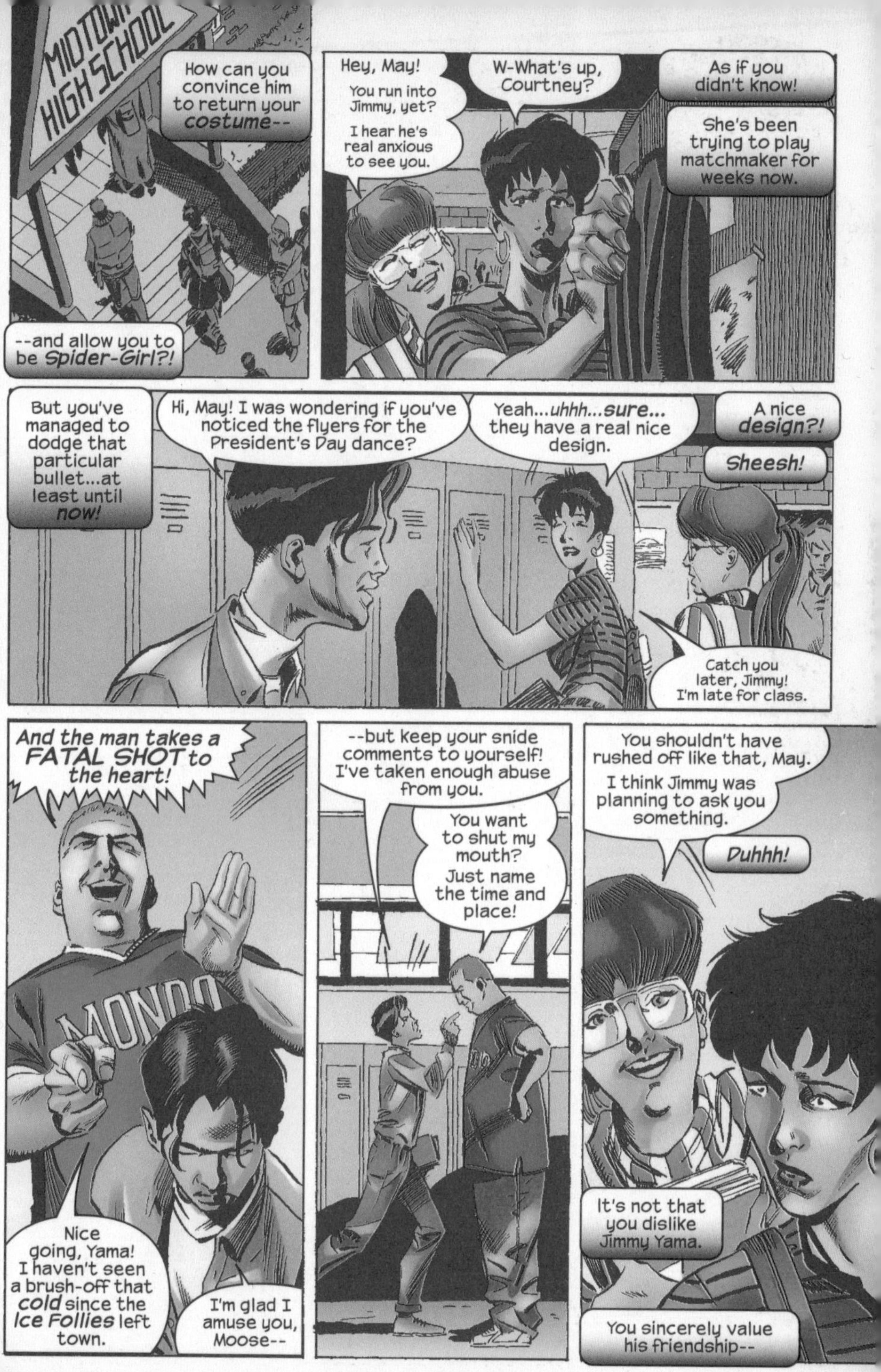
MIDTOWN HIGH SCHOOL
How can you convince him to return your costume--
--and allow you to be Spider-Girl?!
Hey, May! You run into Jimmy, yet? I hear he's real anxious to see you.
W-What's up, Courtney?
As if you didn't know!
She's been trying to play matchmaker for weeks now.
But you've managed to dodge that particular bullet...at least until now!
Hi, May! I was wondering if you've noticed the flyers for the President's Day dance?
Yeah...uhhh...sure... they have a real nice design.
A nice design?!
Sheesh!
Catch you later, Jimmy! I'm late for class.
And the man takes a FATAL SHOT to the heart!
Nice going, Yama! I haven't seen a brush-off that cold since the Ice Follies left town.
I'm glad I amuse you, Moose--
--but keep your snide comments to yourself! I've taken enough abuse from you.
You want to shut my mouth? Just name the time and place!
You shouldn't have rushed off like that, May.
I think Jimmy was planning to ask you something.
Duhhh!
It's not that you dislike Jimmy Yama.
You sincerely value his friendship--

TWAKK!

SNAP!

--but snagging a date for the school dance isn't exactly your highest priority!

Not when you have to prepare for another afternoon *training session* with your Uncle Phil!

One minute, thirty-two seconds...and you got the baby.

Your timing is improving, but you only scored four saves out of ten--

--and that includes the time you dropped the doll.

Still got a way to go, huh?

For practice, you're doing okay.

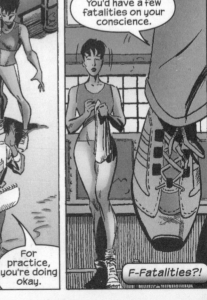

But, if this were actual fieldwork...

You'd have a few fatalities on your conscience.

F-Fatalities?!

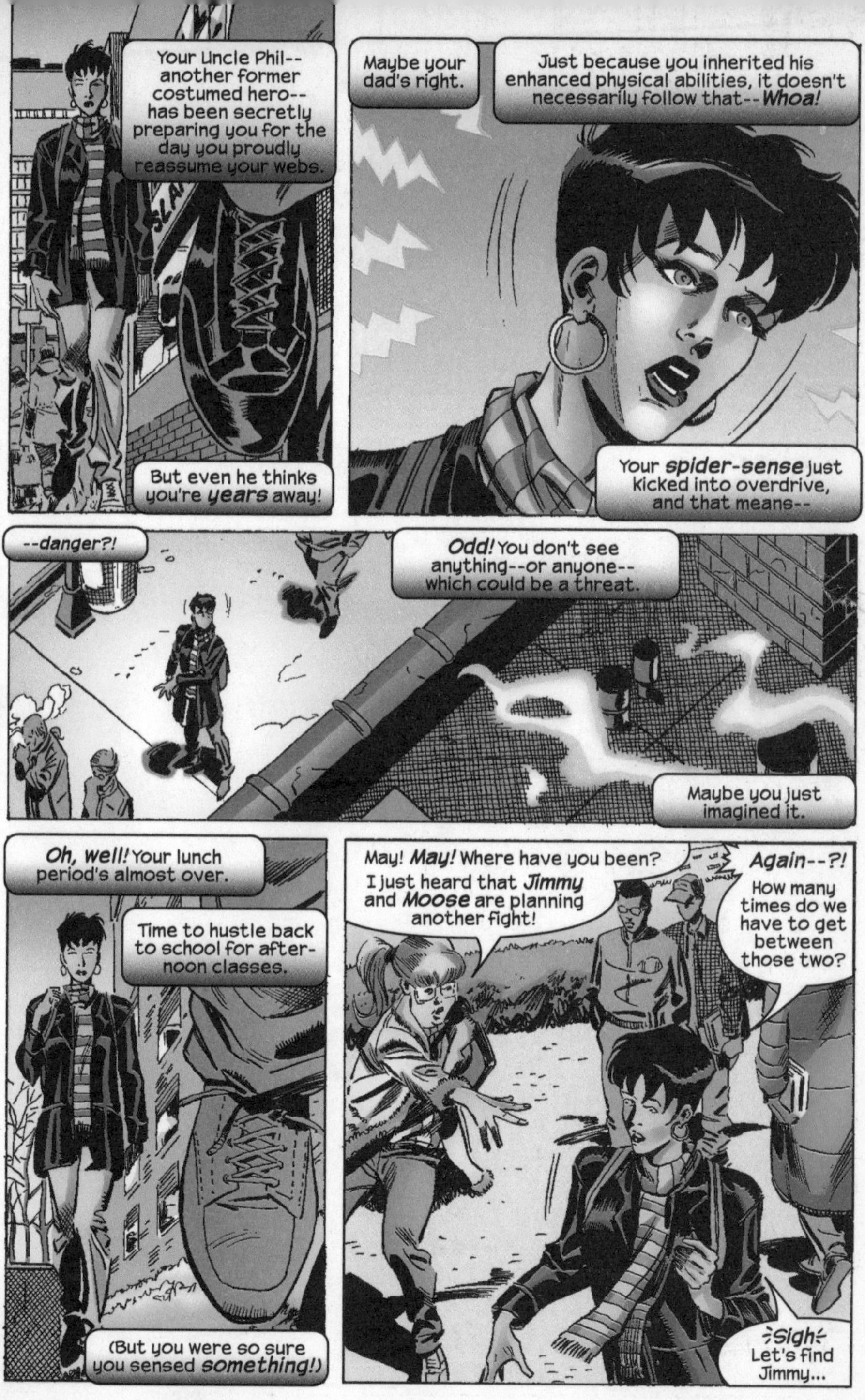

Your Uncle Phil--another former costumed hero--has been secretly preparing you for the day you proudly reassume your webs.
But even he thinks you're *years* away!
Maybe your dad's right.
Just because you inherited his enhanced physical abilities, it doesn't necessarily follow that--*Whoa!*
Your *spider-sense* just kicked into overdrive, and that means--
--*danger?!*
Odd! You don't see anything--or anyone--which could be a threat.
Maybe you just imagined it.
Oh, well! Your lunch period's almost over.
Time to hustle back to school for afternoon classes.
(But you were so sure you sensed *something!*)
May! *May!* Where have you been? I just heard that *Jimmy* and *Moose* are planning another fight!
Again--?! How many times do we have to get between those two?
Sigh Let's find Jimmy...

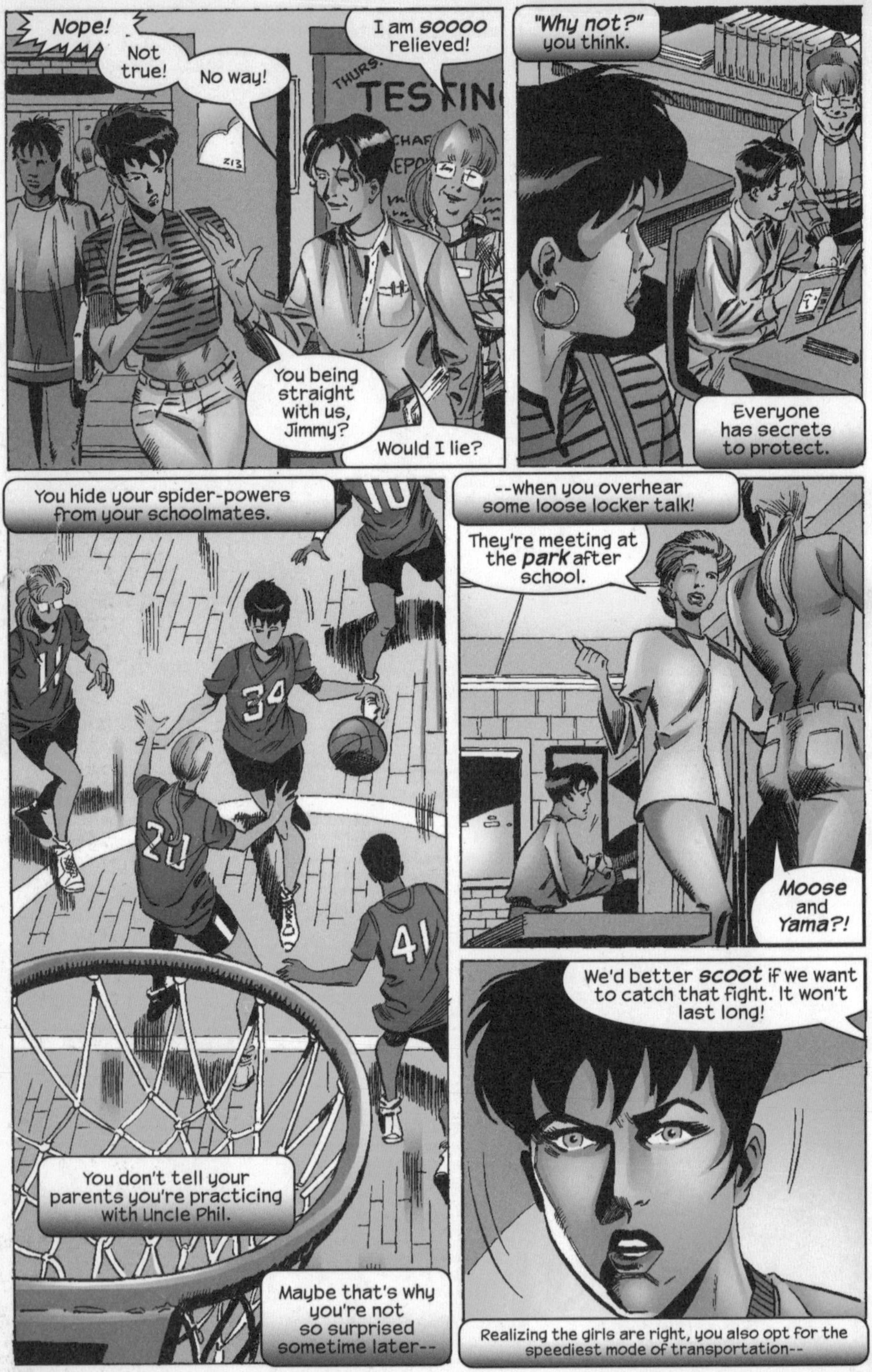
Nope!
Not true!
No way!
I am soooo relieved!
THURS. TESTING
You being straight with us, Jimmy?
Would I lie?
"Why not?" you think.
Everyone has secrets to protect.
You hide your spider-powers from your schoolmates.
You don't tell your parents you're practicing with Uncle Phil.
Maybe that's why you're not so surprised sometime later--
--when you overhear some loose locker talk!
They're meeting at the park after school.
Moose and Yama?!
We'd better scoot if we want to catch that fight. It won't last long!
Realizing the girls are right, you also opt for the speediest mode of transportation--

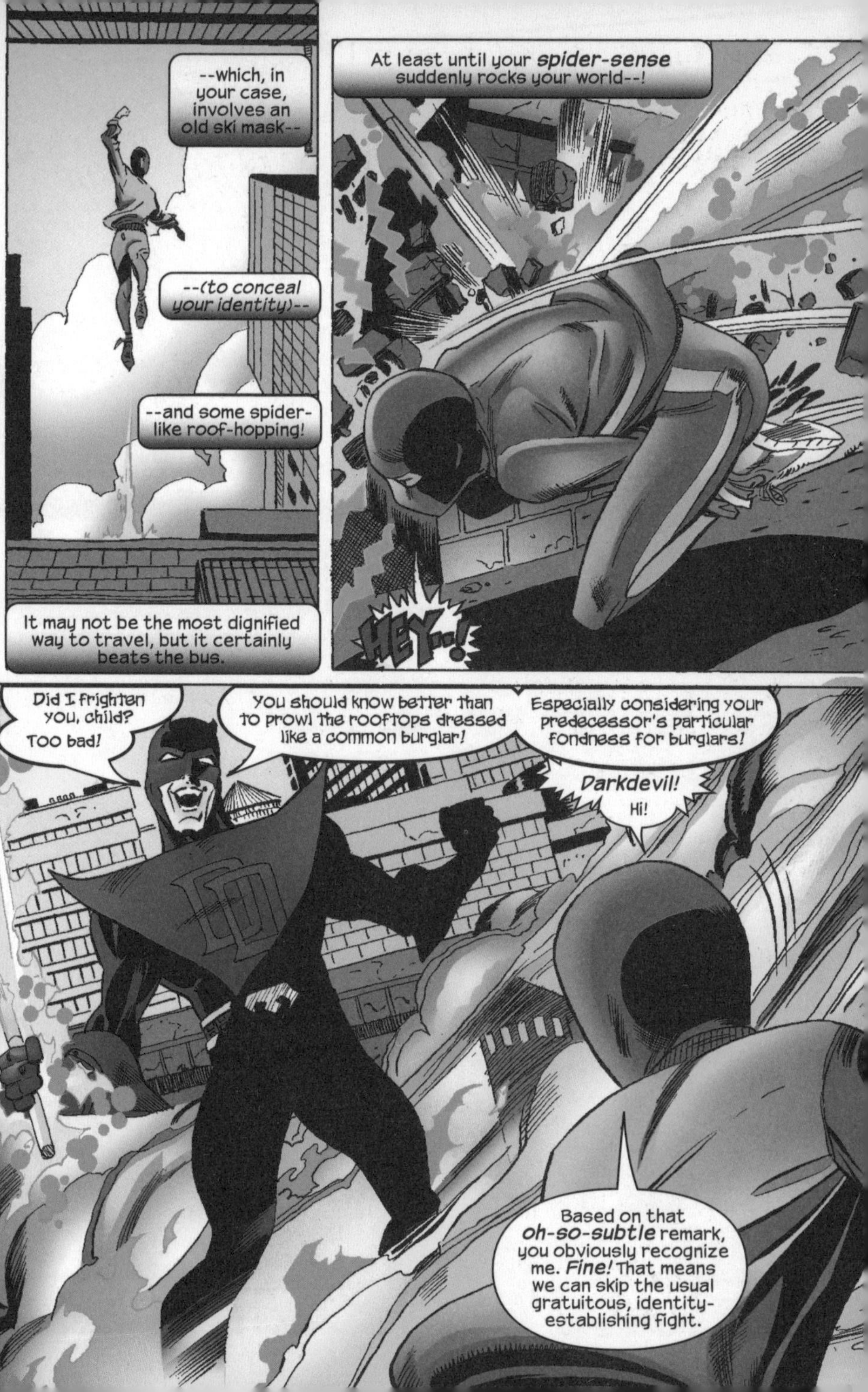
--which, in your case, involves an old ski mask--
--(to conceal your identity)--
--and some spider-like roof-hopping!
It may not be the most dignified way to travel, but it certainly beats the bus.
At least until your *spider-sense* suddenly rocks your world--!
HEY..!
Did I frighten you, child?
TOO bad!
You should know better than to prowl the rooftops dressed like a common burglar!
Especially considering your predecessor's particular fondness for burglars!
Darkdevil!
Hi!
Based on that *oh-so-subtle* remark, you obviously recognize me. *Fine!* That means we can skip the usual gratuitous, identity-establishing fight.

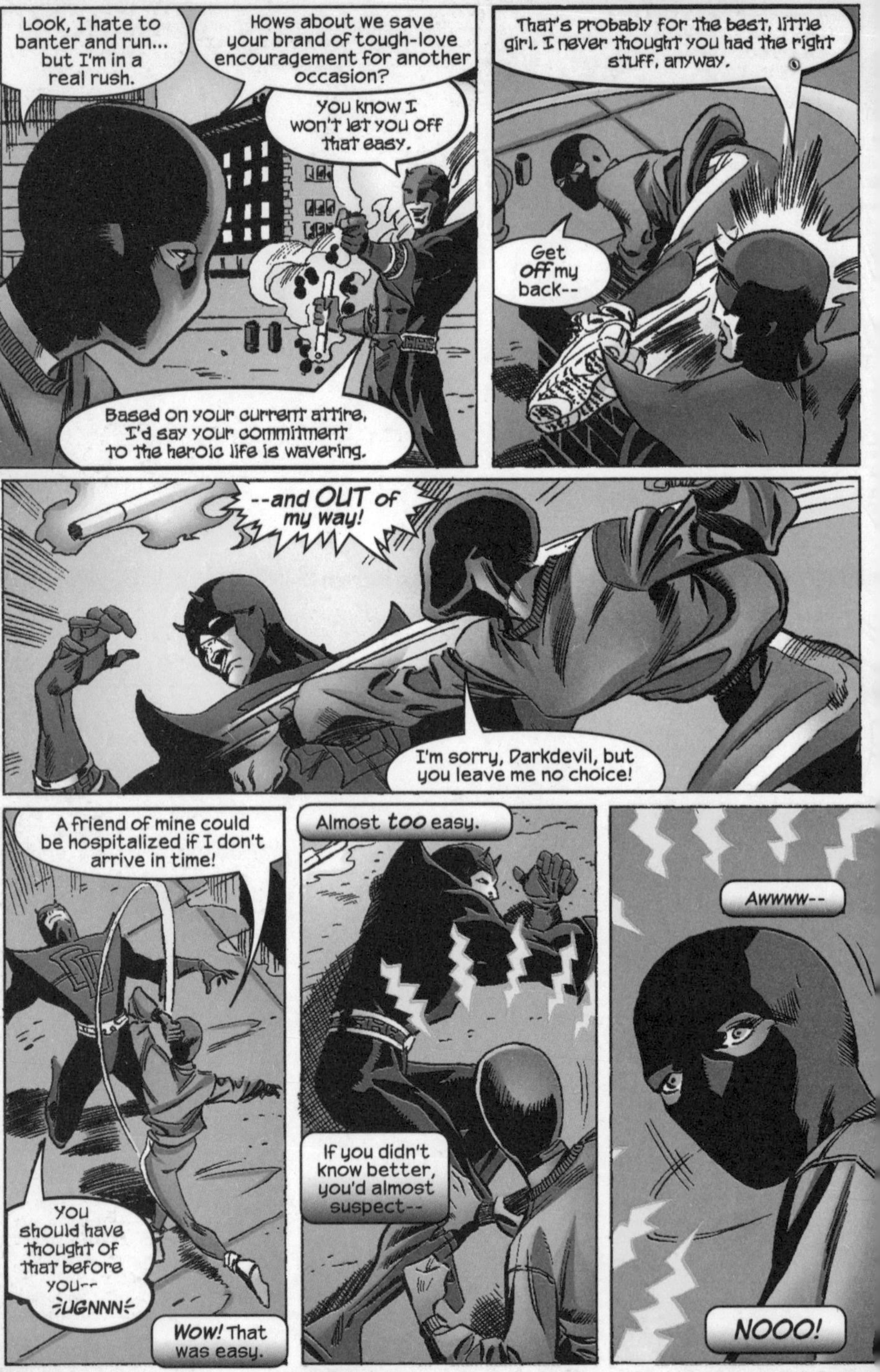
Look, I hate to banter and run... but I'm in a real rush.
Hows about we save your brand of tough-love encouragement for another occasion?
You know I won't let you off that easy.
Based on your current attire, I'd say your commitment to the heroic life is wavering.
That's probably for the best, little girl. I never thought you had the right stuff, anyway.
Get off my back--
--and OUT of my way!
I'm sorry, Darkdevil, but you leave me no choice!
A friend of mine could be hospitalized if I don't arrive in time!
You should have thought of that before you--
UGNNN
WOW! That was easy.
Almost too easy.
If you didn't know better, you'd almost suspect--
Awwww--
NOOO!

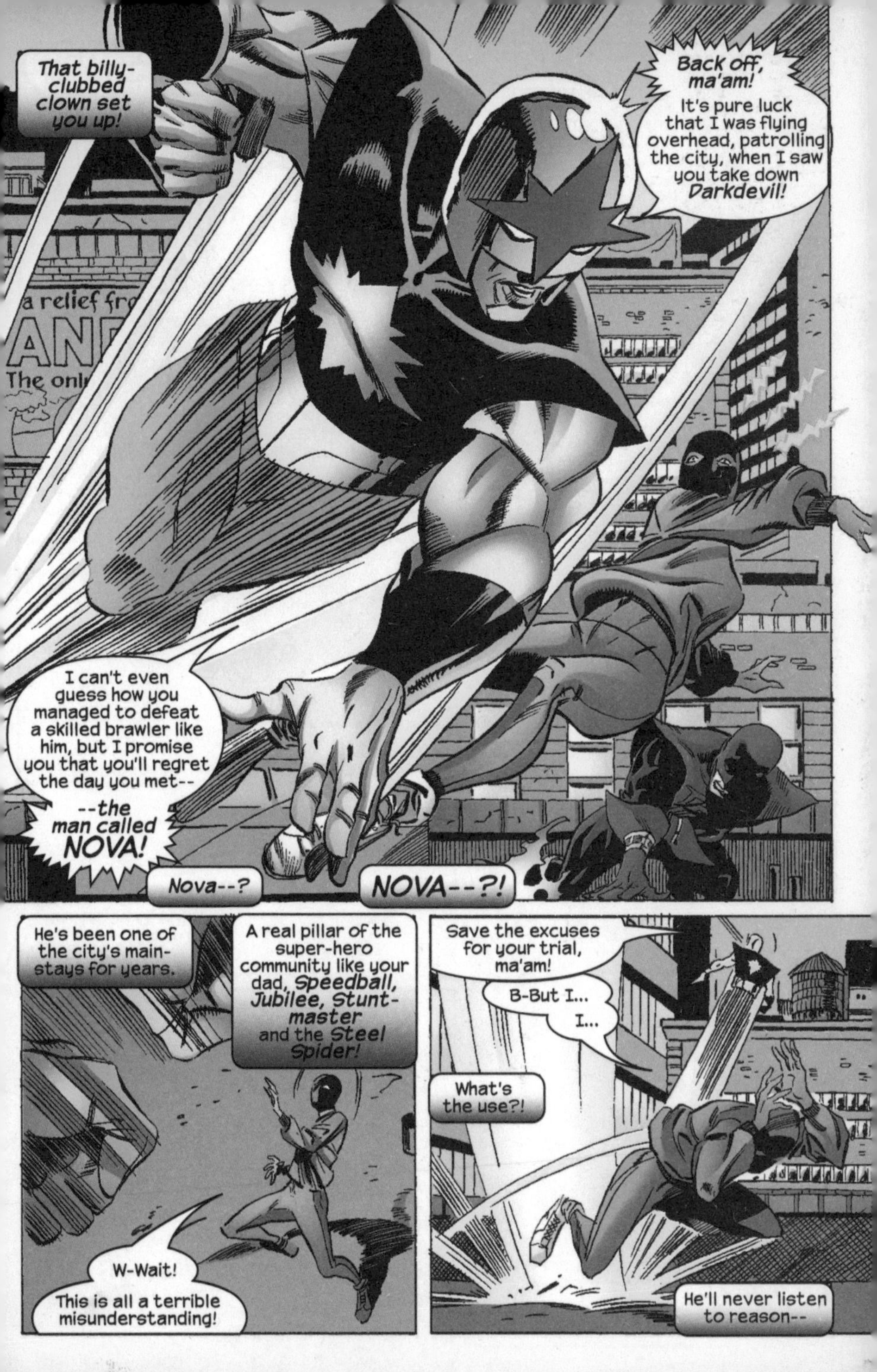
That billy-clubbed clown set you up!
Back off, ma'am!
It's pure luck that I was flying overhead, patrolling the city, when I saw you take down Darkdevil!
a relief fr
AN
The onl
I can't even guess how you managed to defeat a skilled brawler like him, but I promise you that you'll regret the day you met--
--the man called NOVA!
Nova--?
NOVA--?!
He's been one of the city's main-stays for years.
A real pillar of the super-hero community like your dad, Speedball, Jubilee, Stunt-master and the Steel Spider!
W-Wait!
This is all a terrible misunderstanding!
Save the excuses for your trial, ma'am!
B-But I...
I...
What's the use?!
He'll never listen to reason--

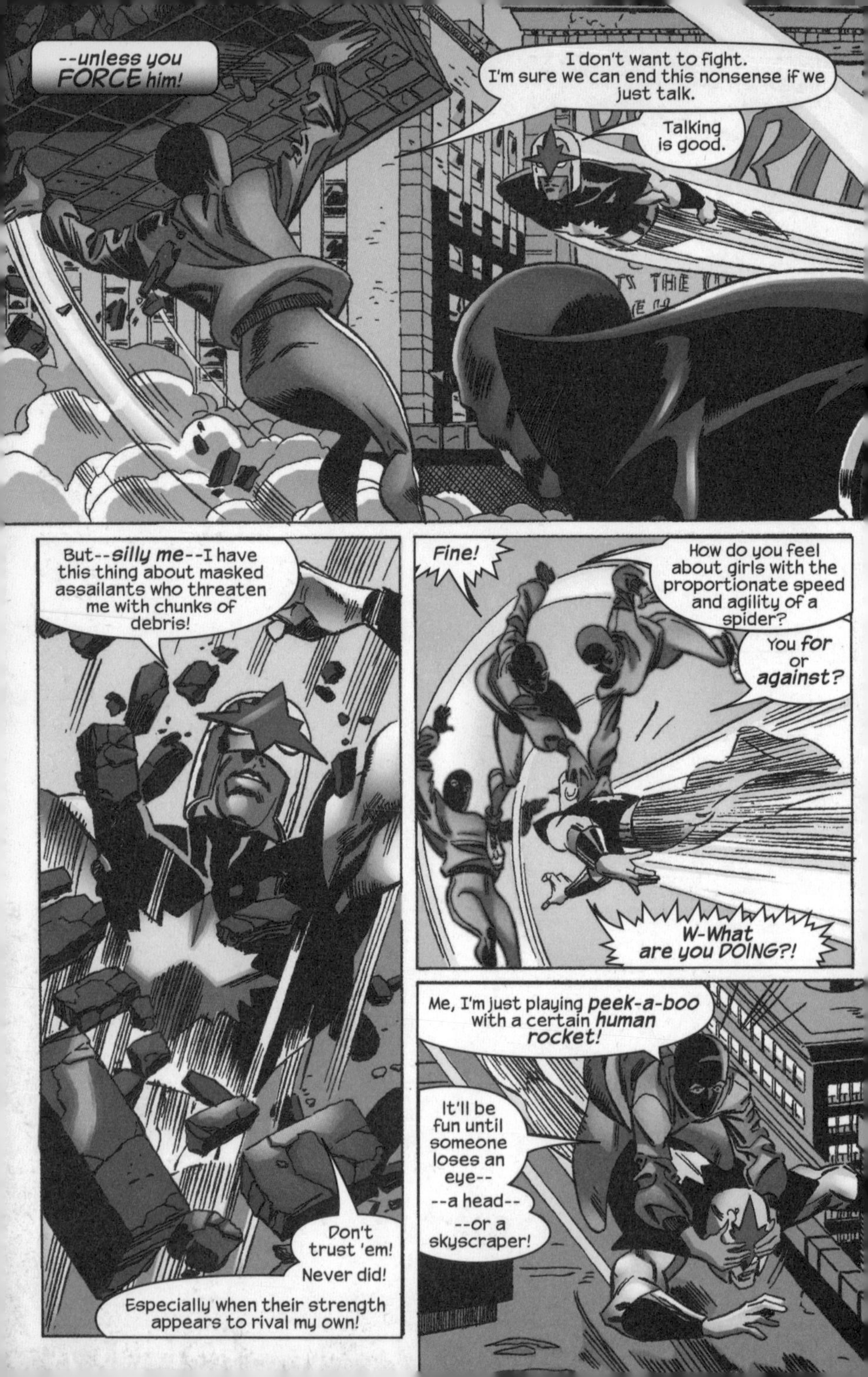
--unless you FORCE him!
I don't want to fight. I'm sure we can end this nonsense if we just talk.
Talking is good.
But--silly me--I have this thing about masked assailants who threaten me with chunks of debris!
Don't trust 'em!
Never did!
Especially when their strength appears to rival my own!
Fine!
How do you feel about girls with the proportionate speed and agility of a spider?
You for or against?
W-What are you DOING?!
Me, I'm just playing peek-a-boo with a certain human rocket!
It'll be fun until someone loses an eye--
--a head--
--or a skyscraper!

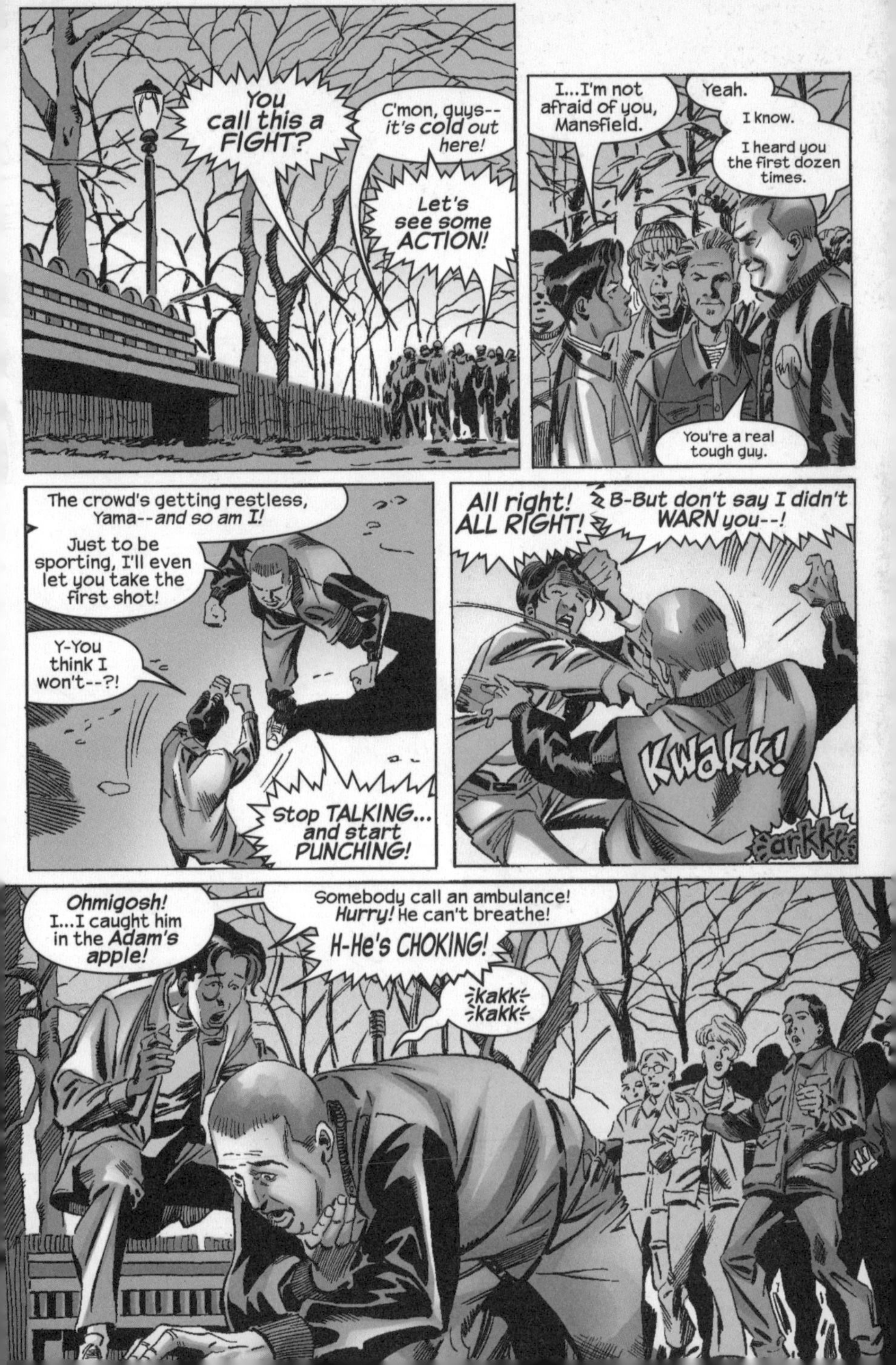
You call this a FIGHT?
C'mon, guys-- it's cold out here!
Let's see some ACTION!
I...I'm not afraid of you, Mansfield.
Yeah.
I know.
I heard you the first dozen times.
You're a real tough guy.
The crowd's getting restless, Yama--and so am I!
Just to be sporting, I'll even let you take the first shot!
Y-You think I won't--?!
Stop TALKING... and start PUNCHING!
All right! ALL RIGHT!
B-But don't say I didn't WARN you--!
KWAKK!
Ohmigosh! I...I caught him in the Adam's apple!
Somebody call an ambulance! Hurry! He can't breathe!
H-He's CHOKING!
kakk kakk

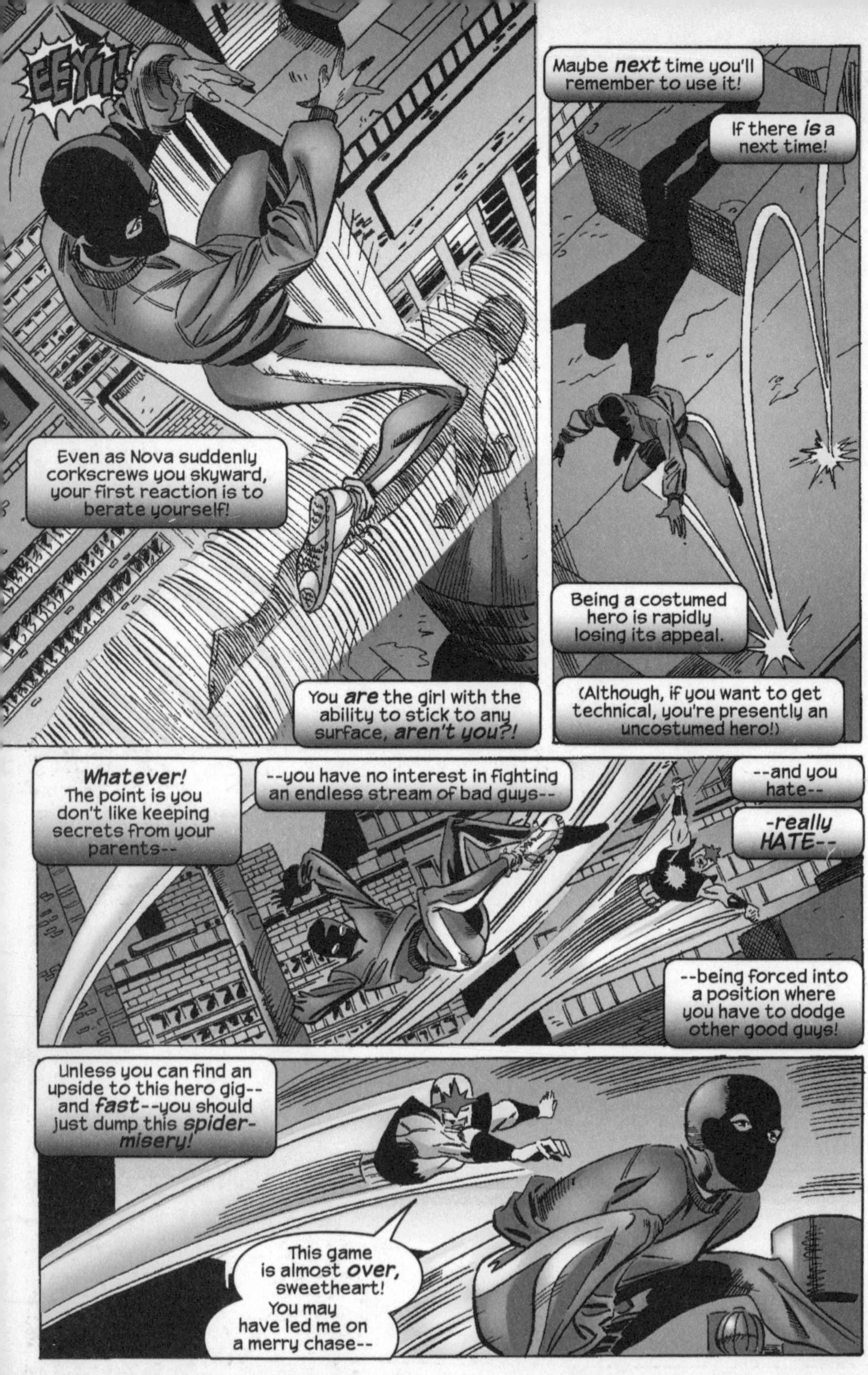
EEYII!
Even as Nova suddenly corkscrews you skyward, your first reaction is to berate yourself!
You are the girl with the ability to stick to any surface, aren't you?!
Maybe next time you'll remember to use it!
If there is a next time!
Being a costumed hero is rapidly losing its appeal.
(Although, if you want to get technical, you're presently an uncostumed hero!)
Whatever! The point is you don't like keeping secrets from your parents--
--you have no interest in fighting an endless stream of bad guys--
--and you hate--
-really HATE--
--being forced into a position where you have to dodge other good guys!
Unless you can find an upside to this hero gig--and fast--you should just dump this spider-misery!
This game is almost over, sweetheart! You may have led me on a merry chase--

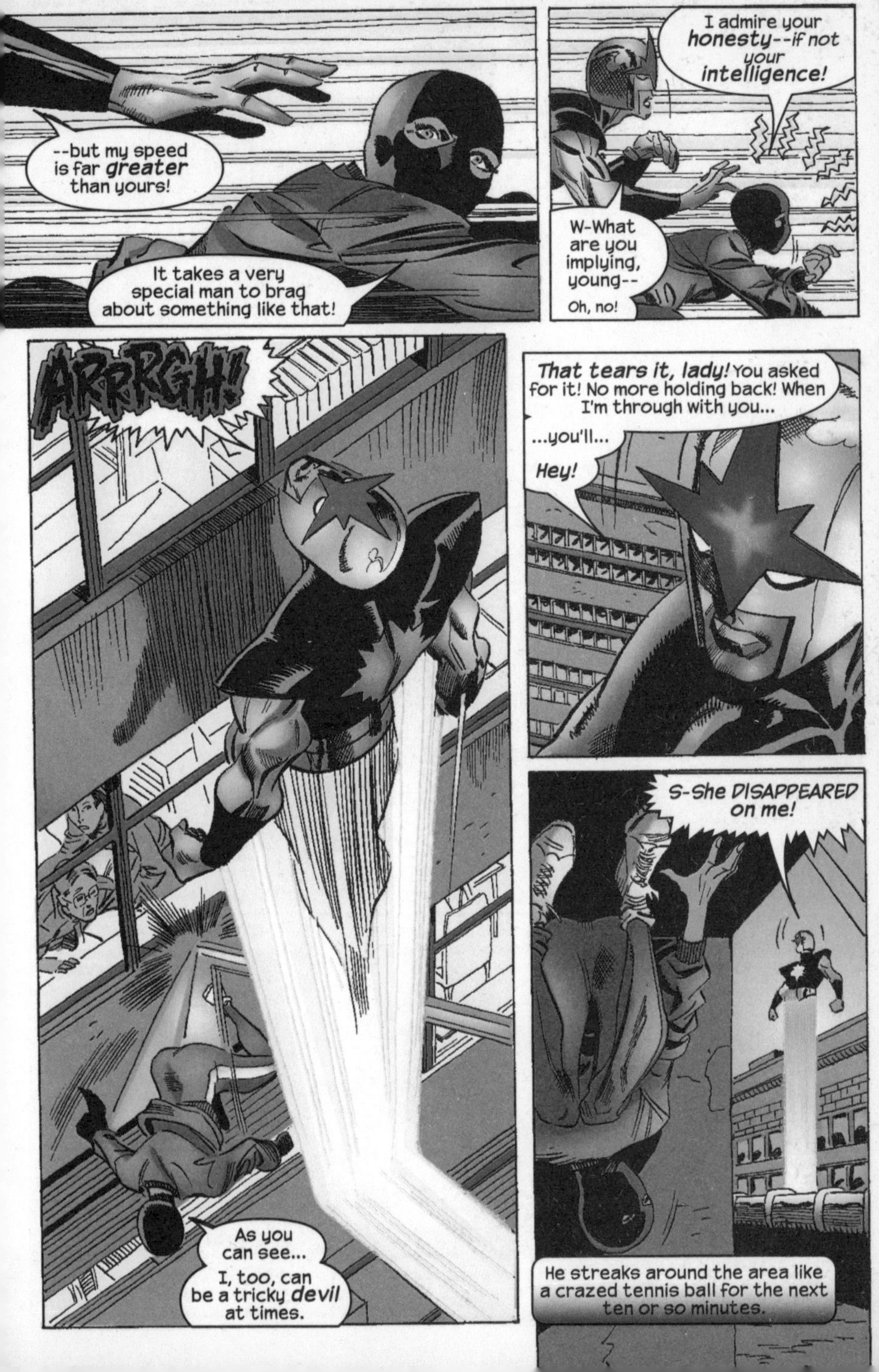

--but my speed is far greater than yours!
It takes a very special man to brag about something like that!
I admire your honesty--if not your intelligence!
W-What are you implying, young--
Oh, no!
ARRRGH!!
As you can see...
I, too, can be a tricky devil at times.
That tears it, lady! You asked for it! No more holding back! When I'm through with you...
...you'll...
Hey!
S-She DISAPPEARED on me!
He streaks around the area like a crazed tennis ball for the next ten or so minutes.

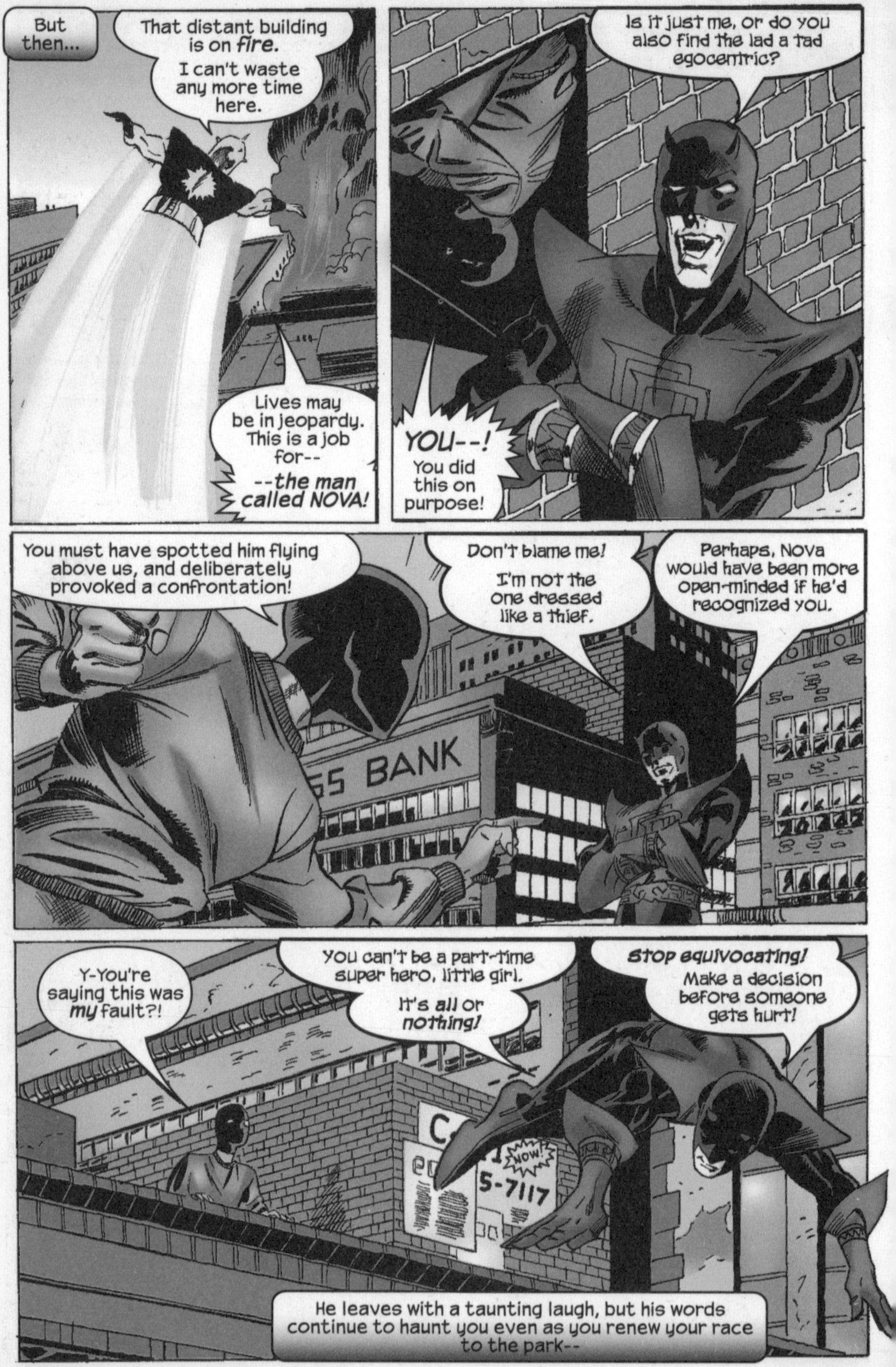
But then...
That distant building is on *fire.* I can't waste any more time here.
Lives may be in jeopardy. This is a job for--
--*the man called NOVA!*
Is it just me, or do you also find the lad a tad egocentric?
YOU--! You did this on purpose!
You must have spotted him flying above us, and deliberately provoked a confrontation!
Don't blame me! I'm not the one dressed like a thief.
Perhaps, Nova would have been more open-minded if he'd recognized you.
GS BANK
Y-You're saying this was *my* fault?!
You can't be a part-time super hero, little girl. It's *all* or *nothing!*
Stop equivocating! Make a decision before someone gets hurt!
NOW!
5-7117
He leaves with a taunting laugh, but his words continue to haunt you even as you renew your race to the park--

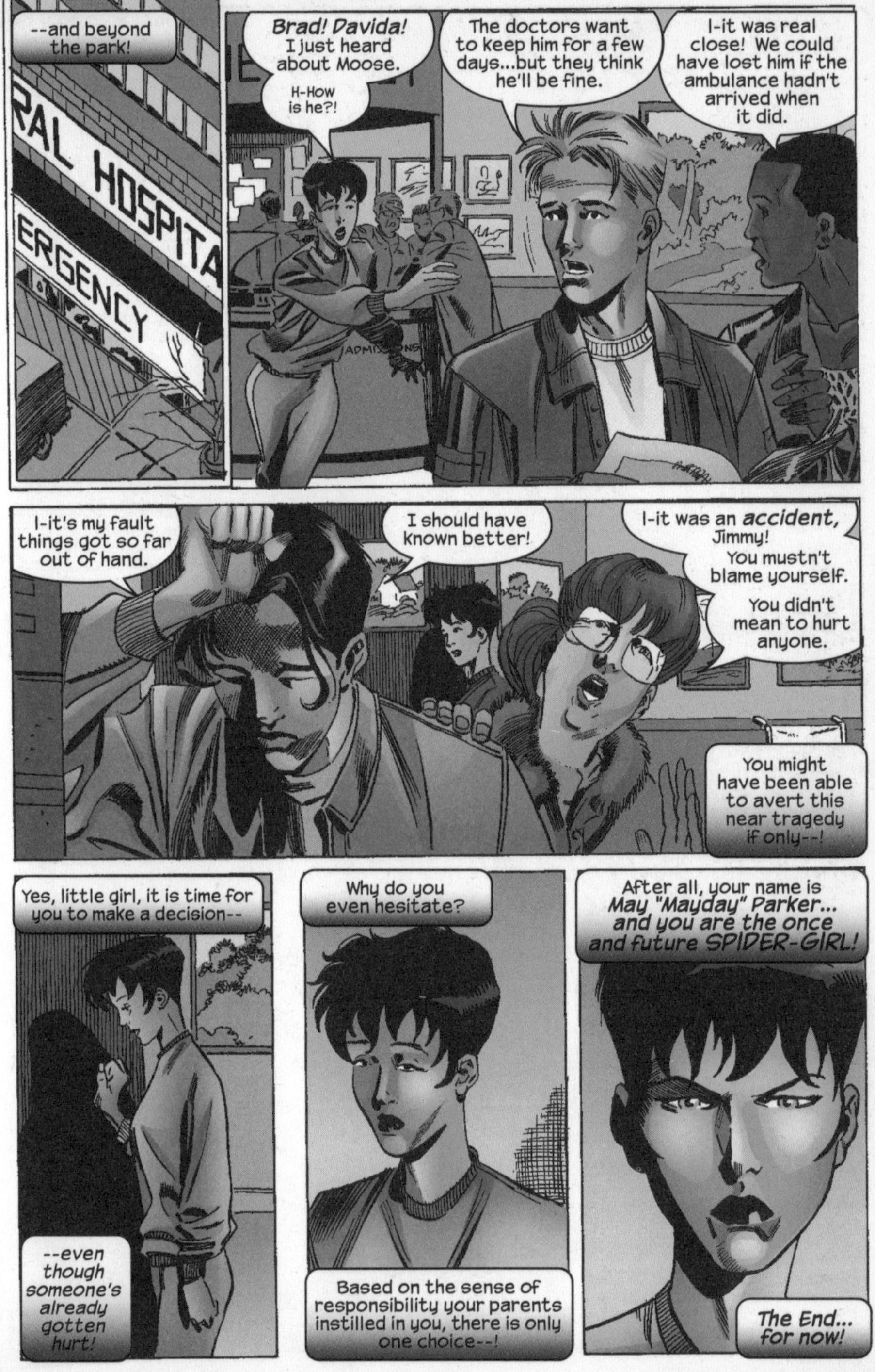

--and beyond the park!
RAL HOSPITA
ERGENCY
Brad! Davida! I just heard about Moose.
H-How is he?!
The doctors want to keep him for a few days...but they think he'll be fine.
I-it was real close! We could have lost him if the ambulance hadn't arrived when it did.
I-it's my fault things got so far out of hand.
I should have known better!
I-it was an accident, Jimmy!
You mustn't blame yourself.
You didn't mean to hurt anyone.
You might have been able to avert this near tragedy if only--!
Yes, little girl, it is time for you to make a decision--
--even though someone's already gotten hurt!
Why do you even hesitate?
Based on the sense of responsibility your parents instilled in you, there is only one choice--!
After all, your name is May "Mayday" Parker... and you are the once and future SPIDER-GIRL!
The End... for now!

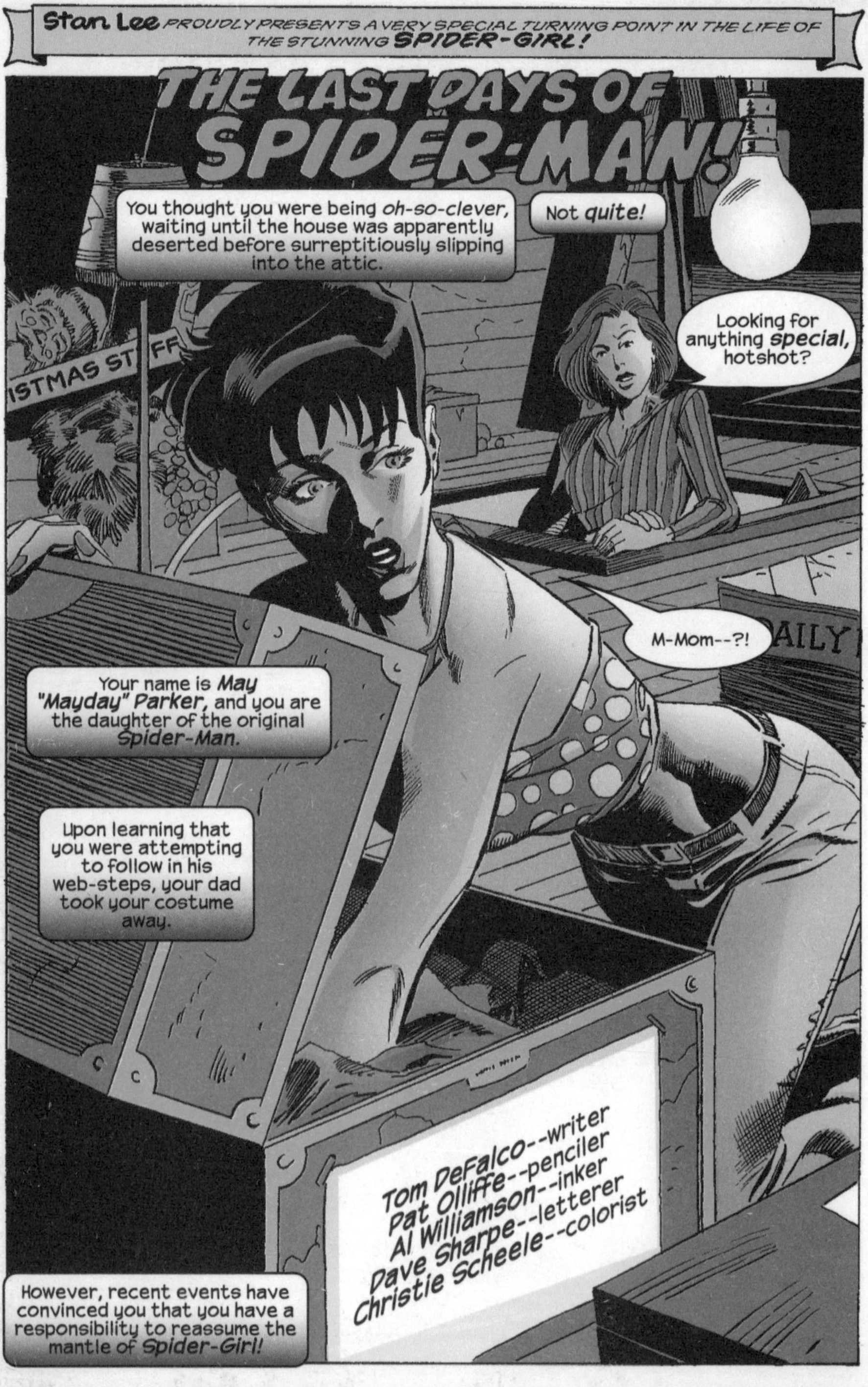

Stan Lee PROUDLY PRESENTS A VERY SPECIAL TURNING POINT IN THE LIFE OF THE STUNNING SPIDER-GIRL!
THE LAST DAYS OF SPIDER-MAN!
You thought you were being oh-so-clever, waiting until the house was apparently deserted before surreptitiously slipping into the attic.
Not quite!
Looking for anything special, hotshot?
ISTMAS STUFF
M-Mom--?!
AILY
Your name is May "Mayday" Parker, and you are the daughter of the original Spider-Man.
Upon learning that you were attempting to follow in his web-steps, your dad took your costume away.
Tom DeFalco--writer
Pat Olliffe--penciler
Al Williamson--inker
Dave Sharpe--letterer
Christie Scheele--colorist
However, recent events have convinced you that you have a responsibility to reassume the mantle of Spider-Girl!

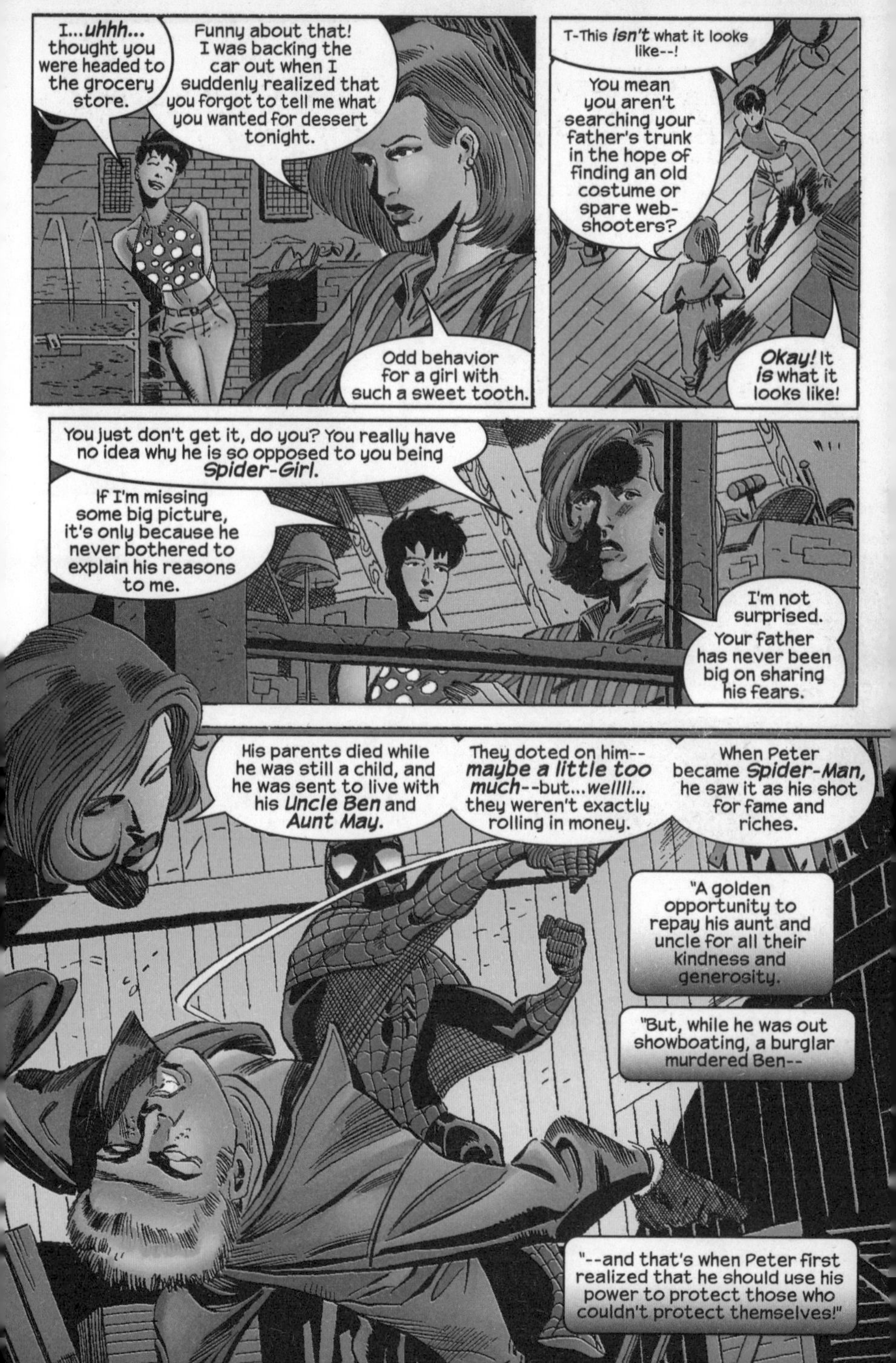
I...uhhh... thought you were headed to the grocery store.
Funny about that! I was backing the car out when I suddenly realized that you forgot to tell me what you wanted for dessert tonight.
Odd behavior for a girl with such a sweet tooth.
T-This isn't what it looks like--!
You mean you aren't searching your father's trunk in the hope of finding an old costume or spare web-shooters?
Okay! It is what it looks like!
You just don't get it, do you? You really have no idea why he is so opposed to you being Spider-Girl.
If I'm missing some big picture, it's only because he never bothered to explain his reasons to me.
I'm not surprised.
Your father has never been big on sharing his fears.
His parents died while he was still a child, and he was sent to live with his Uncle Ben and Aunt May.
They doted on him--maybe a little too much--but...wellll... they weren't exactly rolling in money.
When Peter became Spider-Man, he saw it as his shot for fame and riches.
"A golden opportunity to repay his aunt and uncle for all their kindness and generosity.
"But, while he was out showboating, a burglar murdered Ben--
"--and that's when Peter first realized that he should use his power to protect those who couldn't protect themselves!"

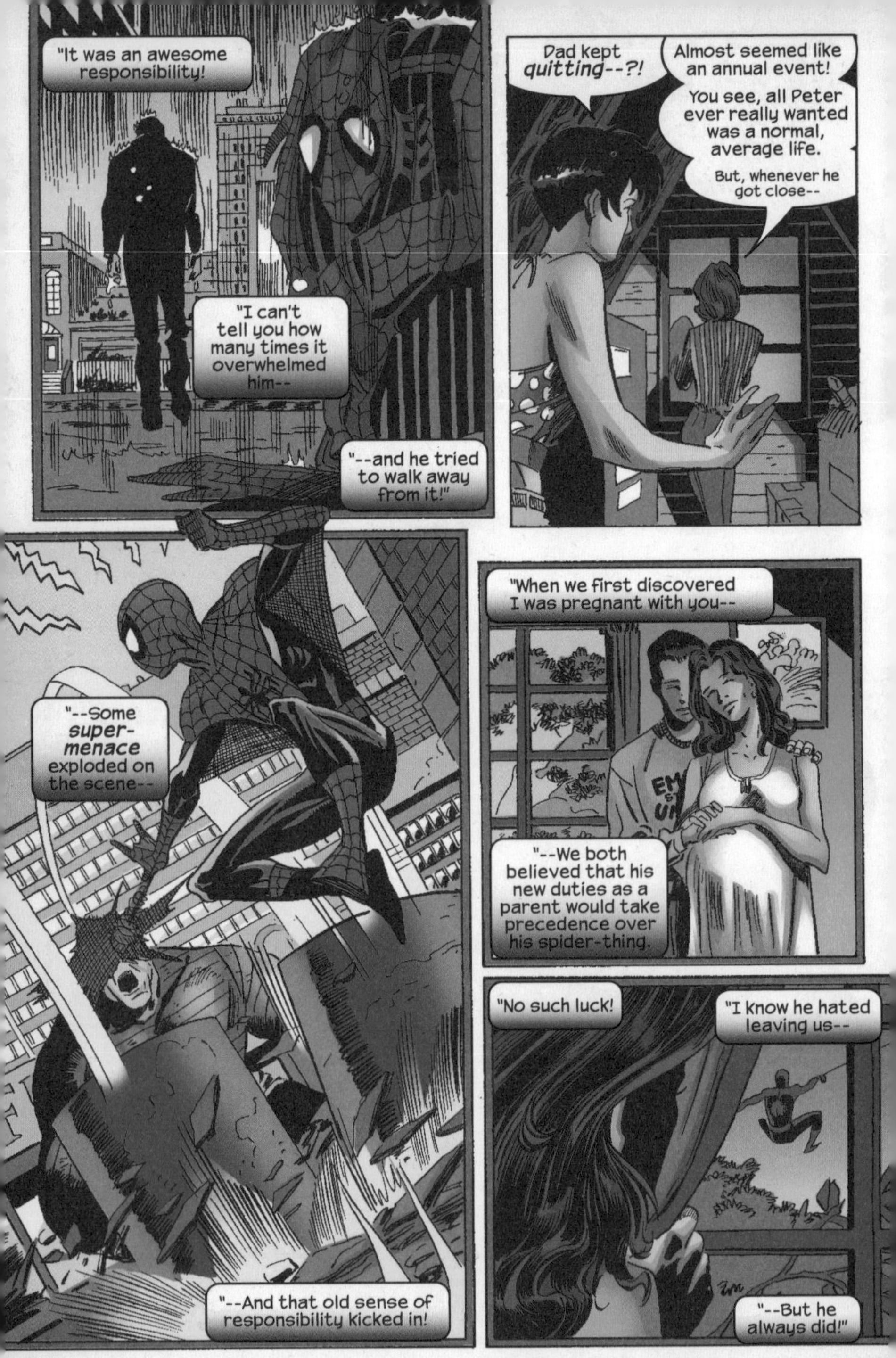
"It was an awesome responsibility!
"I can't tell you how many times it overwhelmed him--
"--and he tried to walk away from it!"
Dad kept *quitting*--?!
Almost seemed like an annual event!
You see, all Peter ever really wanted was a normal, average life.
But, whenever he got close--
"--Some *super-menace* exploded on the scene--
"--And that old sense of responsibility kicked in!
"When we first discovered I was pregnant with you--
"--We both believed that his new duties as a parent would take precedence over his spider-thing.
"No such luck!
"I know he hated leaving us--
"--But he always did!"

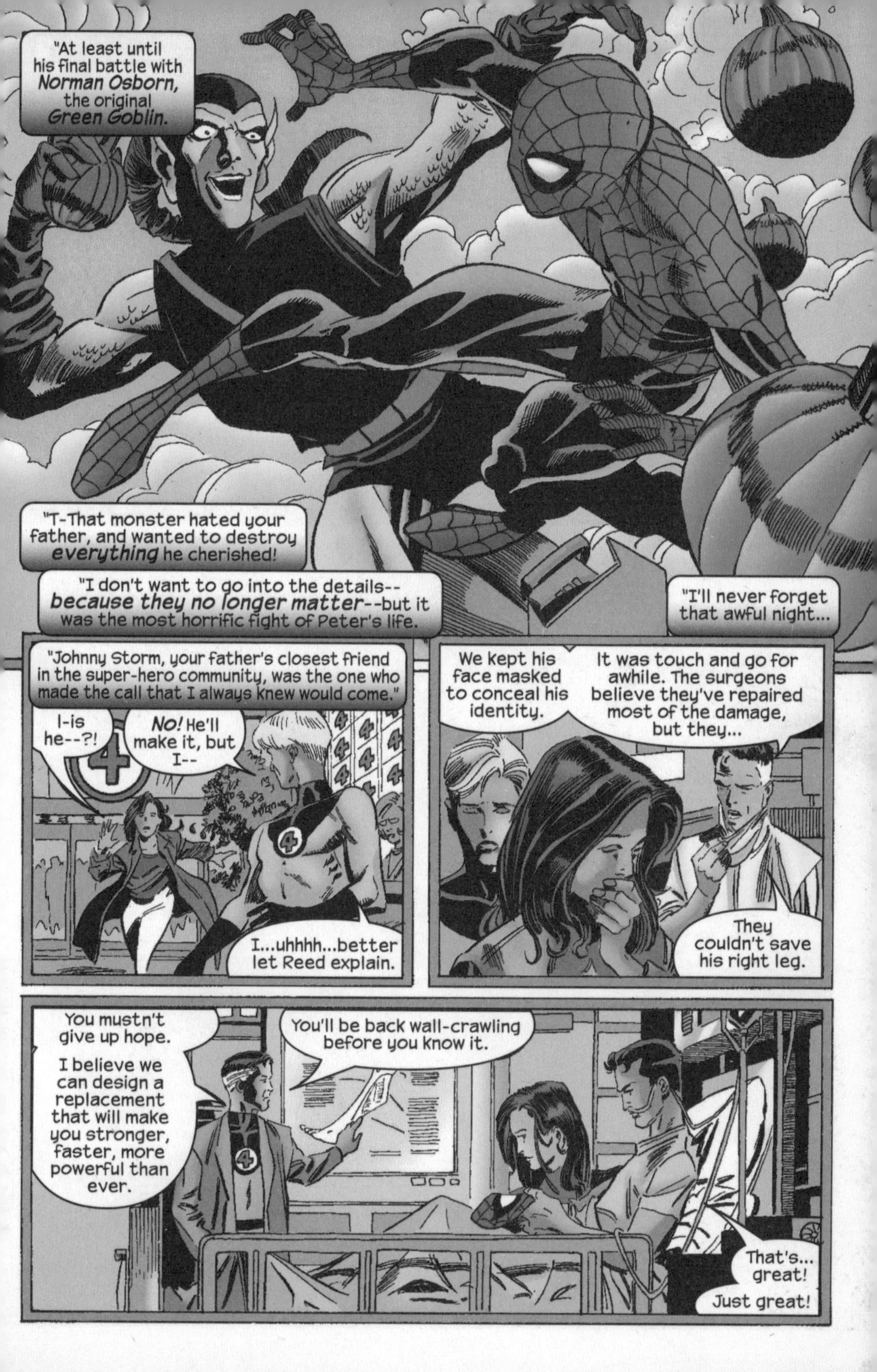
"At least until his final battle with Norman Osborn, the original Green Goblin.
"T-That monster hated your father, and wanted to destroy everything he cherished!
"I don't want to go into the details--because they no longer matter--but it was the most horrific fight of Peter's life.
"I'll never forget that awful night...
"Johnny Storm, your father's closest friend in the super-hero community, was the one who made the call that I always knew would come."
I-is he--?!
No! He'll make it, but I--
I...uhhhh...better let Reed explain.
We kept his face masked to conceal his identity.
It was touch and go for awhile. The surgeons believe they've repaired most of the damage, but they...
They couldn't save his right leg.
You mustn't give up hope.
I believe we can design a replacement that will make you stronger, faster, more powerful than ever.
You'll be back wall-crawling before you know it.
That's... great!
Just great!

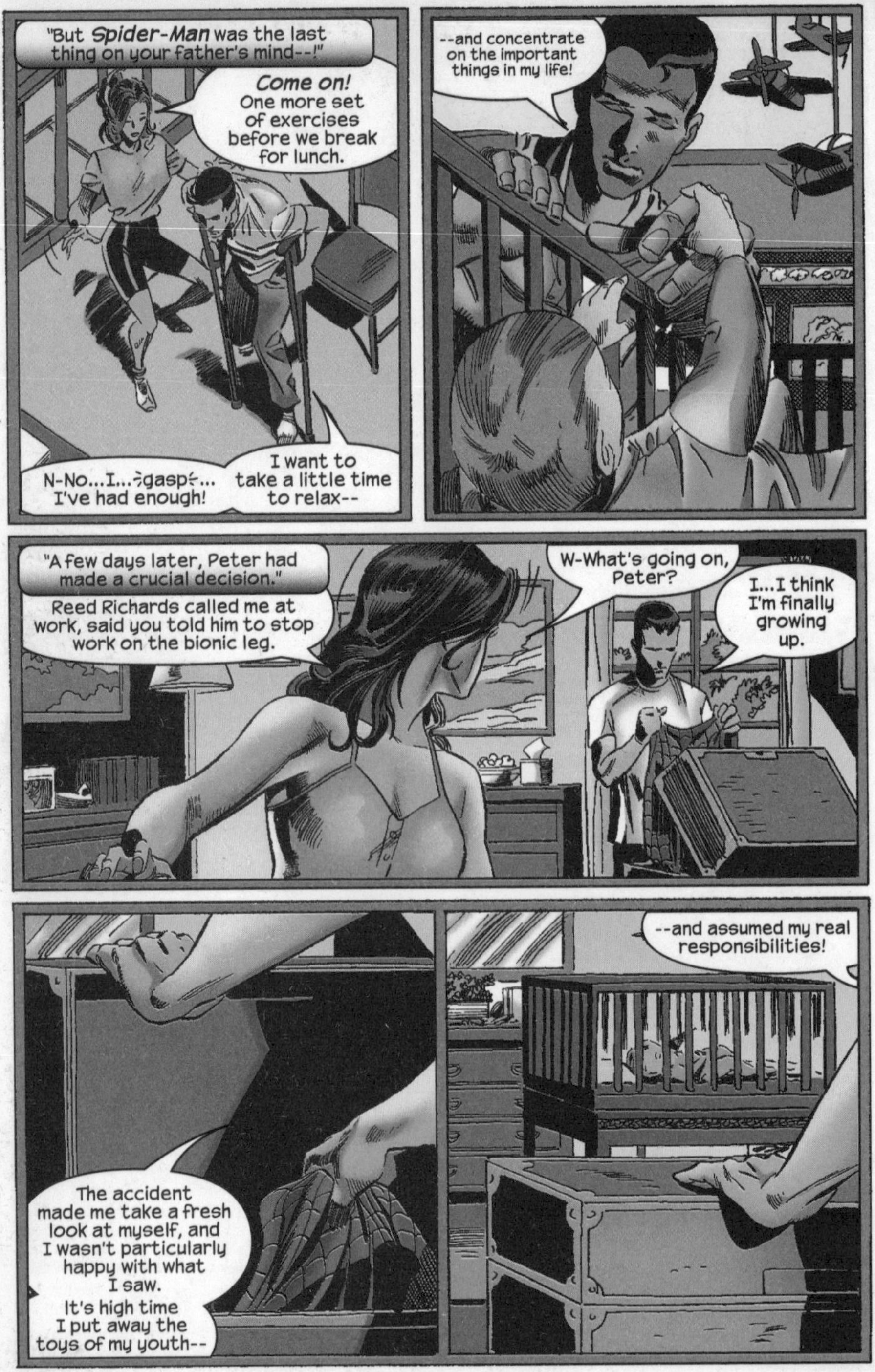
"But Spider-Man was the last thing on your father's mind--!"
Come on! One more set of exercises before we break for lunch.
N-No...I...gasp...I've had enough!
I want to take a little time to relax--
--and concentrate on the important things in my life!
"A few days later, Peter had made a crucial decision."
Reed Richards called me at work, said you told him to stop work on the bionic leg.
W-What's going on, Peter?
I...I think I'm finally growing up.
The accident made me take a fresh look at myself, and I wasn't particularly happy with what I saw.
It's high time I put away the toys of my youth--
--and assumed my real responsibilities!

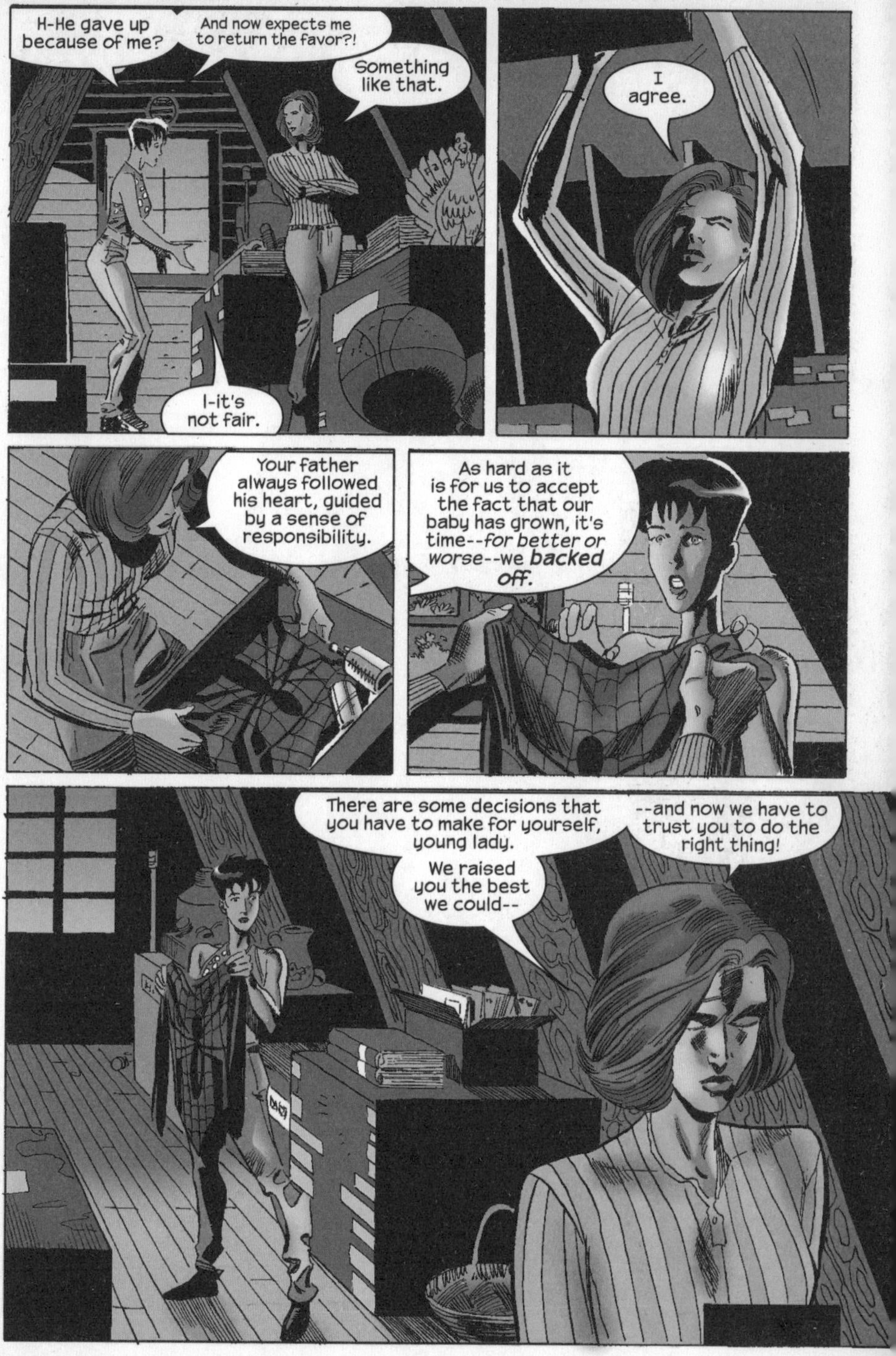
H-He gave up because of me?
And now expects me to return the favor?!
Something like that.
I-it's not fair.
I agree.
Your father always followed his heart, guided by a sense of responsibility.
As hard as it is for us to accept the fact that our baby has grown, it's time--*for better or worse*--we **backed off.**
There are some decisions that you have to make for yourself, young lady.
We raised you the best we could--
--and now we have to trust you to do the right thing!

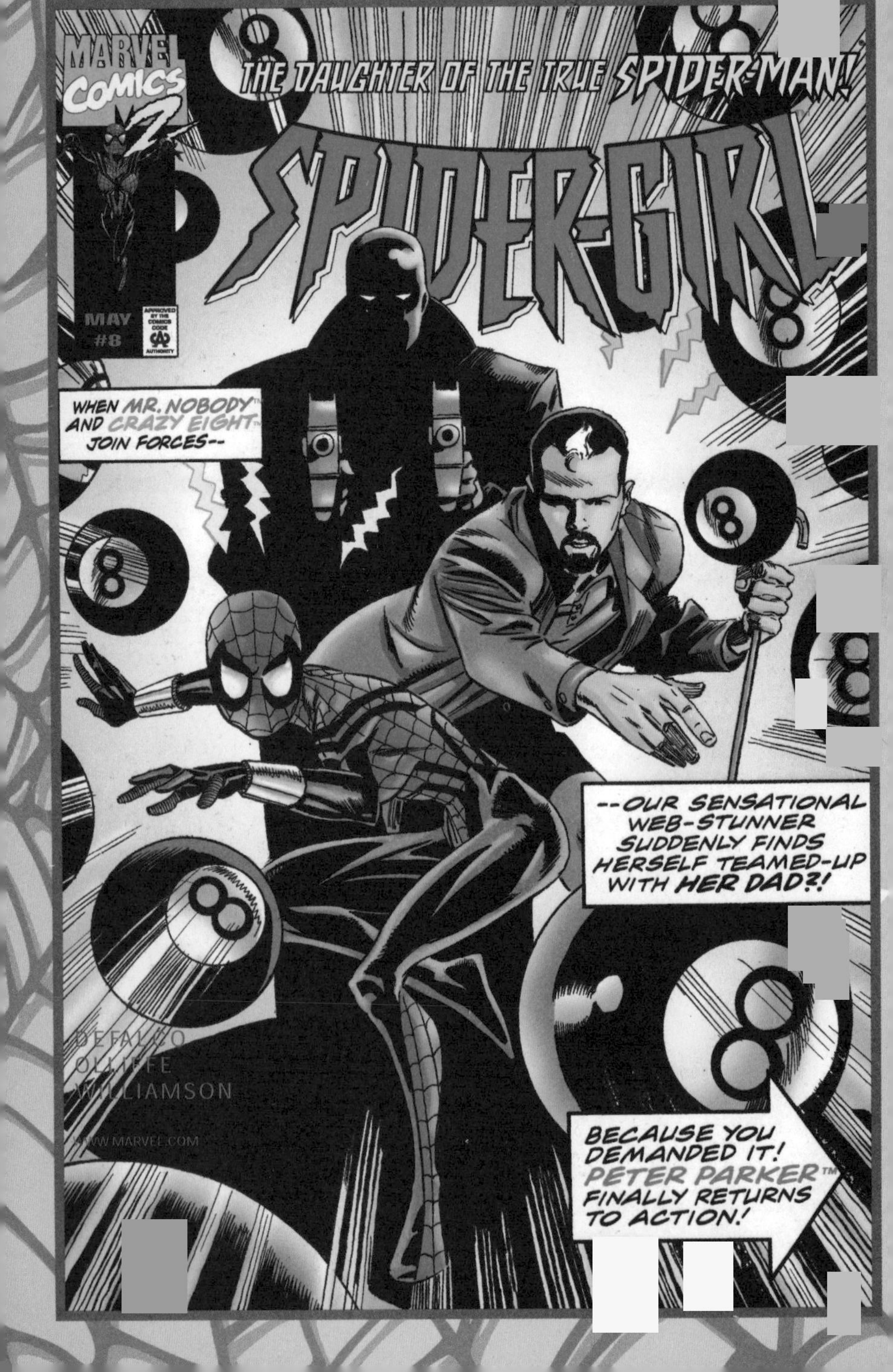
MARVEL COMICS 2
THE DAUGHTER OF THE TRUE SPIDER-MAN!
SPIDER-GIRL
MAY #8
APPROVED BY THE COMICS CODE AUTHORITY
WHEN MR. NOBODY™ AND CRAZY EIGHT™ JOIN FORCES--
--OUR SENSATIONAL WEB-STUNNER SUDDENLY FINDS HERSELF TEAMED-UP WITH HER DAD?!
BECAUSE YOU DEMANDED IT! PETER PARKER™ FINALLY RETURNS TO ACTION!
DEFALCO
OLLIFFE
WILLIAMSON
WWW.MARVEL.COM

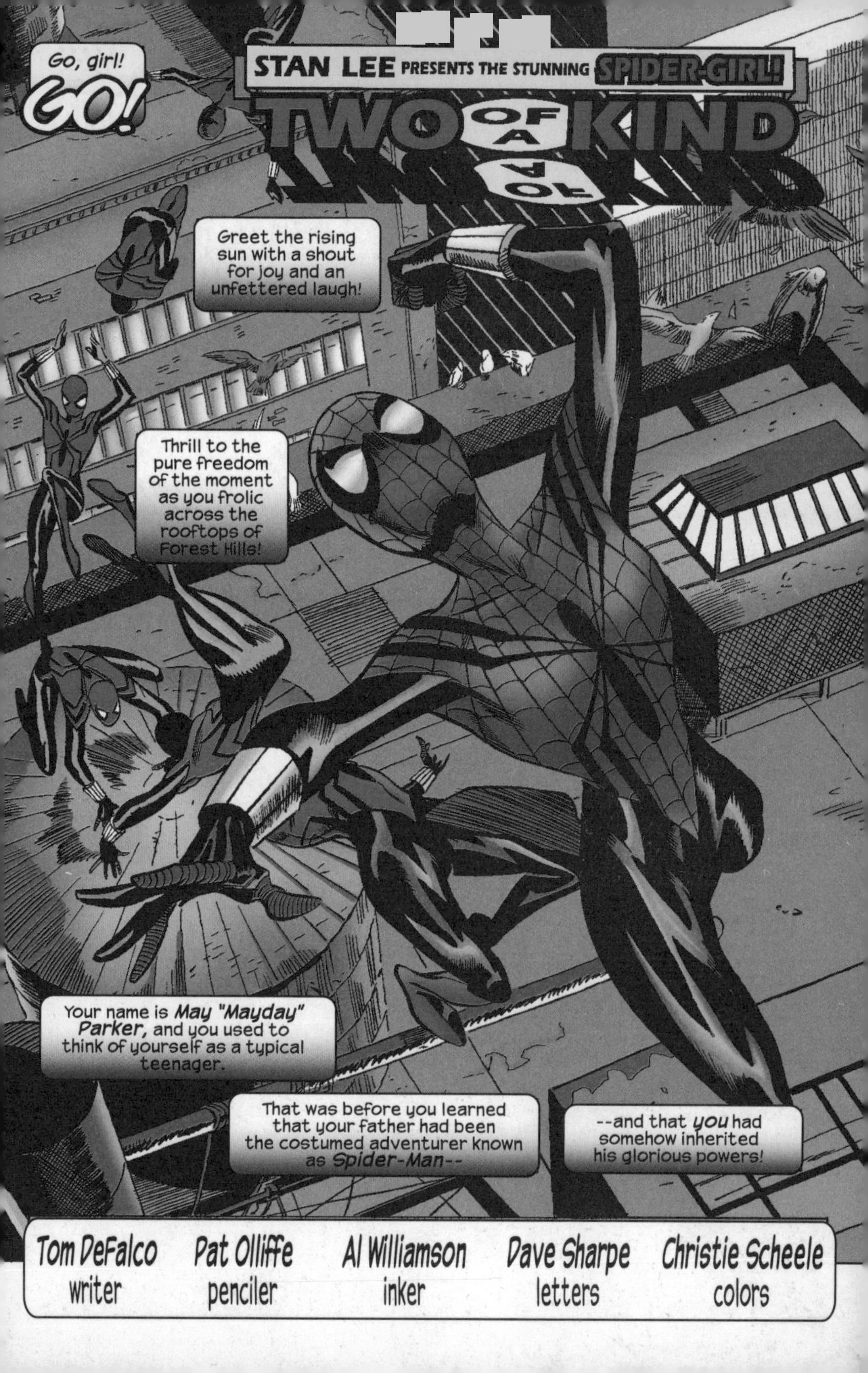
Go, girl! GO!
STAN LEE PRESENTS THE STUNNING SPIDER-GIRL!
TWO OF A KIND
Greet the rising sun with a shout for joy and an unfettered laugh!
Thrill to the pure freedom of the moment as you frolic across the rooftops of Forest Hills!
Your name is *May "Mayday" Parker,* and you used to think of yourself as a typical teenager.
That was before you learned that your father had been the costumed adventurer known as *Spider-Man--*
--and that *you* had somehow inherited his glorious powers!
Tom DeFalco writer
Pat Olliffe penciler
Al Williamson inker
Dave Sharpe letters
Christie Scheele colors

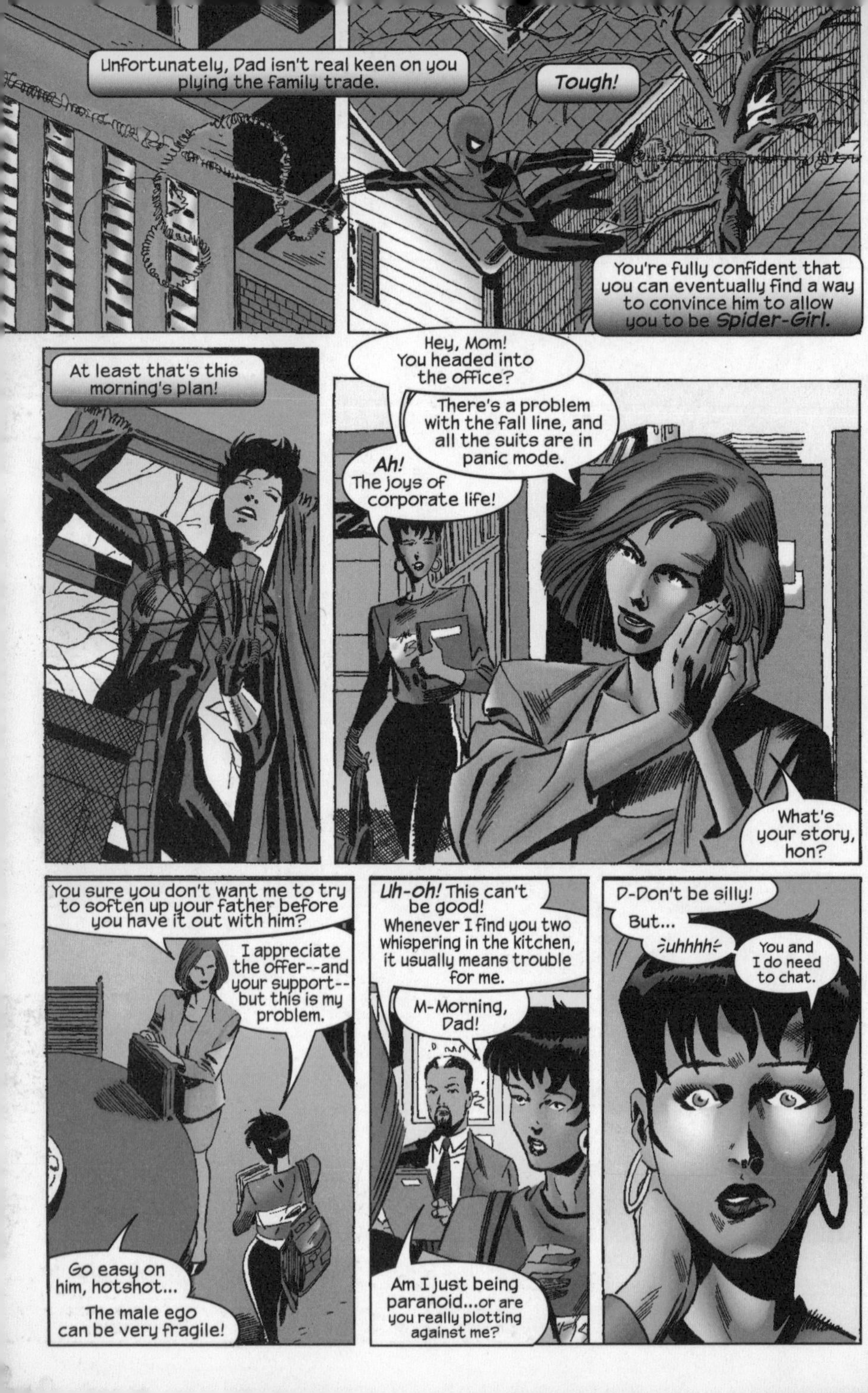
Unfortunately, Dad isn't real keen on you plying the family trade.
Tough!
You're fully confident that you can eventually find a way to convince him to allow you to be Spider-Girl.
At least that's this morning's plan!
Hey, Mom! You headed into the office?
There's a problem with the fall line, and all the suits are in panic mode.
Ah! The joys of corporate life!
What's your story, hon?
You sure you don't want me to try to soften up your father before you have it out with him?
I appreciate the offer--and your support--but this is my problem.
Go easy on him, hotshot...
The male ego can be very fragile!
Uh-oh! This can't be good!
Whenever I find you two whispering in the kitchen, it usually means trouble for me.
M-Morning, Dad!
Am I just being paranoid...or are you really plotting against me?
D-Don't be silly!
But...
uhhhh
You and I do need to chat.

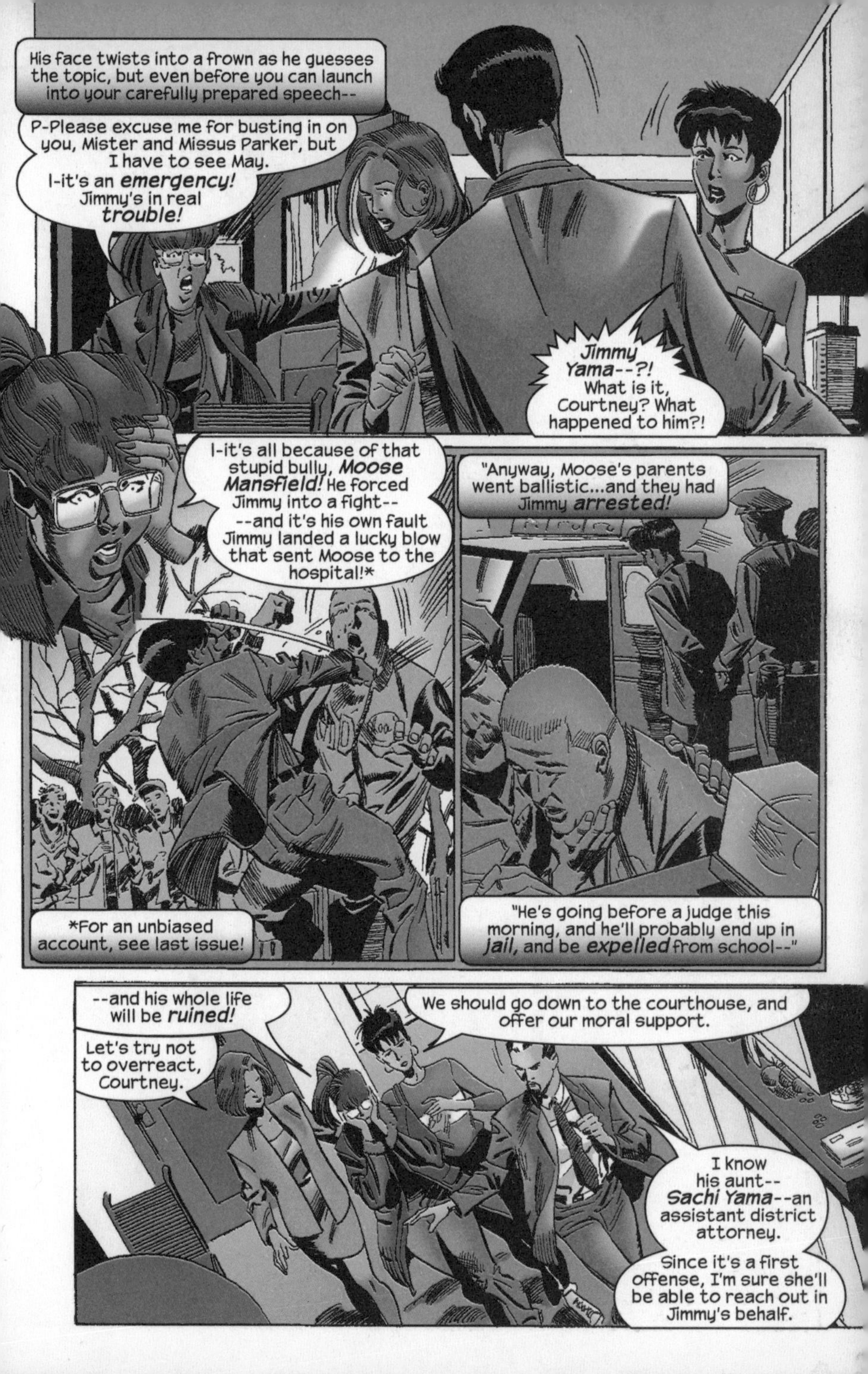
His face twists into a frown as he guesses the topic, but even before you can launch into your carefully prepared speech--
P-Please excuse me for busting in on you, Mister and Missus Parker, but I have to see May.
I-it's an emergency! Jimmy's in real trouble!
Jimmy Yama--?! What is it, Courtney? What happened to him?!
I-it's all because of that stupid bully, Moose Mansfield! He forced Jimmy into a fight--
--and it's his own fault Jimmy landed a lucky blow that sent Moose to the hospital!*
*For an unbiased account, see last issue!
"Anyway, Moose's parents went ballistic...and they had Jimmy arrested!
"He's going before a judge this morning, and he'll probably end up in jail, and be expelled from school--"
--and his whole life will be ruined!
Let's try not to overreact, Courtney.
We should go down to the courthouse, and offer our moral support.
I know his aunt--Sachi Yama--an assistant district attorney.
Since it's a first offense, I'm sure she'll be able to reach out in Jimmy's behalf.

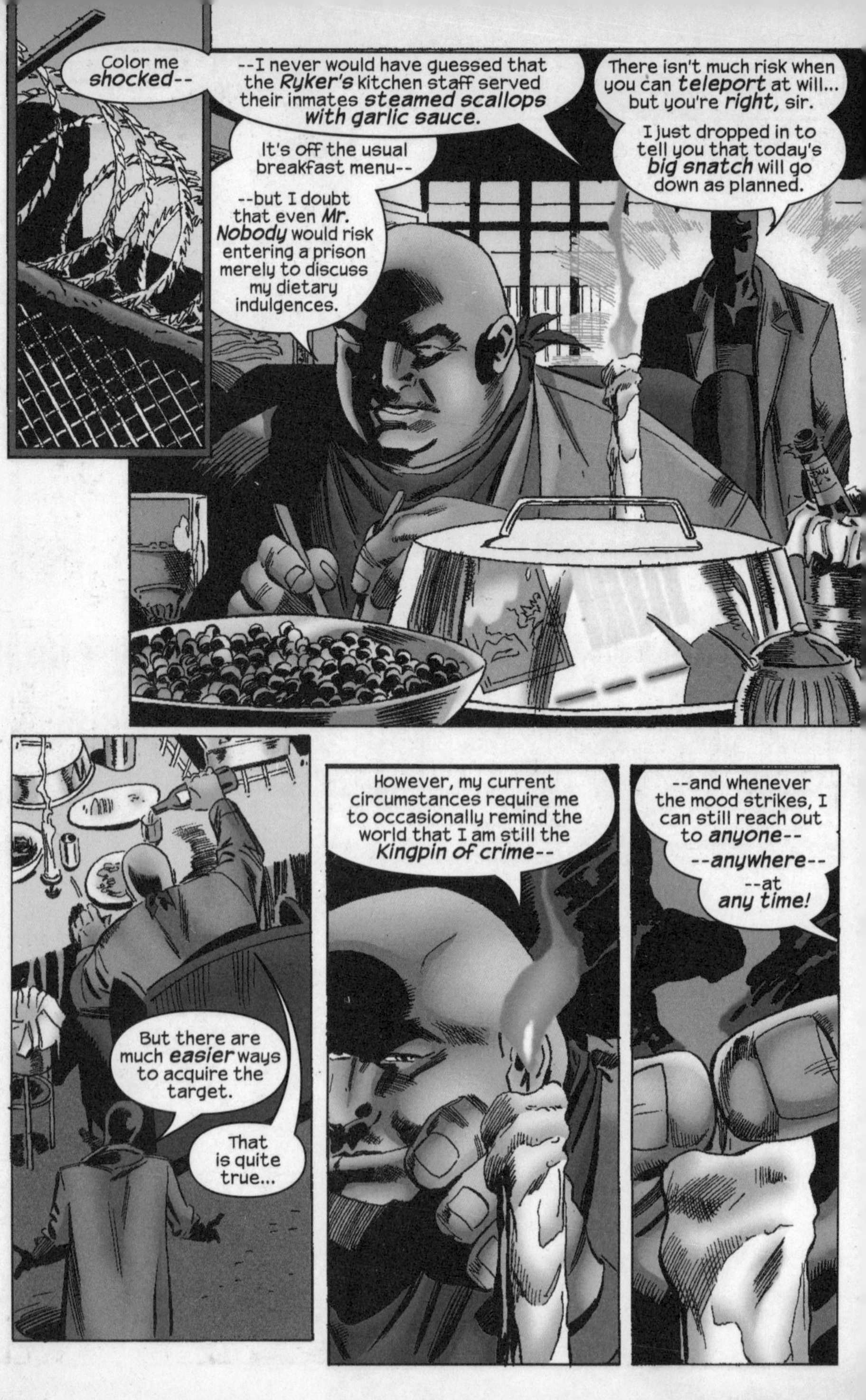
Color me shocked--
--I never would have guessed that the Ryker's kitchen staff served their inmates steamed scallops with garlic sauce.
It's off the usual breakfast menu--
--but I doubt that even Mr. Nobody would risk entering a prison merely to discuss my dietary indulgences.
There isn't much risk when you can teleport at will... but you're right, sir.
I just dropped in to tell you that today's big snatch will go down as planned.
But there are much easier ways to acquire the target.
That is quite true...
However, my current circumstances require me to occasionally remind the world that I am still the Kingpin of crime--
--and whenever the mood strikes, I can still reach out to anyone--
--anywhere--
--at any time!

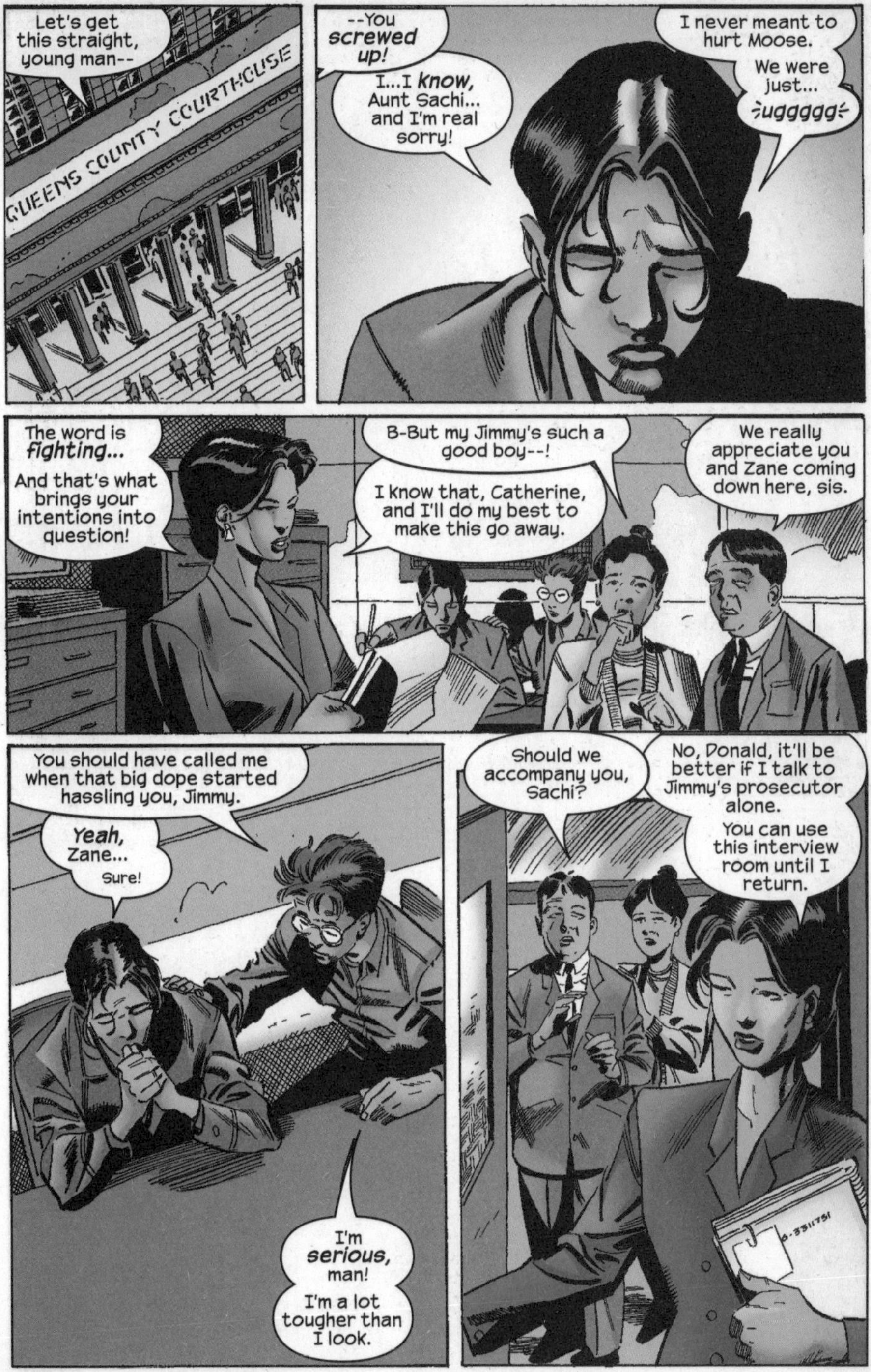
QUEENS COUNTY COURTHOUSE
Let's get this straight, young man--
--You *screwed up!*
I...I *know,* Aunt Sachi... and I'm real sorry!
I never meant to hurt Moose.
We were just... *uggggg*
The word is *fighting...*
And that's what brings your intentions into question!
B-But my Jimmy's such a good boy--!
I know that, Catherine, and I'll do my best to make this go away.
We really appreciate you and Zane coming down here, sis.
You should have called me when that big dope started hassling you, Jimmy.
Yeah, Zane...
Sure!
I'm *serious,* man!
I'm a lot tougher than I look.
Should we accompany you, Sachi?
No, Donald, it'll be better if I talk to Jimmy's prosecutor alone.
You can use this interview room until I return.

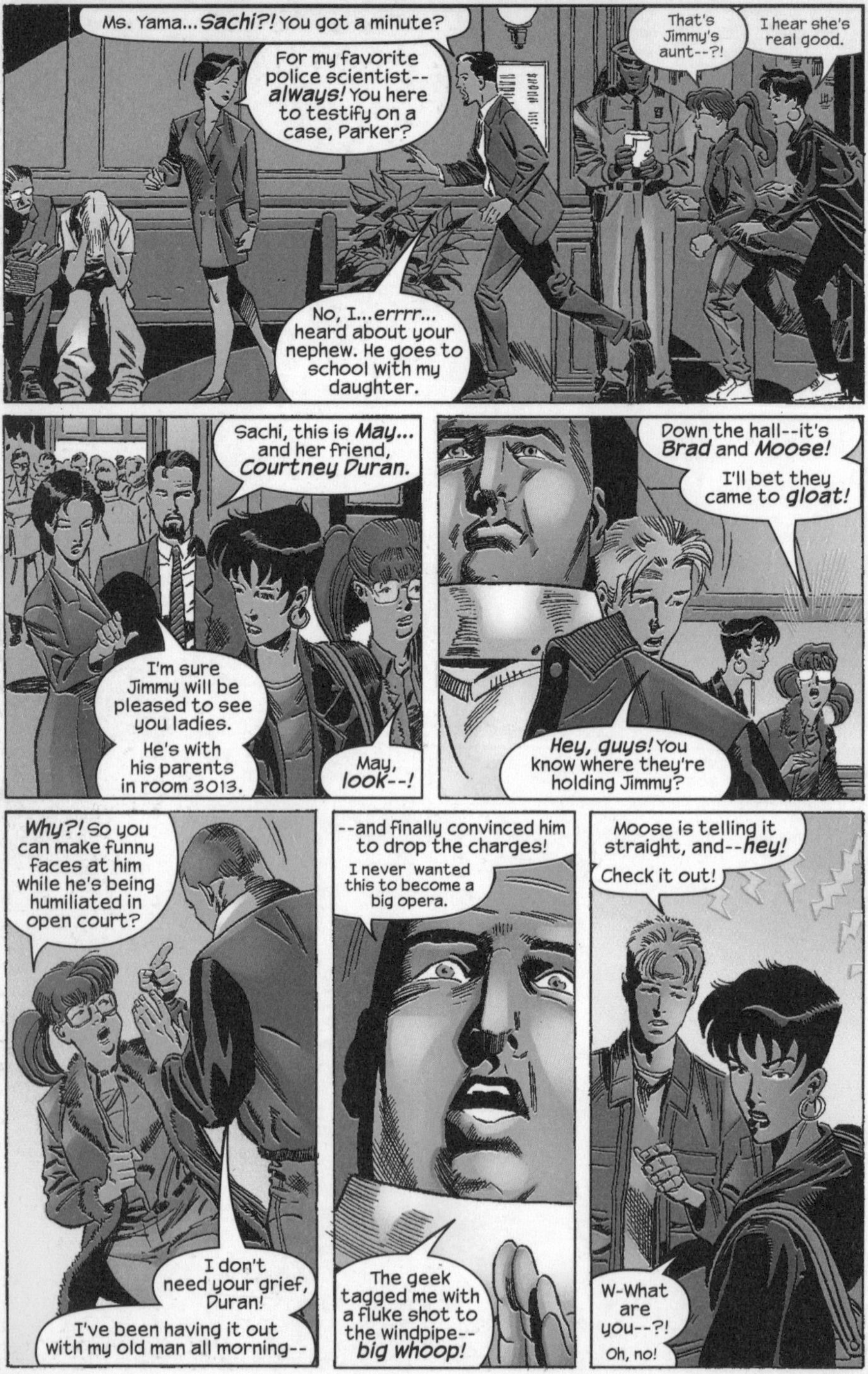
Ms. Yama... Sachi?! You got a minute?
For my favorite police scientist-- always! You here to testify on a case, Parker?
No, I...errrr... heard about your nephew. He goes to school with my daughter.
That's Jimmy's aunt--?!
I hear she's real good.
Sachi, this is May... and her friend, Courtney Duran.
I'm sure Jimmy will be pleased to see you ladies.
He's with his parents in room 3013.
May, look--!
Down the hall--it's Brad and Moose!
I'll bet they came to gloat!
Hey, guys! You know where they're holding Jimmy?
Why?! So you can make funny faces at him while he's being humiliated in open court?
I don't need your grief, Duran!
I've been having it out with my old man all morning--
--and finally convinced him to drop the charges!
I never wanted this to become a big opera.
The geek tagged me with a fluke shot to the windpipe-- big whoop!
Moose is telling it straight, and--hey!
Check it out!
W-What are you--?!
Oh, no!

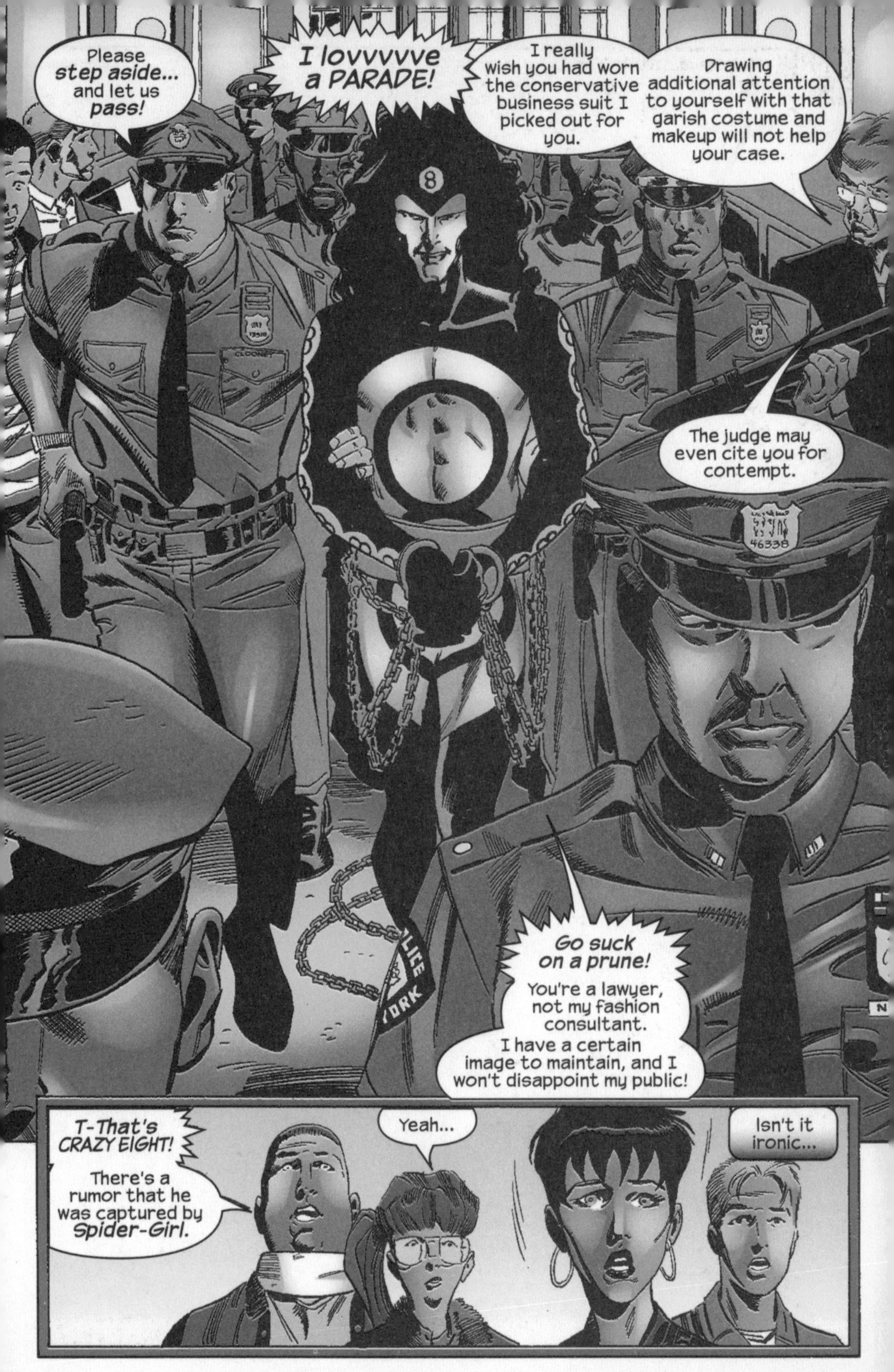

Please step aside... and let us pass!
I lovvvvve a PARADE!
I really wish you had worn the conservative business suit I picked out for you.
Drawing additional attention to yourself with that garish costume and makeup will not help your case.
The judge may even cite you for contempt.
Go suck on a prune!
You're a lawyer, not my fashion consultant.
I have a certain image to maintain, and I won't disappoint my public!
T-That's CRAZY EIGHT!
There's a rumor that he was captured by Spider-Girl.
Yeah...
Isn't it ironic...

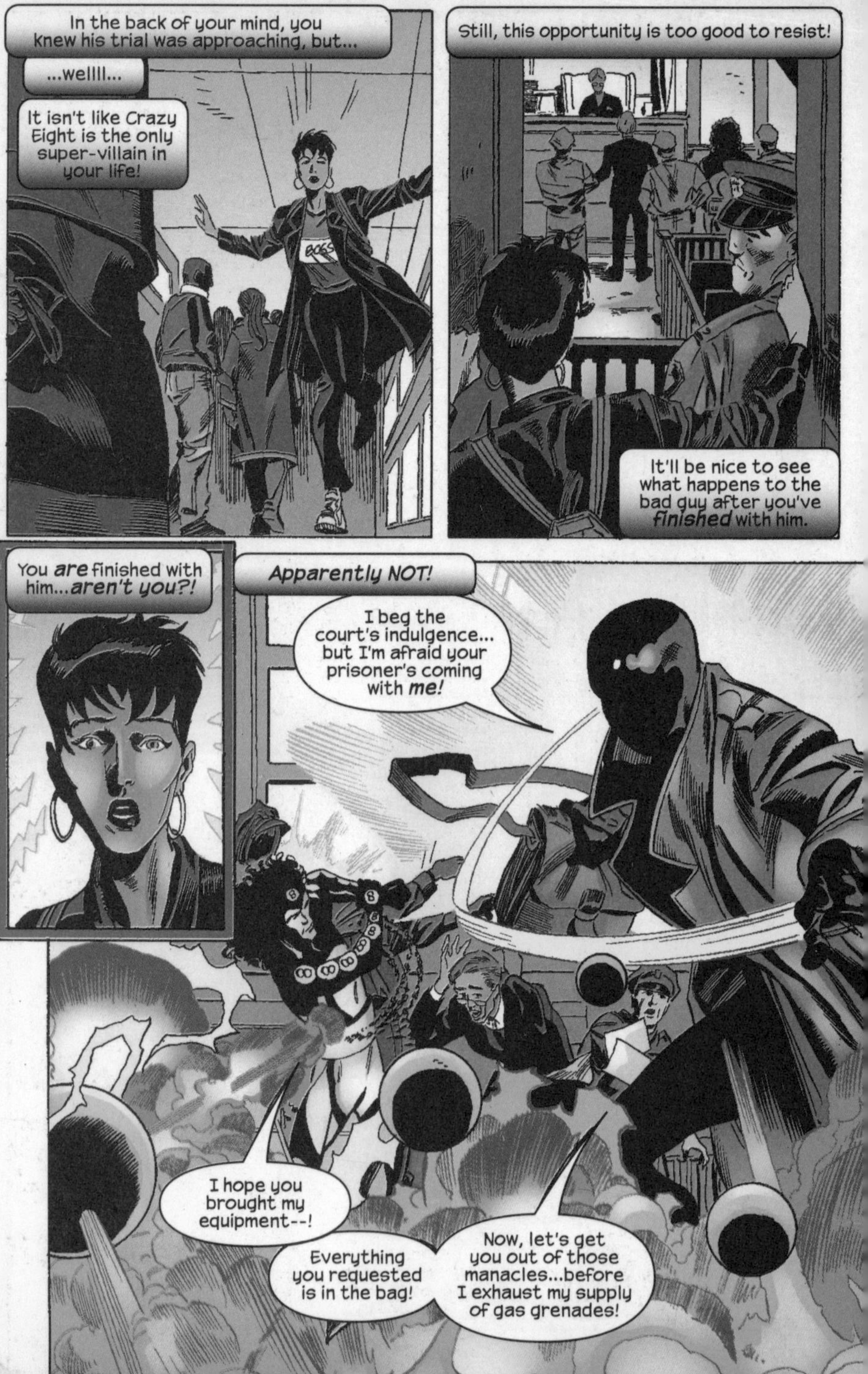
In the back of your mind, you knew his trial was approaching, but...
...wellll...
It isn't like Crazy Eight is the only super-villain in your life!
BOSS
Still, this opportunity is too good to resist!
It'll be nice to see what happens to the bad guy after you've *finished* with him.
You **are** finished with him...***aren't you?!***
Apparently NOT!
I beg the court's indulgence... but I'm afraid your prisoner's coming with ***me!***
I hope you brought my equipment--!
Everything you requested is in the bag!
Now, let's get you out of those manacles...before I exhaust my supply of gas grenades!

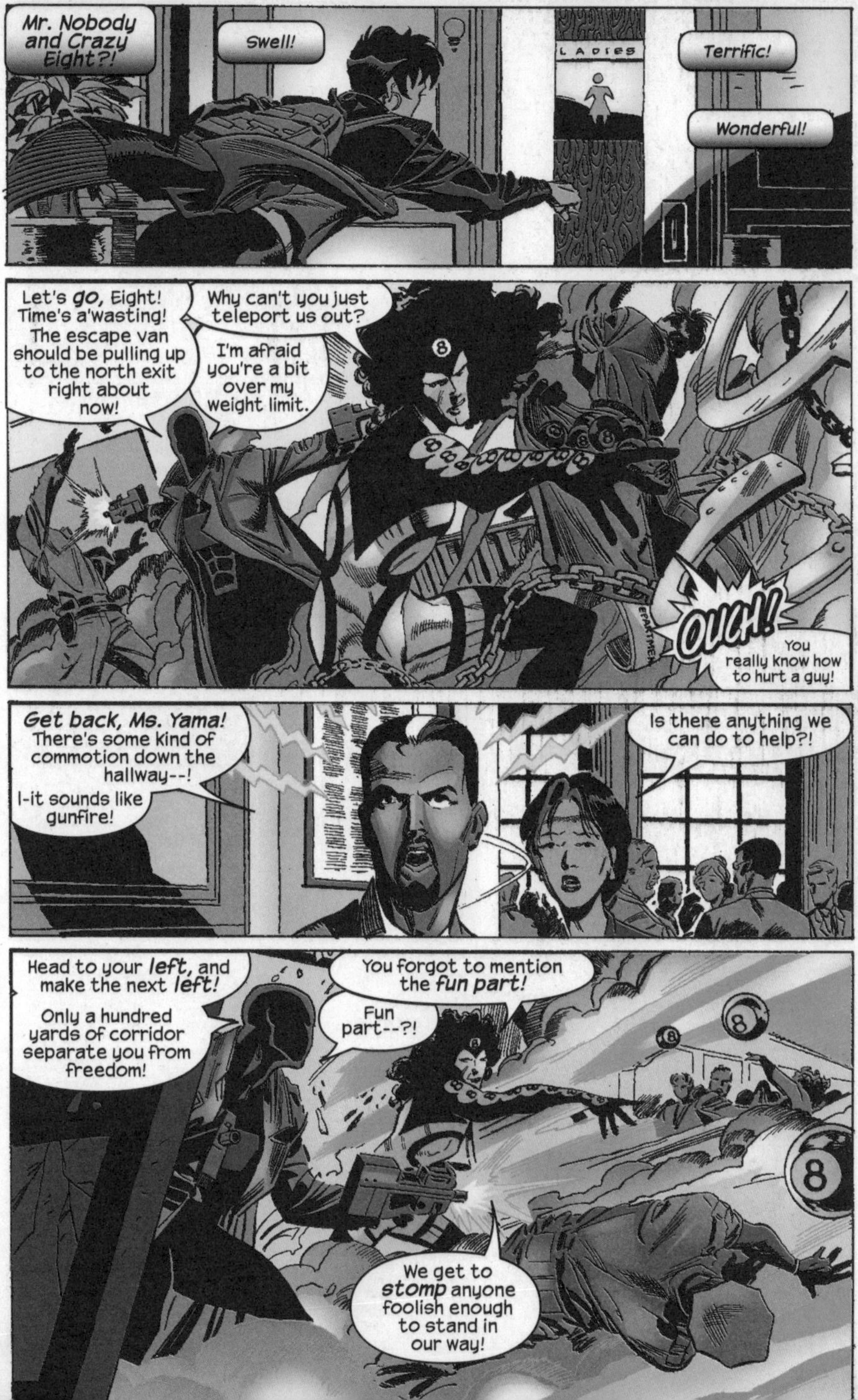
Mr. Nobody and Crazy Eight?!
Swell!
LADIES
Terrific!
Wonderful!
Let's go, Eight! Time's a'wasting! The escape van should be pulling up to the north exit right about now!
Why can't you just teleport us out?
I'm afraid you're a bit over my weight limit.
OUCH!
You really know how to hurt a guy!
Get back, Ms. Yama! There's some kind of commotion down the hallway--!
I-it sounds like gunfire!
Is there anything we can do to help?!
Head to your left, and make the next left!
Only a hundred yards of corridor separate you from freedom!
You forgot to mention the fun part!
Fun part--?!
We get to stomp anyone foolish enough to stand in our way!

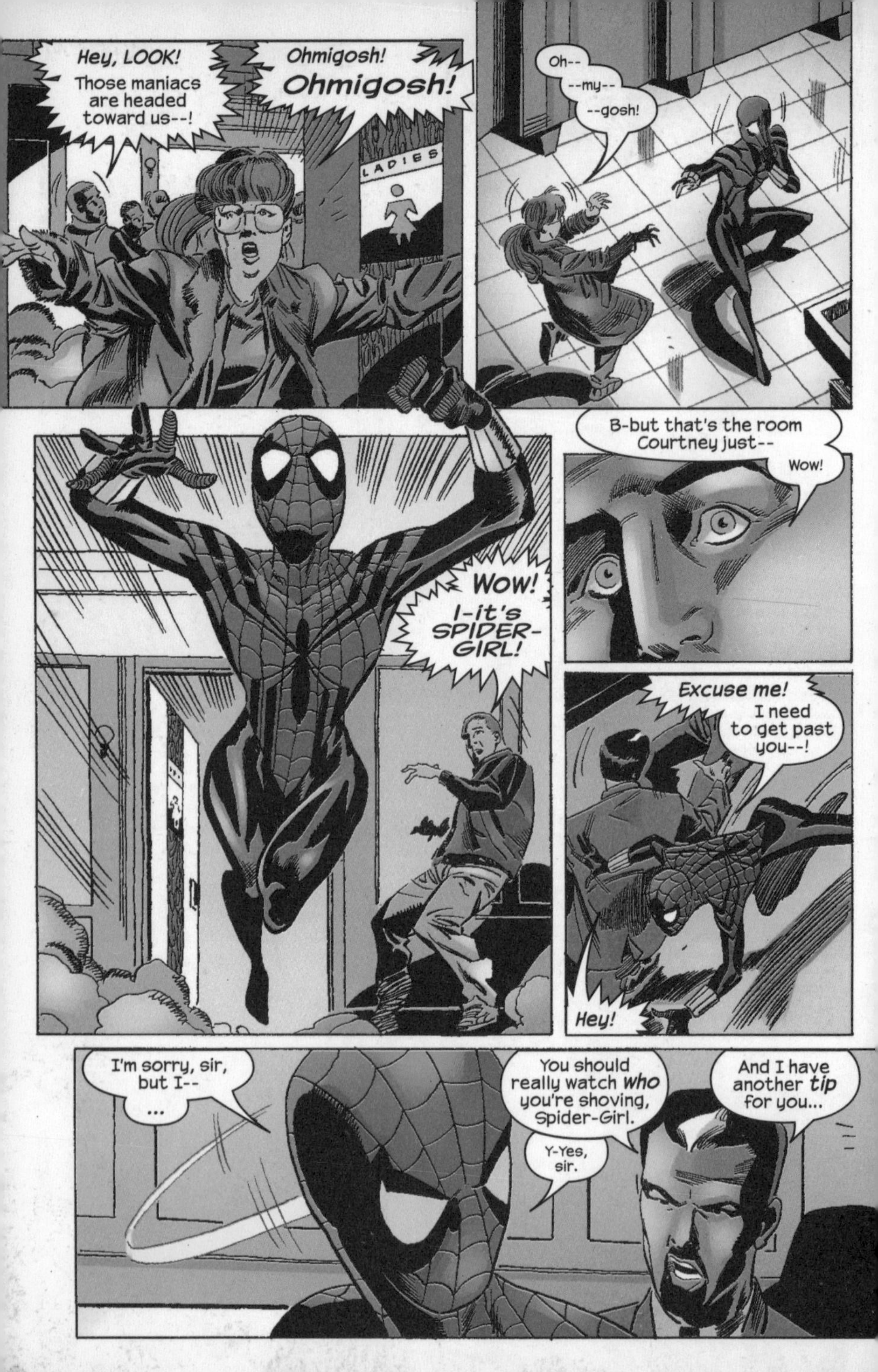
Hey, LOOK! Those maniacs are headed toward us--!
Ohmigosh! Ohmigosh!
LADIES
Oh--
--my--
--gosh!
WOW! I-it's SPIDER-GIRL!
B-but that's the room Courtney just--
Wow!
Excuse me! I need to get past you--!
Hey!
I'm sorry, sir, but I-- ...
You should really watch who you're shoving, Spider-Girl.
Y-Yes, sir.
And I have another tip for you...

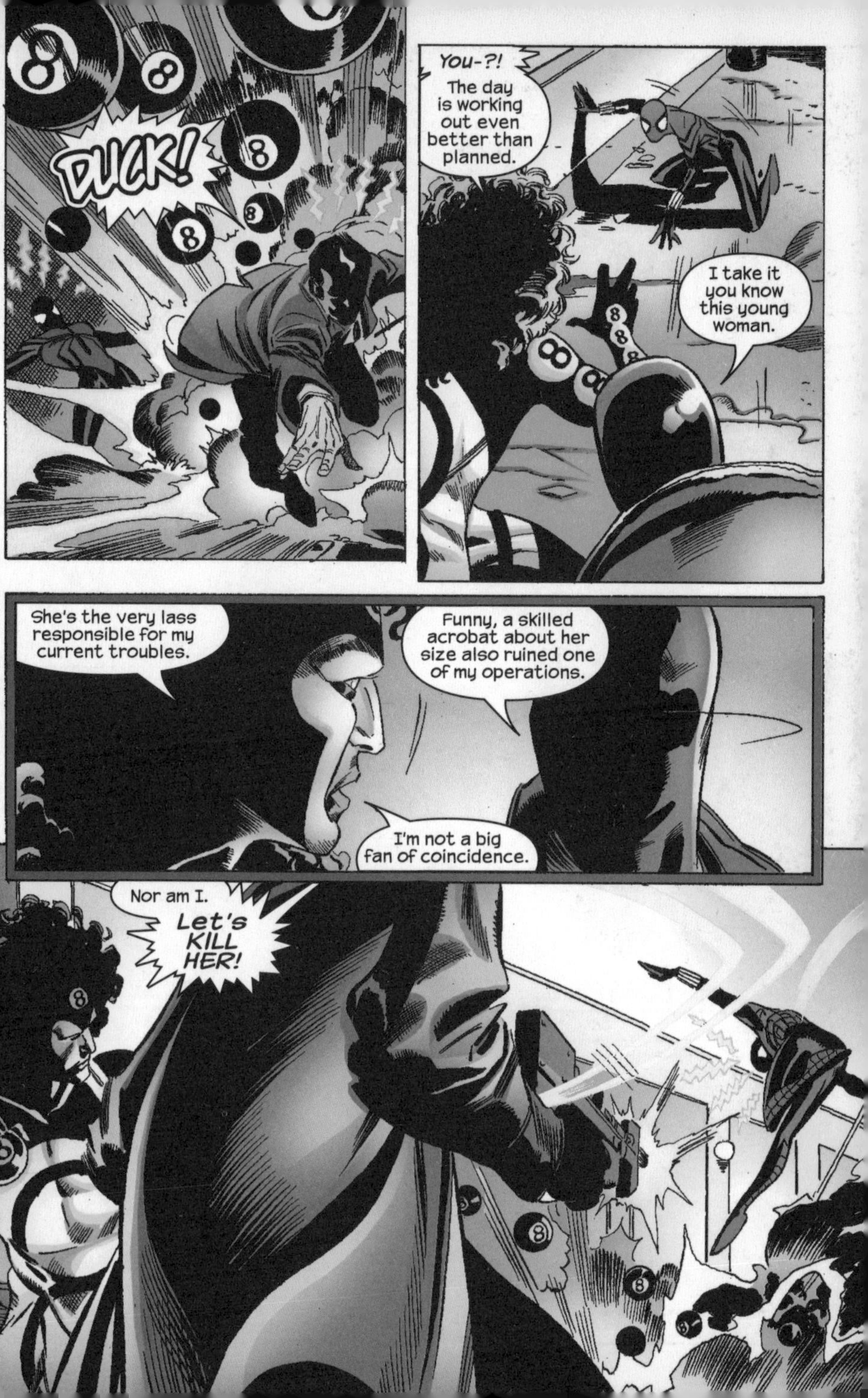
DUCK!
You-?!
The day is working out even better than planned.
I take it you know this young woman.
She's the very lass responsible for my current troubles.
Funny, a skilled acrobat about her size also ruined one of my operations.
I'm not a big fan of coincidence.
Nor am I.
Let's KILL HER!

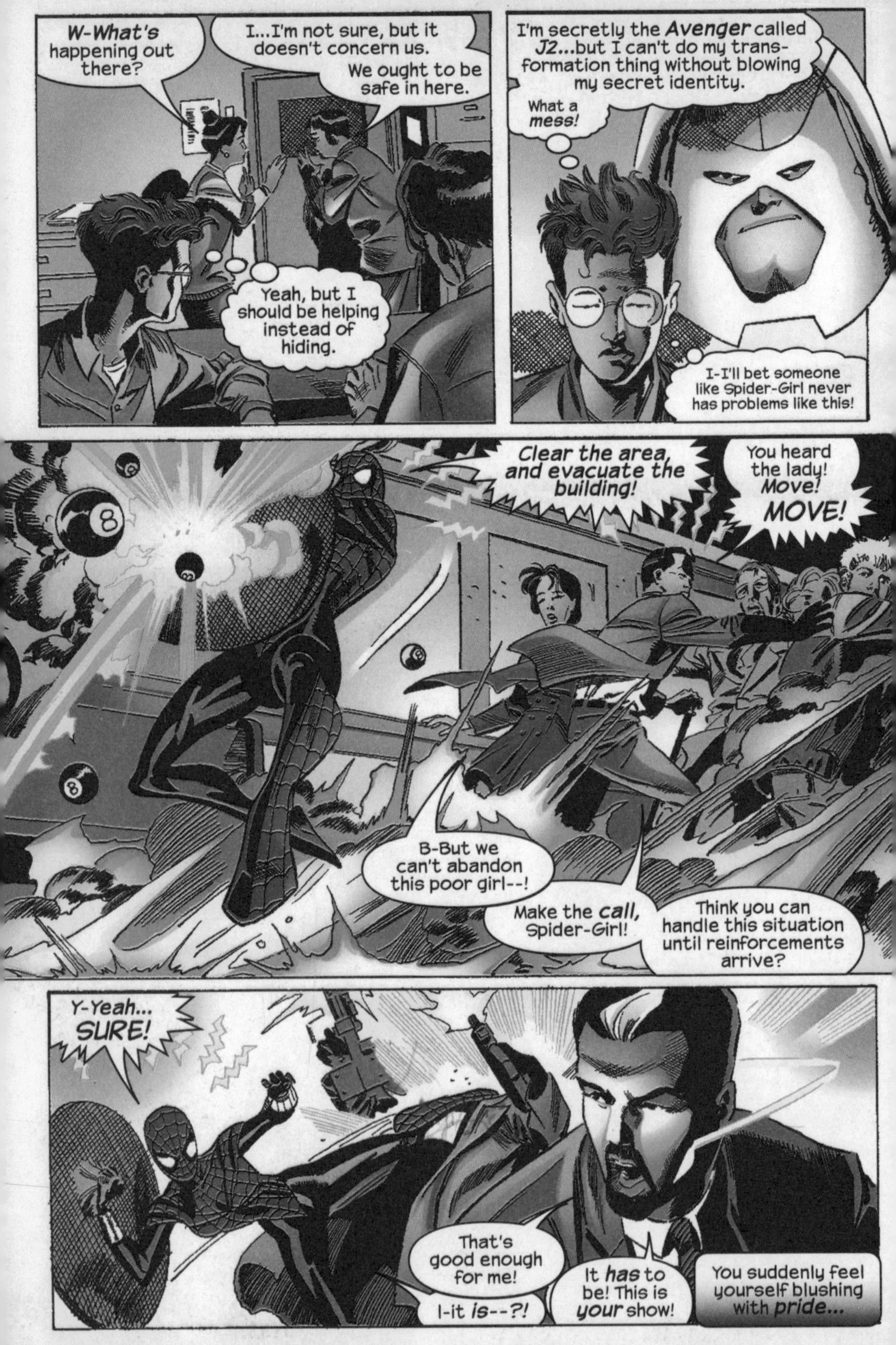
W-What's happening out there?
I...I'm not sure, but it doesn't concern us.
We ought to be safe in here.
Yeah, but I should be helping instead of hiding.
I'm secretly the Avenger called J2...but I can't do my transformation thing without blowing my secret identity.
What a mess!
I-I'll bet someone like Spider-Girl never has problems like this!
Clear the area, and evacuate the building!
You heard the lady! Move! MOVE!
B-But we can't abandon this poor girl--!
Make the call, Spider-Girl!
Think you can handle this situation until reinforcements arrive?
Y-Yeah... SURE!
That's good enough for me!
I-it is--?!
It has to be! This is your show!
You suddenly feel yourself blushing with pride...

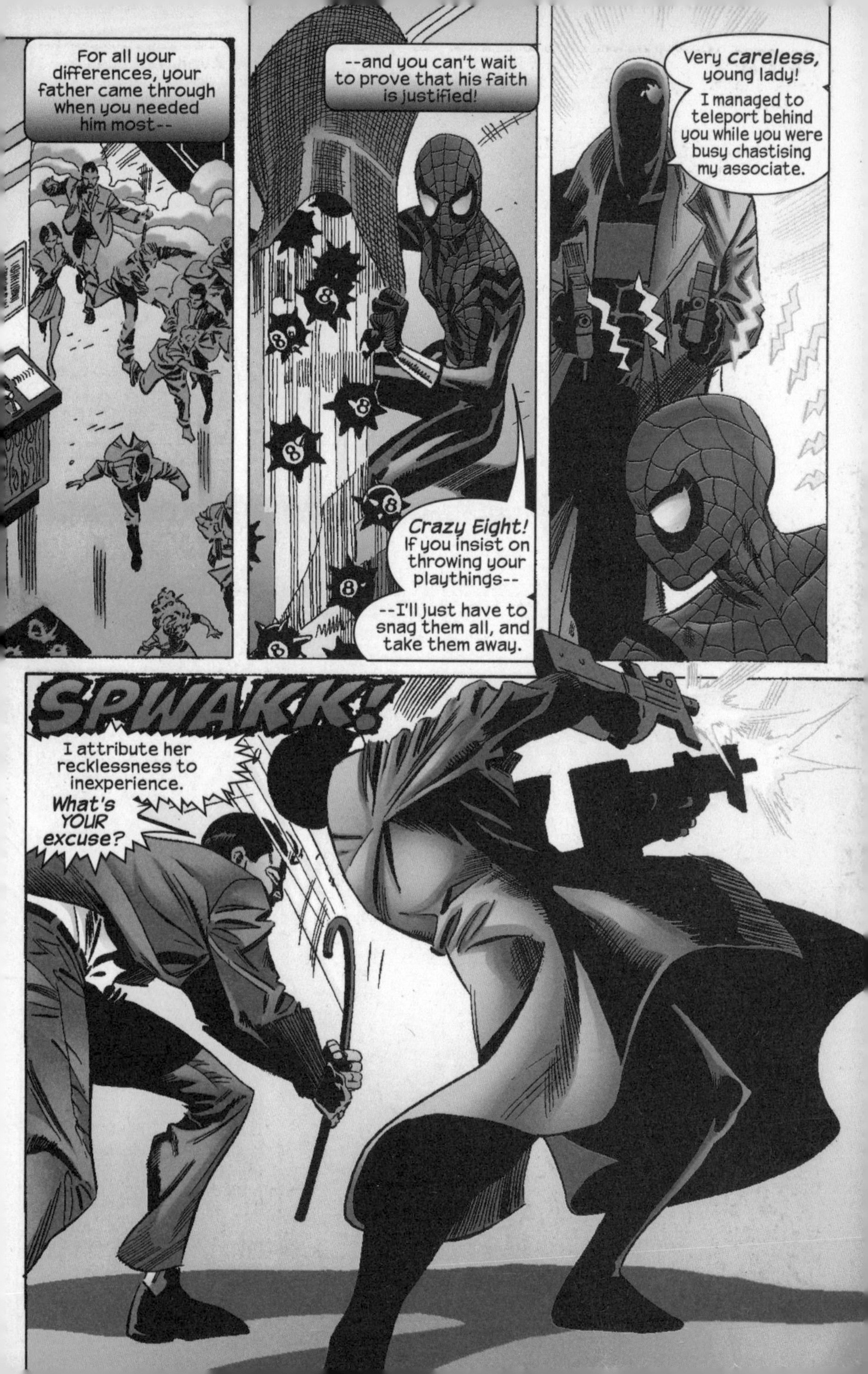
For all your differences, your father came through when you needed him most--
--and you can't wait to prove that his faith is justified!
Crazy Eight! If you insist on throwing your playthings--
--I'll just have to snag them all, and take them away.
Very careless, young lady!
I managed to teleport behind you while you were busy chastising my associate.
SPWAKK!
I attribute her recklessness to inexperience.
What's YOUR excuse?

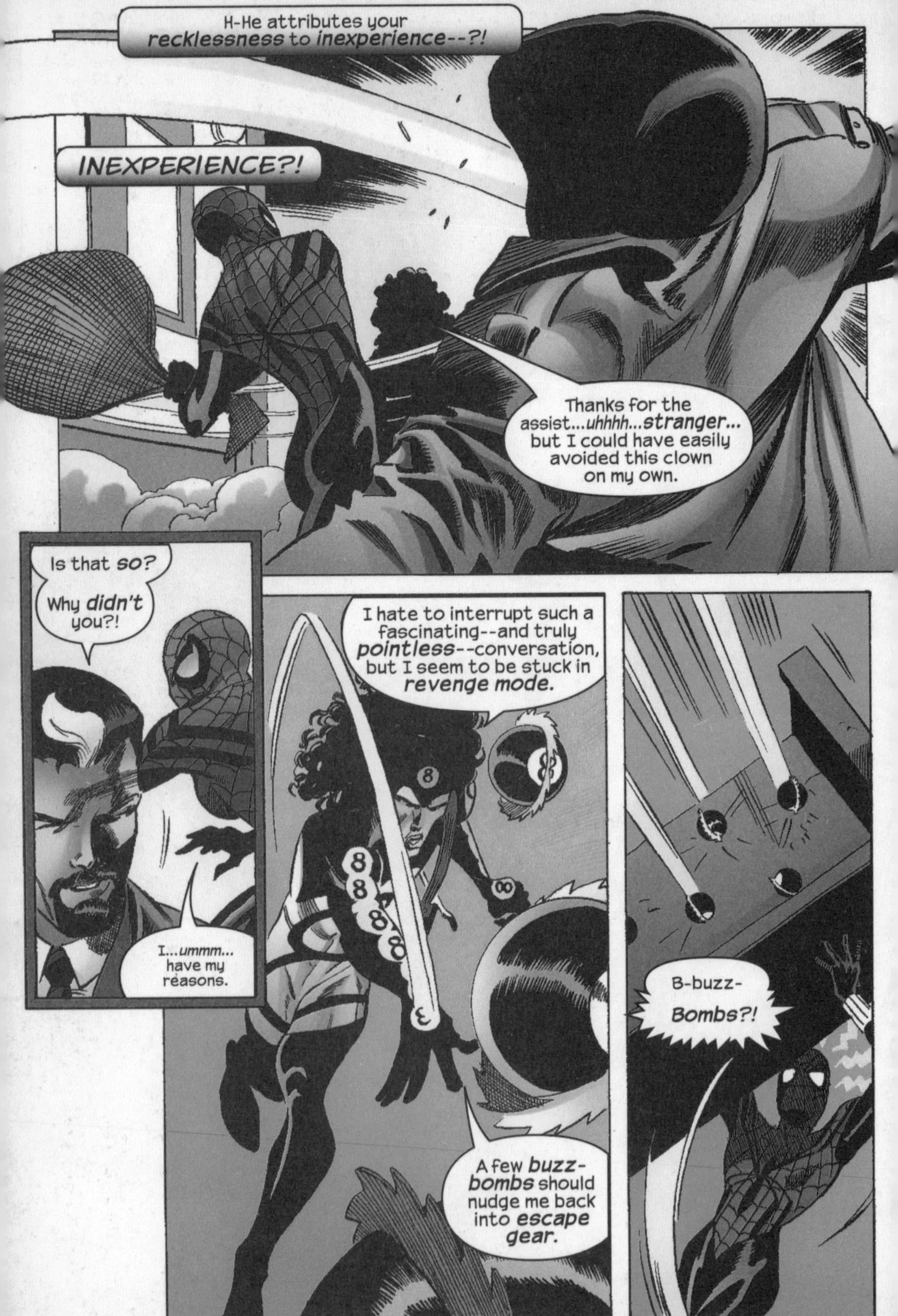

H-He attributes your recklessness to inexperience--?!
INEXPERIENCE?!
Thanks for the assist...uhhhh...stranger... but I could have easily avoided this clown on my own.
Is that so?
Why didn't you?!
I...ummm... have my reasons.
I hate to interrupt such a fascinating--and truly pointless--conversation, but I seem to be stuck in revenge mode.
A few buzz-bombs should nudge me back into escape gear.
B-buzz-Bombs?!

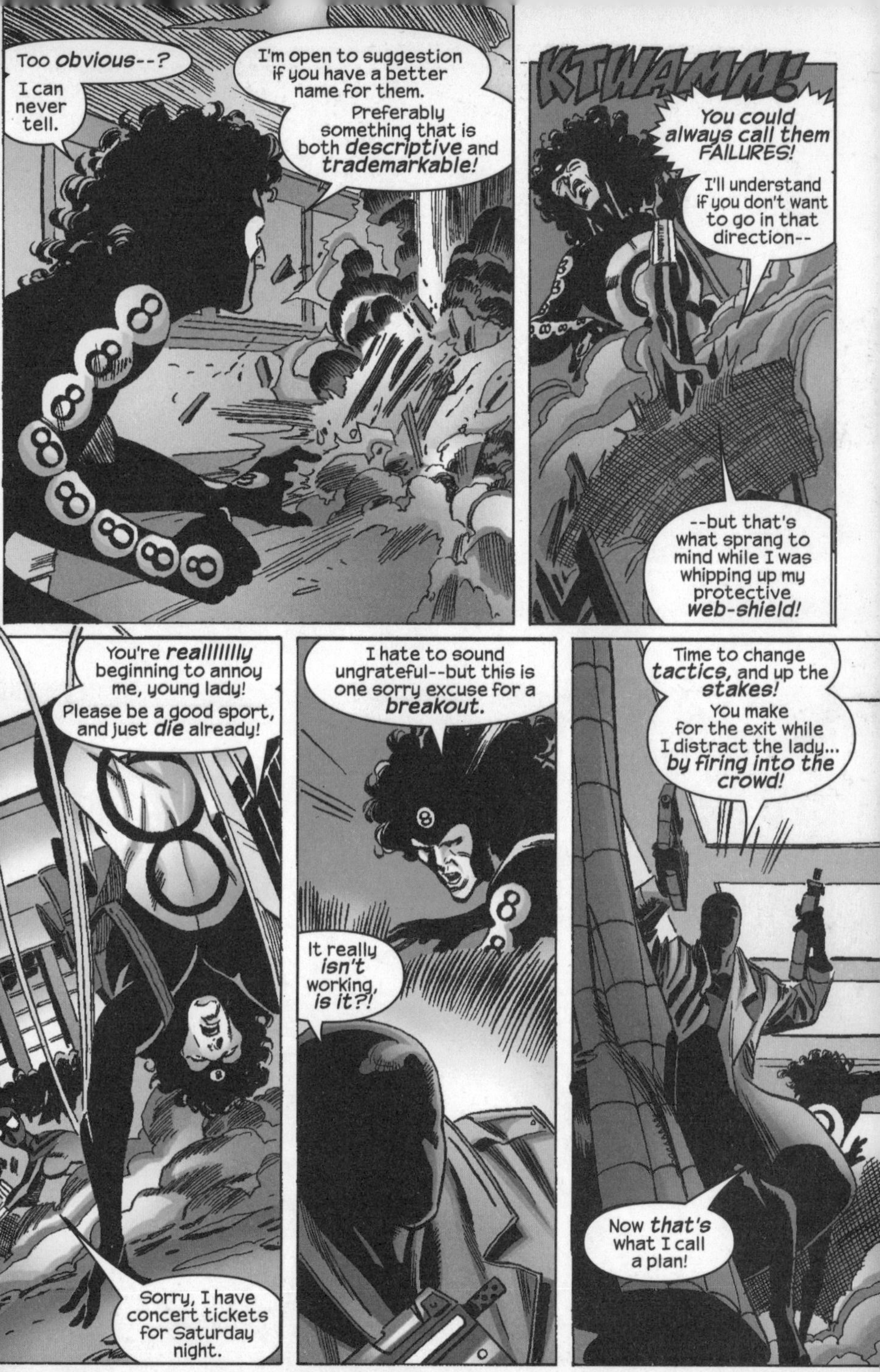
Too obvious--?
I can never tell.
I'm open to suggestion if you have a better name for them.
Preferably something that is both descriptive and trademarkable!
KTWAMM!
You could always call them FAILURES!
I'll understand if you don't want to go in that direction--
--but that's what sprang to mind while I was whipping up my protective web-shield!
You're reallllllly beginning to annoy me, young lady!
Please be a good sport, and just die already!
Sorry, I have concert tickets for Saturday night.
I hate to sound ungrateful--but this is one sorry excuse for a breakout.
It really isn't working, is it?!
Time to change tactics, and up the stakes!
You make for the exit while I distract the lady... by firing into the crowd!
Now that's what I call a plan!

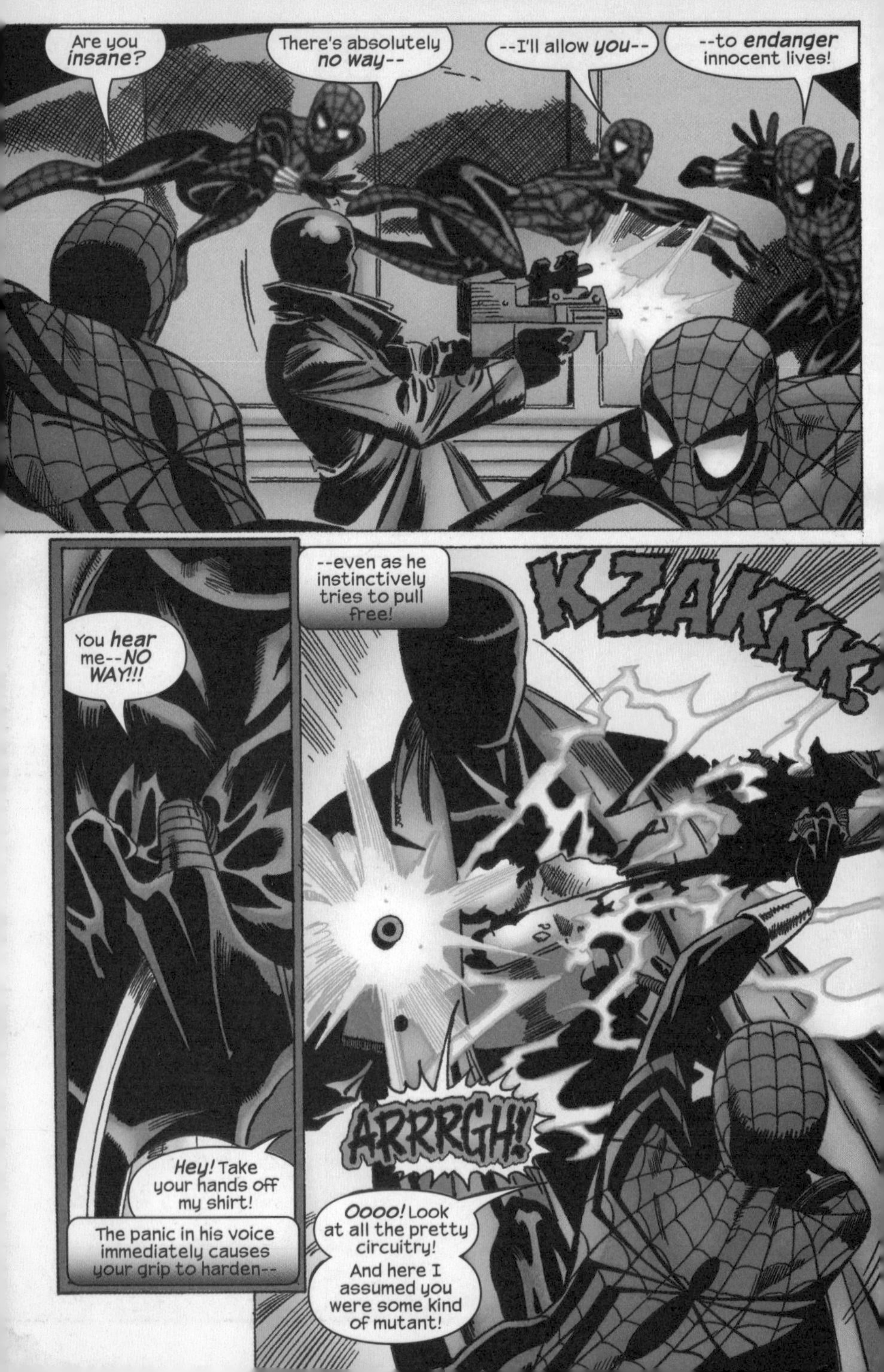

Are you *insane?*
There's absolutely *no way--*
--I'll allow *you--*
--to *endanger* innocent lives!
You *hear* me--*NO WAY!!!*
Hey! Take your hands off my shirt!
The panic in his voice immediately causes your grip to harden--
--even as he instinctively tries to pull free!
KZAKKK!
ARRRGH!
Oooo! Look at all the pretty circuitry!
And here I assumed you were some kind of mutant!

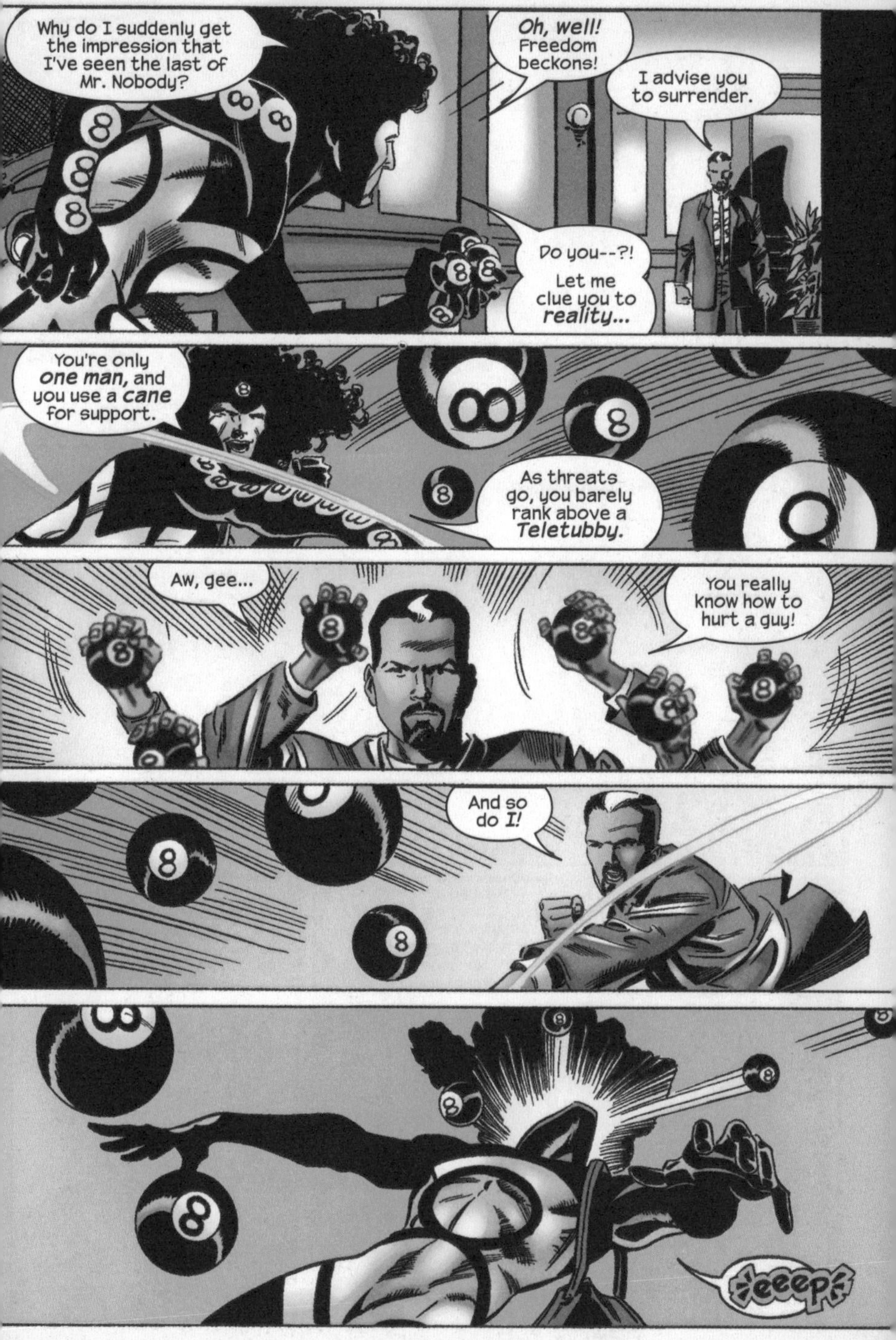
Why do I suddenly get the impression that I've seen the last of Mr. Nobody?
Oh, well! Freedom beckons!
I advise you to surrender.
Do you--?! Let me clue you to reality...
You're only one man, and you use a cane for support.
As threats go, you barely rank above a Teletubby.
Aw, gee...
You really know how to hurt a guy!
And so do I!
eeep

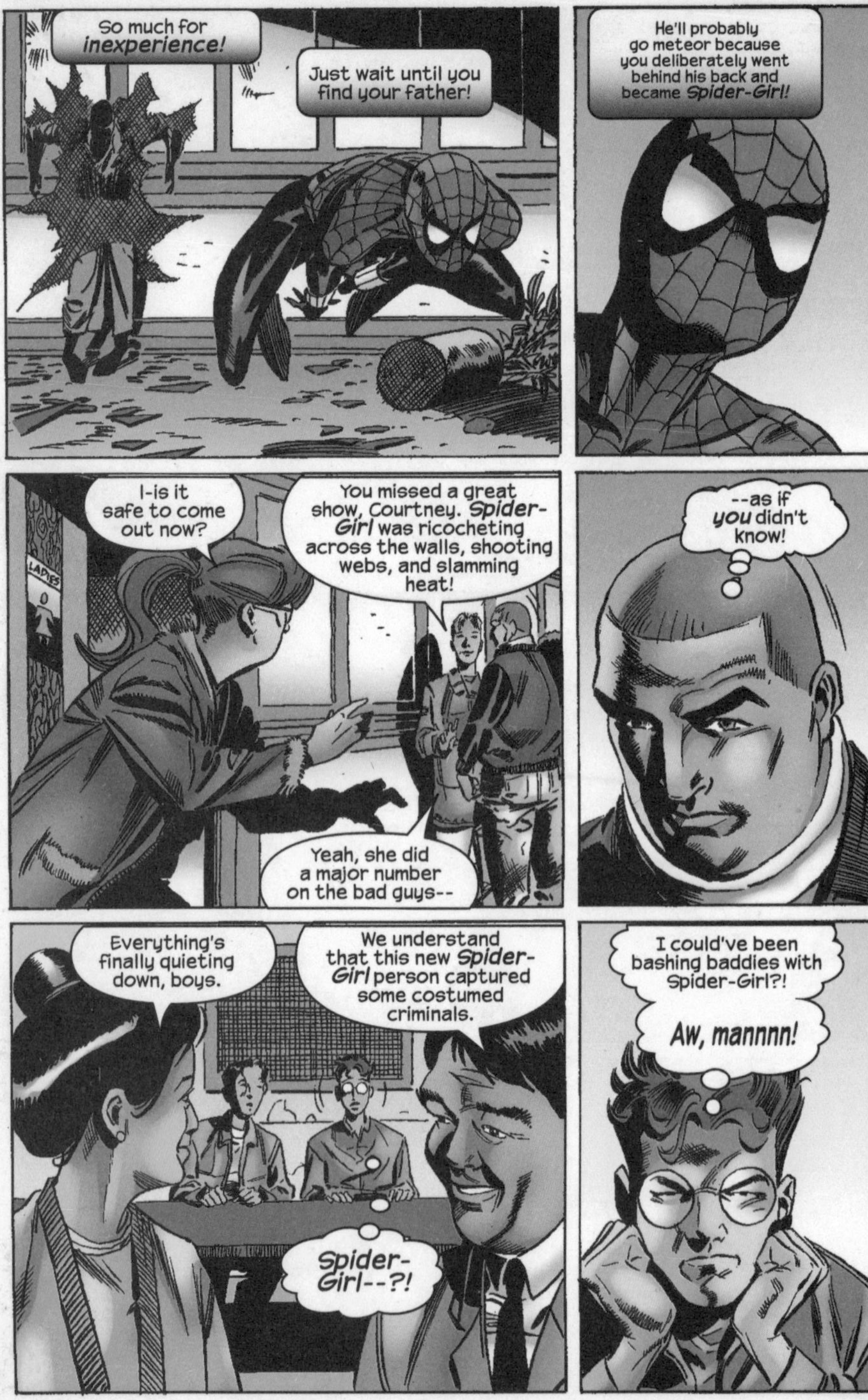
So much for inexperience!
Just wait until you find your father!
He'll probably go meteor because you deliberately went behind his back and became Spider-Girl!
I-is it safe to come out now?
You missed a great show, Courtney. Spider-Girl was ricocheting across the walls, shooting webs, and slamming heat!
Yeah, she did a major number on the bad guys--
--as if you didn't know!
Everything's finally quieting down, boys.
We understand that this new Spider-Girl person captured some costumed criminals.
Spider-Girl--?!
I could've been bashing baddies with Spider-Girl?!
Aw, mannnn!

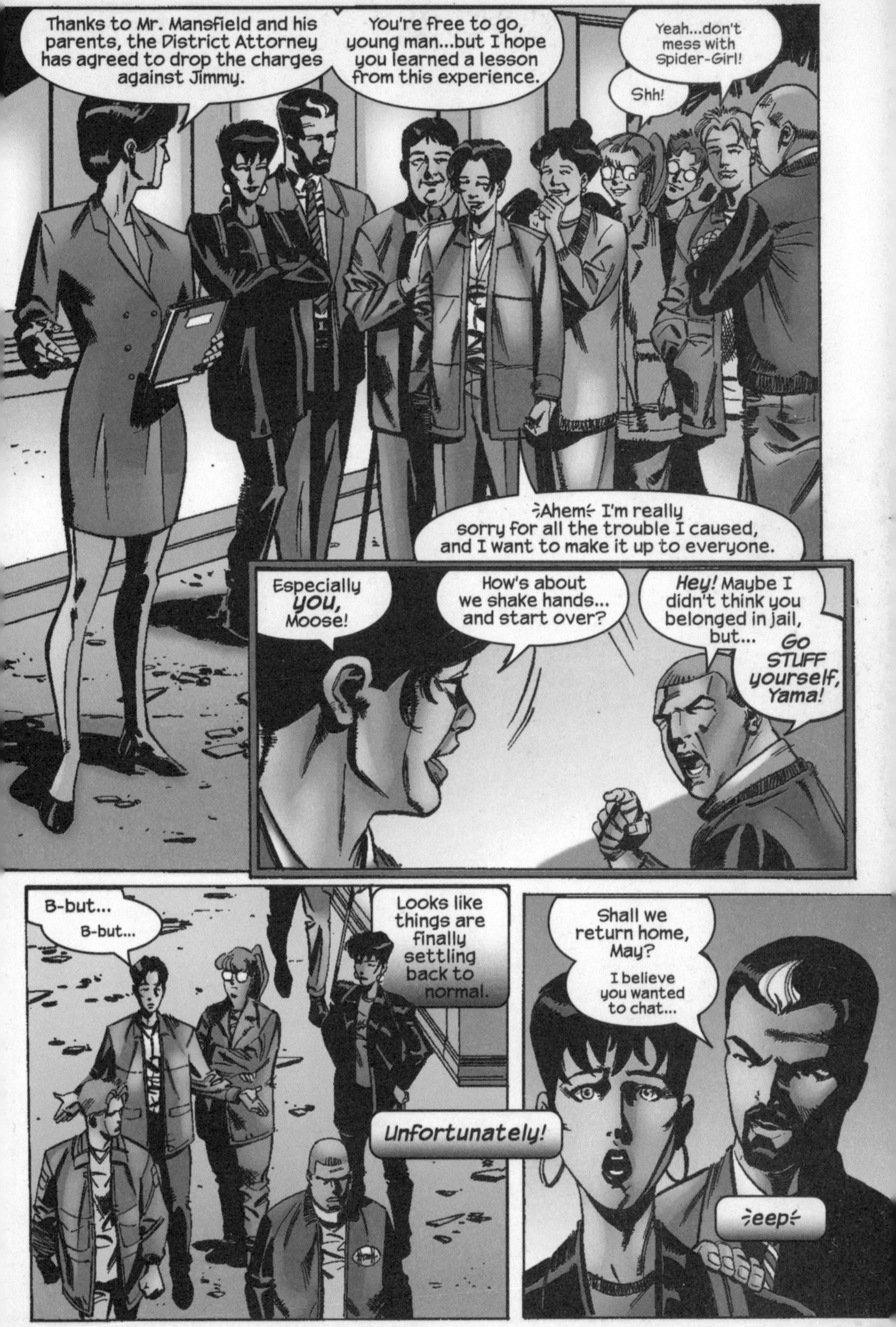

Thanks to Mr. Mansfield and his parents, the District Attorney has agreed to drop the charges against Jimmy.
You're free to go, young man...but I hope you learned a lesson from this experience.
Yeah...don't mess with Spider-Girl!
Shh!
Ahem I'm really sorry for all the trouble I caused, and I want to make it up to everyone.
Especially YOU, Moose!
How's about we shake hands... and start over?
Hey! Maybe I didn't think you belonged in jail, but...
Go STUFF yourself, Yama!
B-but...
B-but...
Looks like things are finally settling back to normal.
Unfortunately!
Shall we return home, May?
I believe you wanted to chat...
eep

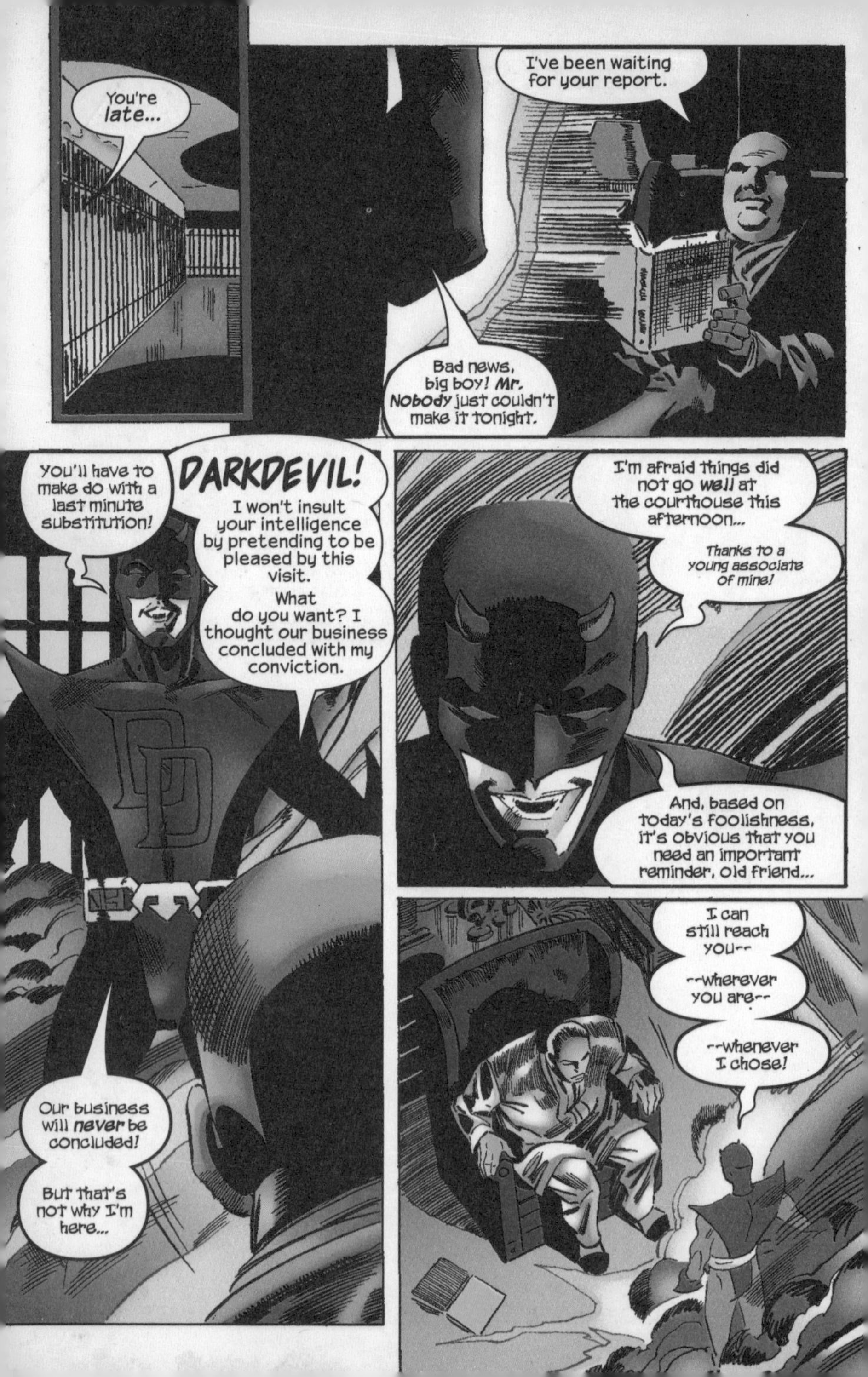
You're late...
I've been waiting for your report.
Bad news, big boy! Mr. Nobody just couldn't make it tonight.
You'll have to make do with a last minute substitution!
DARKDEVIL!
I won't insult your intelligence by pretending to be pleased by this visit.
What do you want? I thought our business concluded with my conviction.
Our business will never be concluded!
But that's not why I'm here...
I'm afraid things did not go well at the courthouse this afternoon...
Thanks to a young associate of mine!
And, based on today's foolishness, it's obvious that you need an important reminder, old friend...
I can still reach you--
--wherever you are--
--whenever I chose!

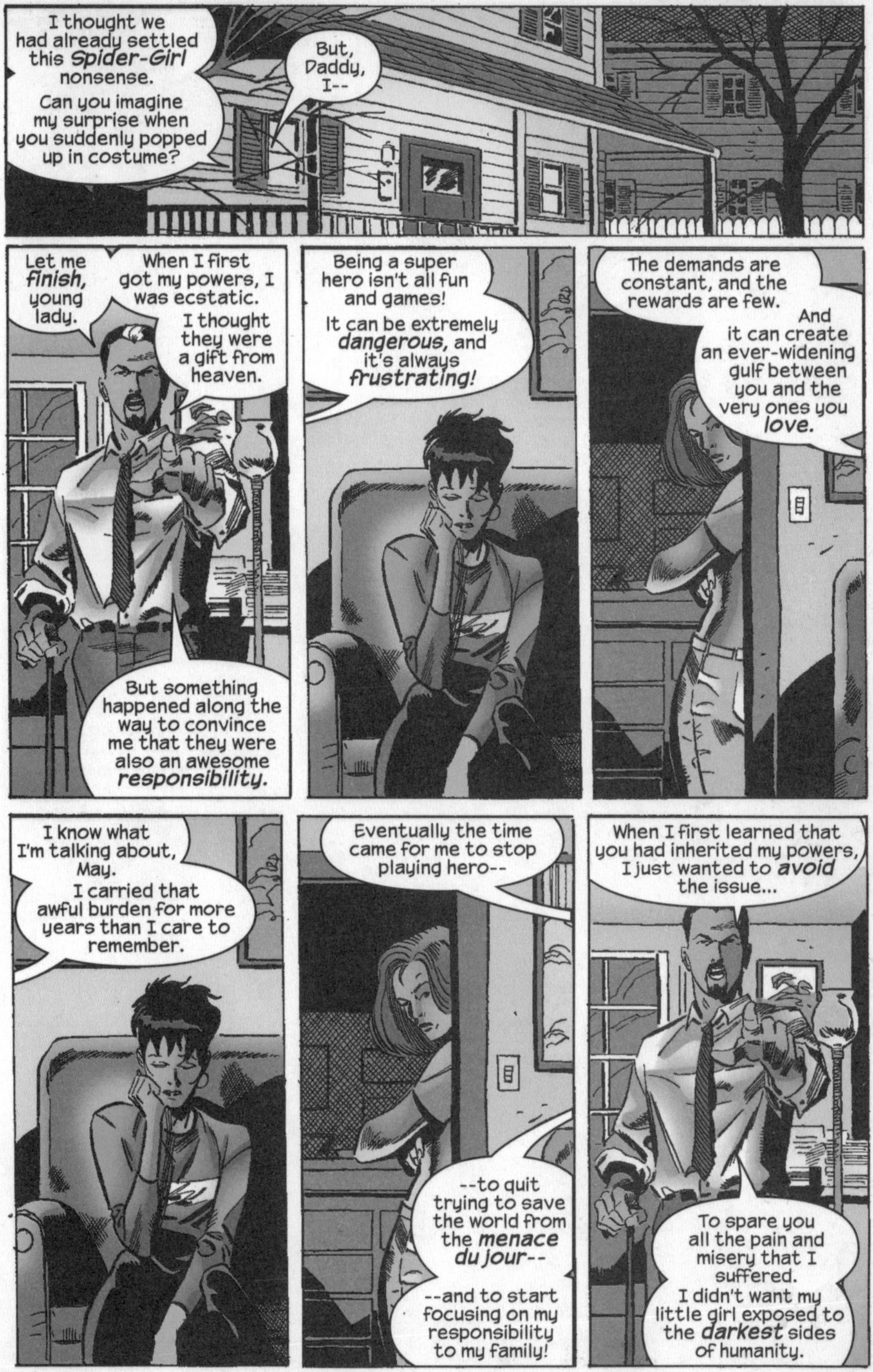

I thought we had already settled this Spider-Girl nonsense.
Can you imagine my surprise when you suddenly popped up in costume?
But, Daddy, I--
Let me finish, young lady.
When I first got my powers, I was ecstatic.
I thought they were a gift from heaven.
But something happened along the way to convince me that they were also an awesome responsibility.
Being a super hero isn't all fun and games!
It can be extremely dangerous, and it's always frustrating!
The demands are constant, and the rewards are few.
And it can create an ever-widening gulf between you and the very ones you love.
I know what I'm talking about, May.
I carried that awful burden for more years than I care to remember.
Eventually the time came for me to stop playing hero--
--to quit trying to save the world from the menace du jour--
--and to start focusing on my responsibility to my family!
When I first learned that you had inherited my powers, I just wanted to avoid the issue...
To spare you all the pain and misery that I suffered.
I didn't want my little girl exposed to the darkest sides of humanity.

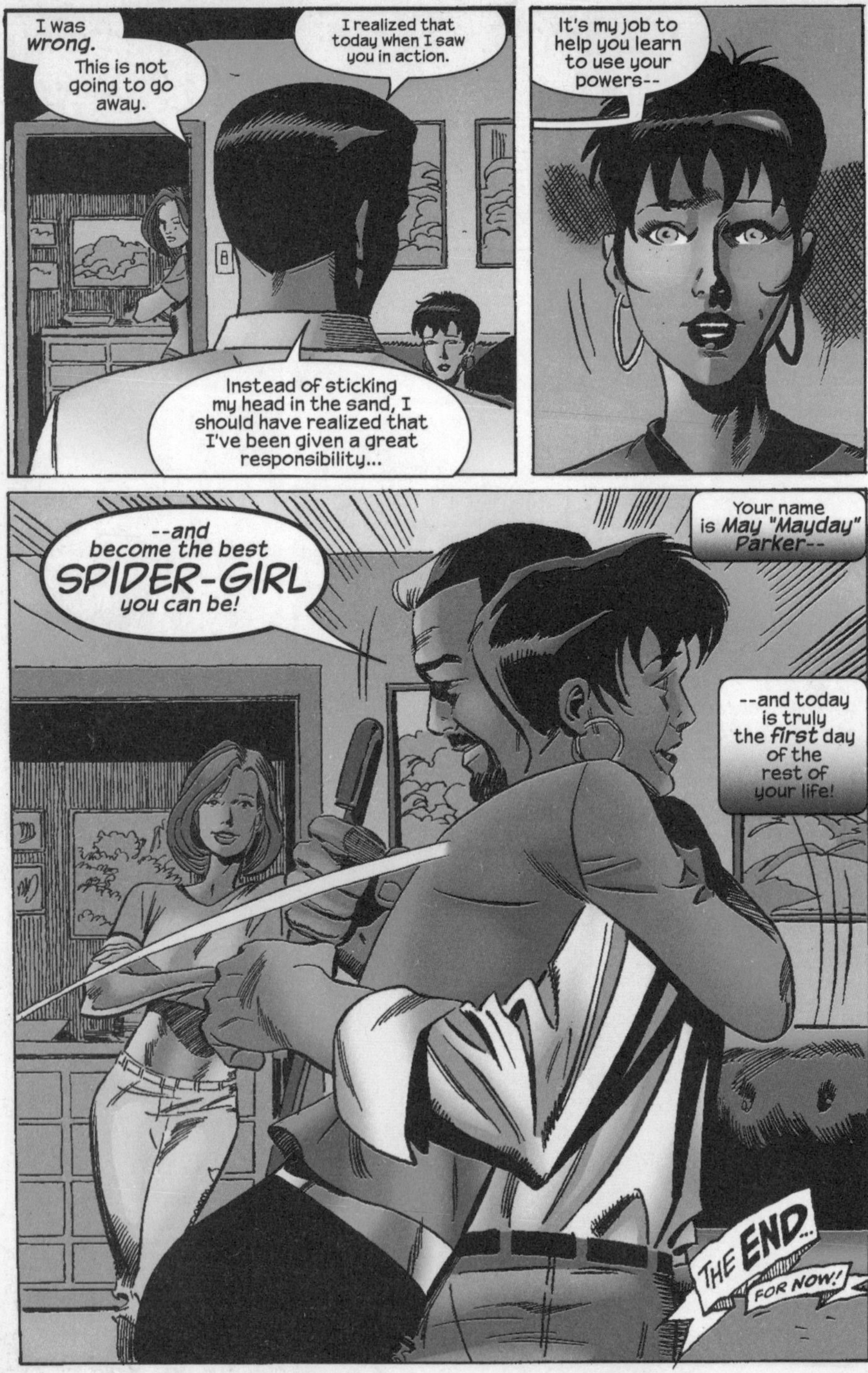
I was *wrong.*
This is not going to go away.
I realized that today when I saw you in action.
Instead of sticking my head in the sand, I should have realized that I've been given a great responsibility...
It's my job to help you learn to use your powers--
--and become the best SPIDER-GIRL you can be!
Your name is *May "Mayday"* Parker--
--and today is truly the *first* day of the rest of your life!
THE END... FOR NOW!

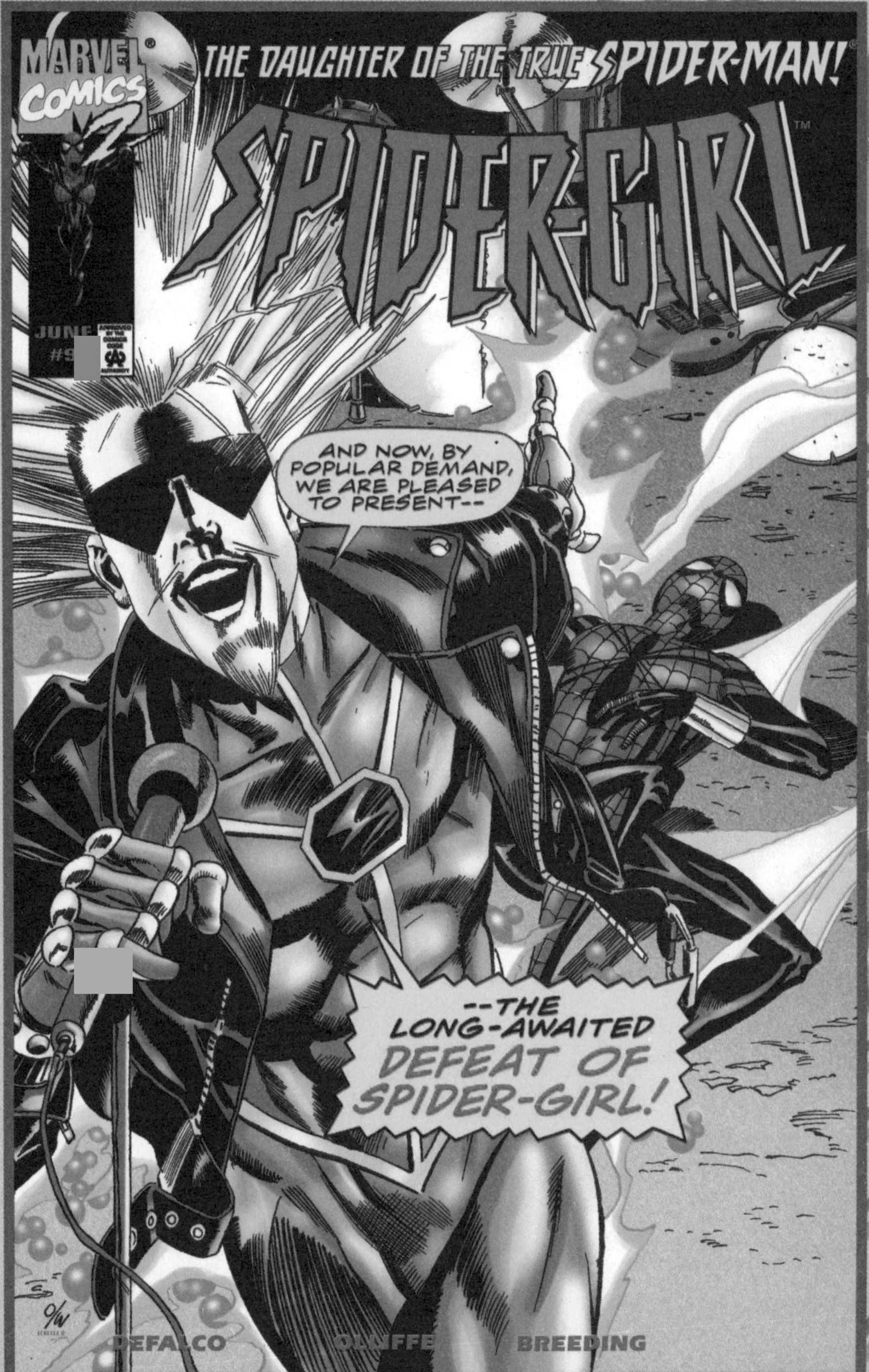
MARVEL COMICS
THE DAUGHTER OF THE TRUE SPIDER-MAN!
SPIDER-GIRL
JUNE
AND NOW, BY POPULAR DEMAND, WE ARE PLEASED TO PRESENT--
--THE LONG-AWAITED DEFEAT OF SPIDER-GIRL!
DEFALCO
OLIFFE
BREEDING

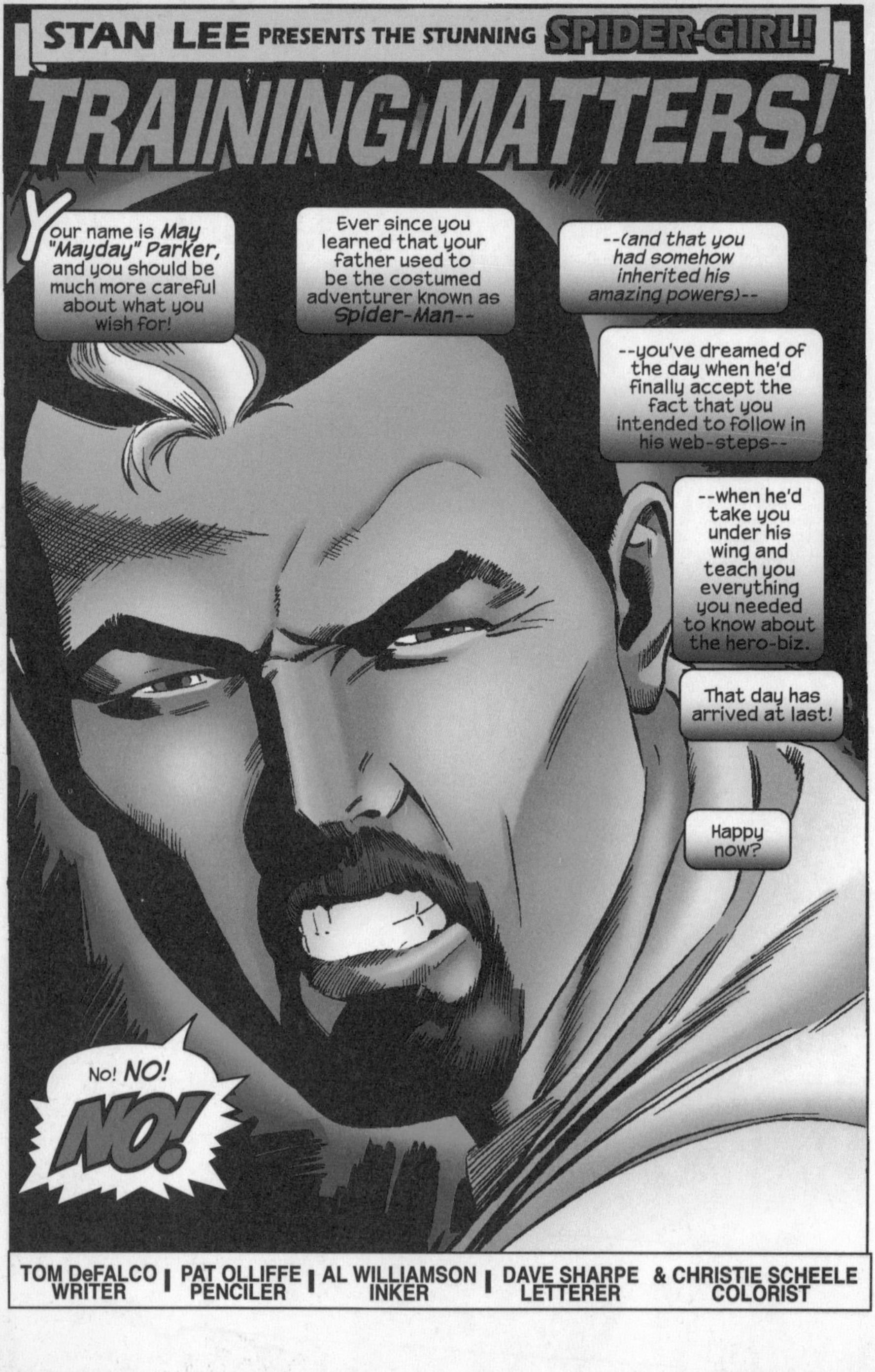
STAN LEE PRESENTS THE STUNNING SPIDER-GIRL!
TRAINING MATTERS!
Your name is May "Mayday" Parker, and you should be much more careful about what you wish for!
Ever since you learned that your father used to be the costumed adventurer known as Spider-Man--
--(and that you had somehow inherited his amazing powers)--
--you've dreamed of the day when he'd finally accept the fact that you intended to follow in his web-steps--
--when he'd take you under his wing and teach you everything you needed to know about the hero-biz.
That day has arrived at last!
Happy now?
No! NO! NO!
TOM DeFALCO WRITER | PAT OLLIFFE PENCILER | AL WILLIAMSON INKER | DAVE SHARPE LETTERER & CHRISTIE SCHEELE COLORIST

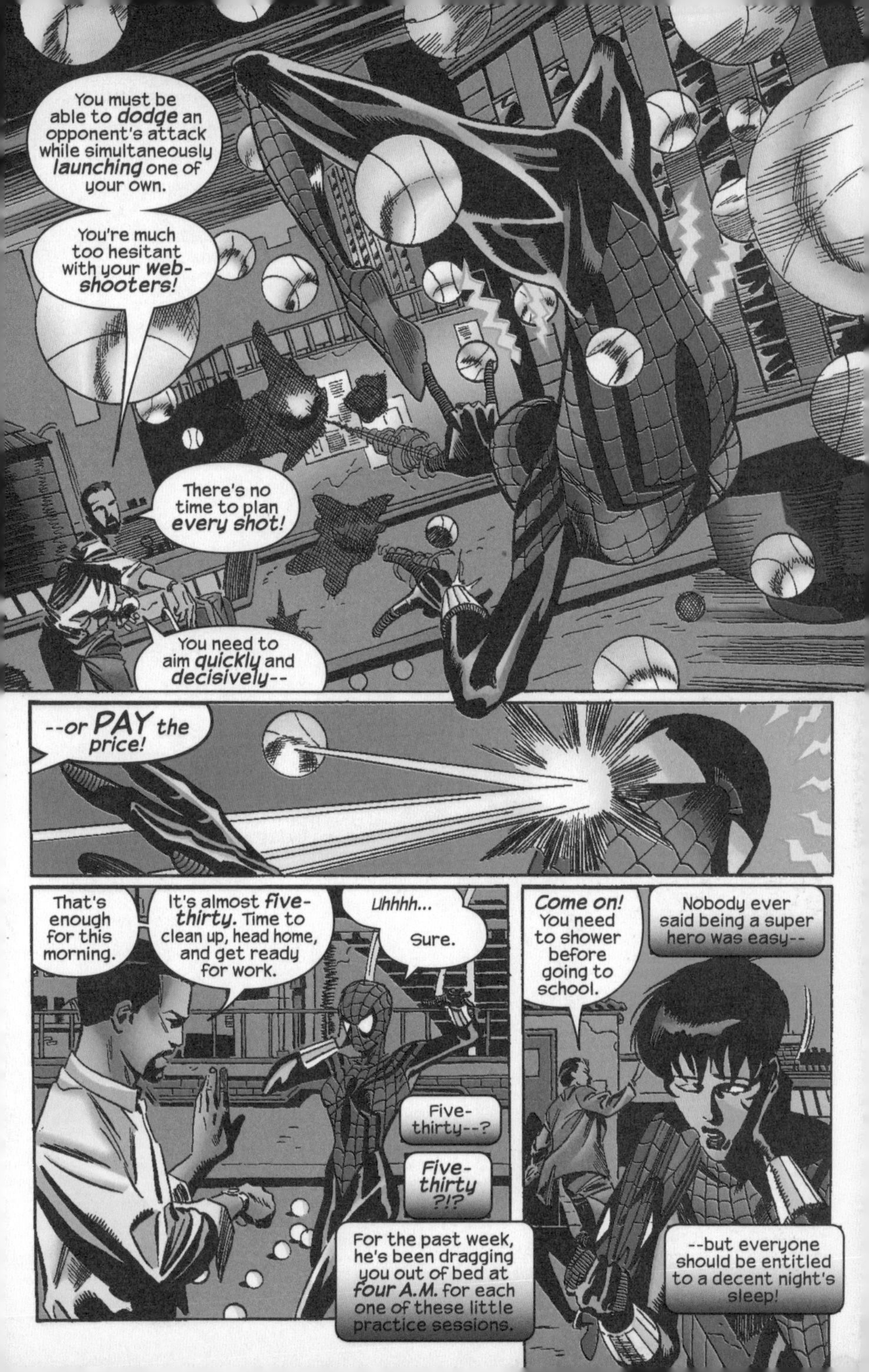

You must be able to *dodge* an opponent's attack while simultaneously *launching* one of your own.
You're much too hesitant with your *web-shooters!*
There's no time to plan *every shot!*
You need to aim *quickly* and *decisively*--
--or *PAY* the price!
That's enough for this morning.
It's almost *five-thirty.* Time to clean up, head home, and get ready for work.
Uhhhh...
Sure.
Five-thirty--?
Five-thirty ?!?
For the past week, he's been dragging you out of bed at *four A.M.* for each one of these little practice sessions.
Come on! You need to shower before going to school.
Nobody ever said being a super hero was easy--
--but everyone should be entitled to a decent night's sleep!

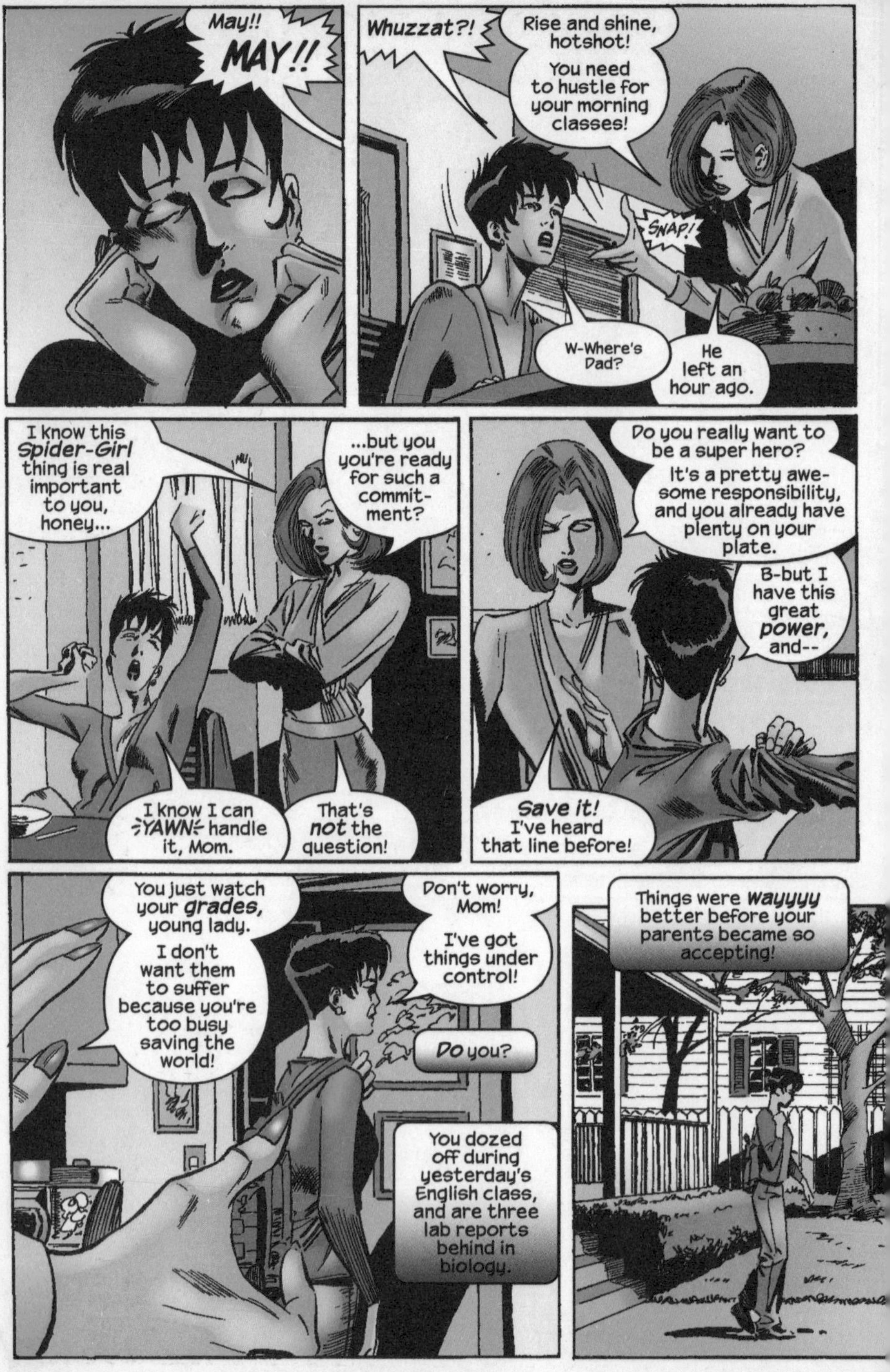
May!! MAY!!
Whuzzat?!
Rise and shine, hotshot!
You need to hustle for your morning classes!
SNAP!
W-Where's Dad?
He left an hour ago.
I know this Spider-Girl thing is real important to you, honey...
...but you you're ready for such a commit-ment?
I know I can ≈YAWN≈ handle it, Mom.
That's not the question!
Do you really want to be a super hero?
It's a pretty awe-some responsibility, and you already have plenty on your plate.
B-but I have this great power, and--
Save it! I've heard that line before!
You just watch your grades, young lady.
I don't want them to suffer because you're too busy saving the world!
Don't worry, Mom!
I've got things under control!
Do you?
You dozed off during yesterday's English class, and are three lab reports behind in biology.
Things were wayyyy better before your parents became so accepting!

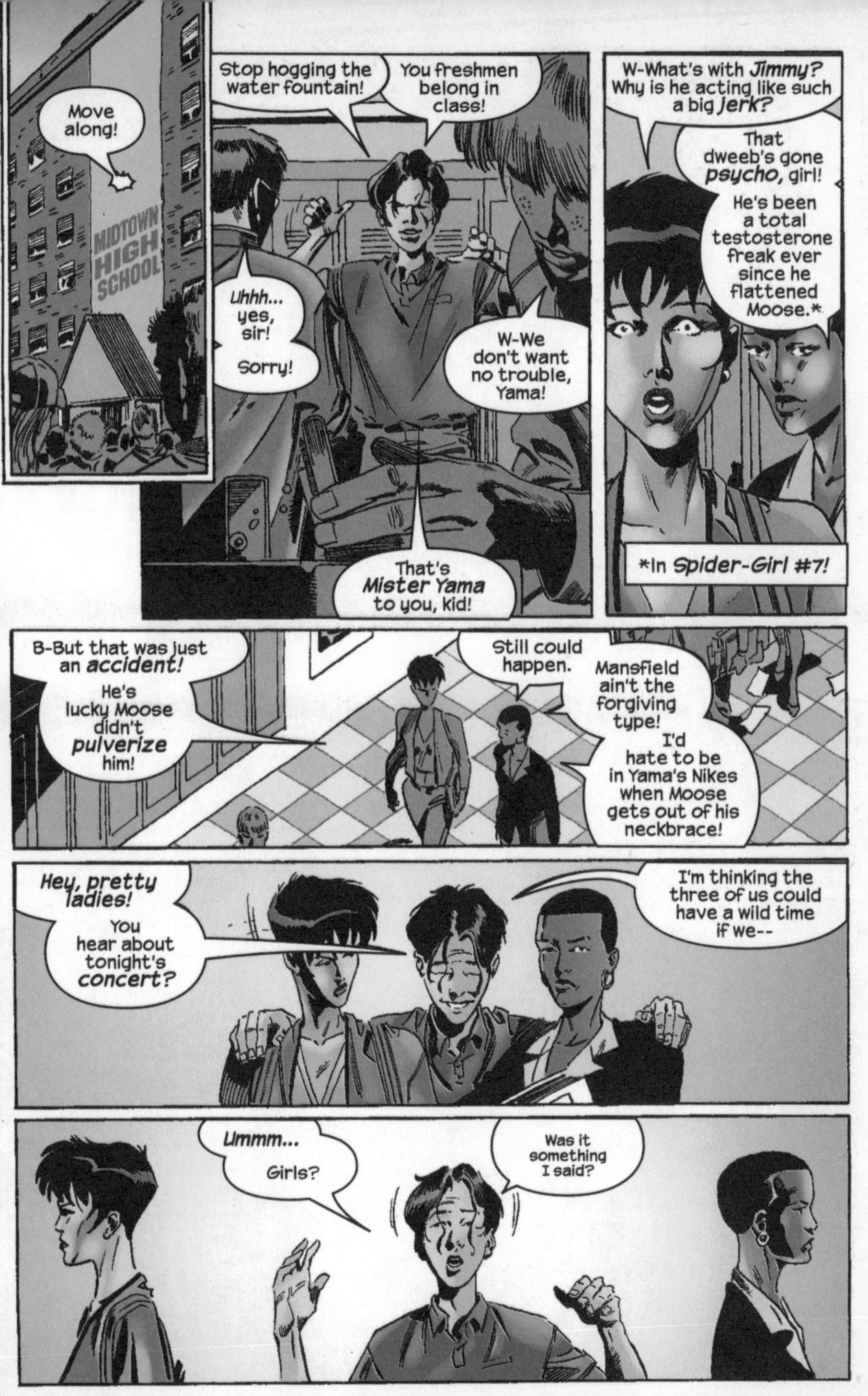
Move along!
MIDTOWN HIGH SCHOOL
Stop hogging the water fountain!
You freshmen belong in class!
Uhhh... yes, sir!
Sorry!
W-We don't want no trouble, Yama!
That's Mister Yama to you, kid!
W-What's with Jimmy? Why is he acting like such a big jerk?
That dweeb's gone psycho, girl!
He's been a total testosterone freak ever since he flattened Moose.*
*In Spider-Girl #7!
B-But that was just an accident!
He's lucky Moose didn't pulverize him!
Still could happen.
Mansfield ain't the forgiving type!
I'd hate to be in Yama's Nikes when Moose gets out of his neckbrace!
Hey, pretty ladies!
You hear about tonight's concert?
I'm thinking the three of us could have a wild time if we--
Ummm...
Girls?
Was it something I said?

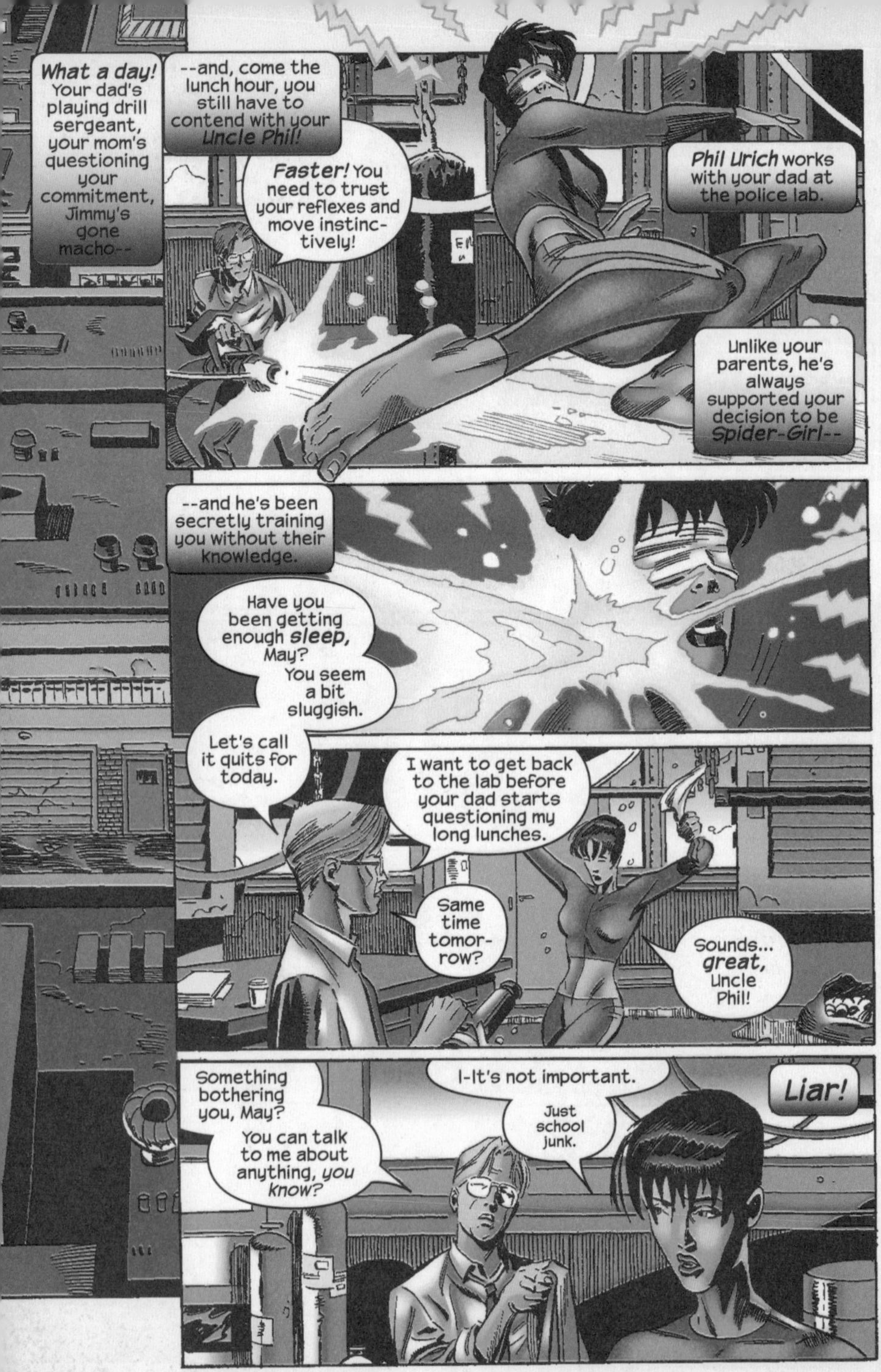
What a day! Your dad's playing drill sergeant, your mom's questioning your commitment, Jimmy's gone macho--
--and, come the lunch hour, you still have to contend with your Uncle Phil!
Faster! You need to trust your reflexes and move instinctively!
Phil Urich works with your dad at the police lab.
Unlike your parents, he's always supported your decision to be Spider-Girl--
--and he's been secretly training you without their knowledge.
Have you been getting enough sleep, May?
You seem a bit sluggish.
Let's call it quits for today.
I want to get back to the lab before your dad starts questioning my long lunches.
Same time tomorrow?
Sounds... great, Uncle Phil!
Something bothering you, May?
You can talk to me about anything, you know?
I-It's not important.
Just school junk.
Liar!

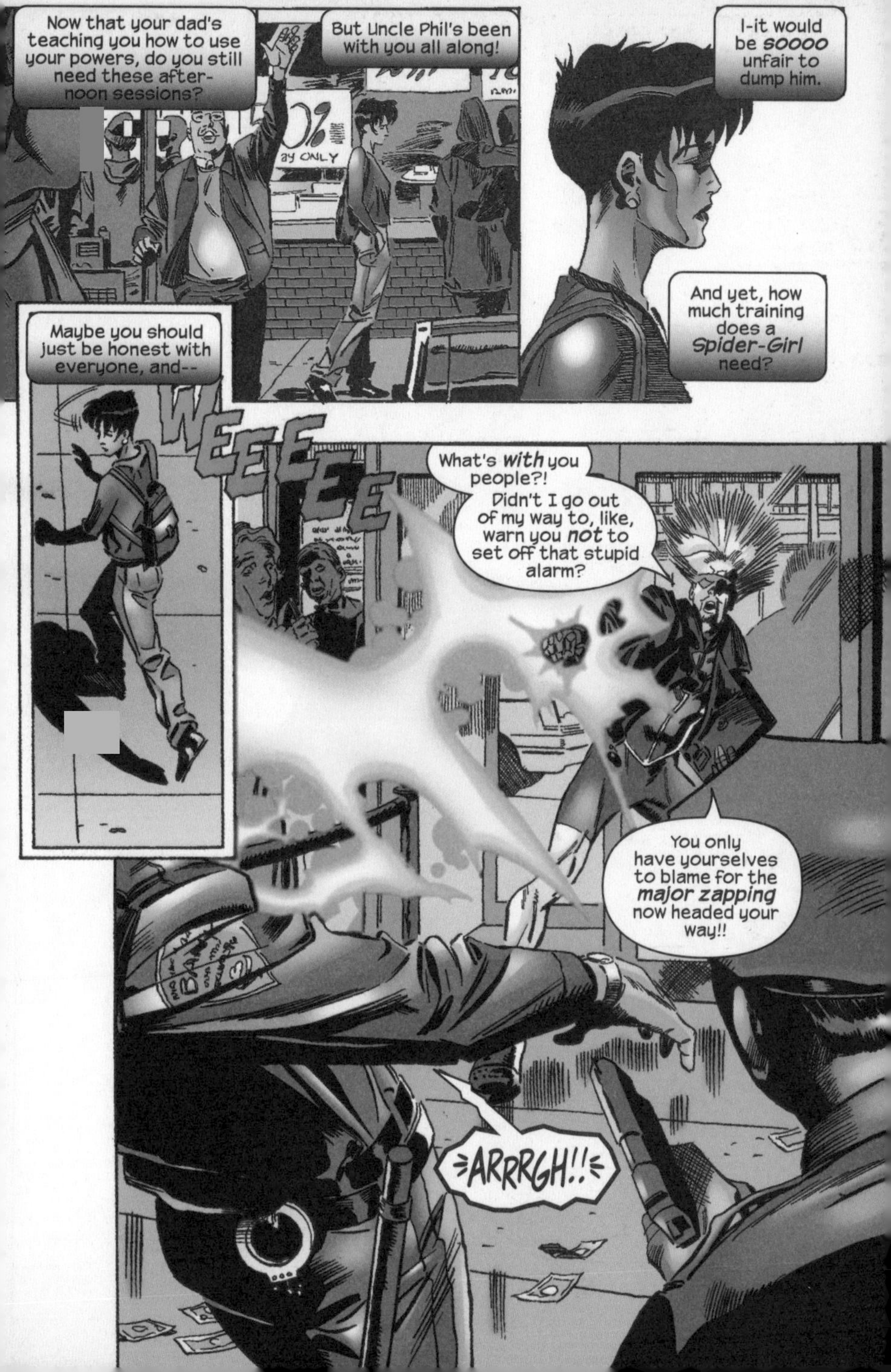

Now that your dad's teaching you how to use your powers, do you still need these after-noon sessions?
But Uncle Phil's been with you all along!
I-it would be *soooo* unfair to dump him.
And yet, how much training does a *Spider-Girl* need?
Maybe you should just be honest with everyone, and--
WEEEEEE
What's *with* you people?!
Didn't I go out of my way to, like, warn you *not* to set off that stupid alarm?
You only have yourselves to blame for the *major zapping* now headed your way!!
ARRRGH!!

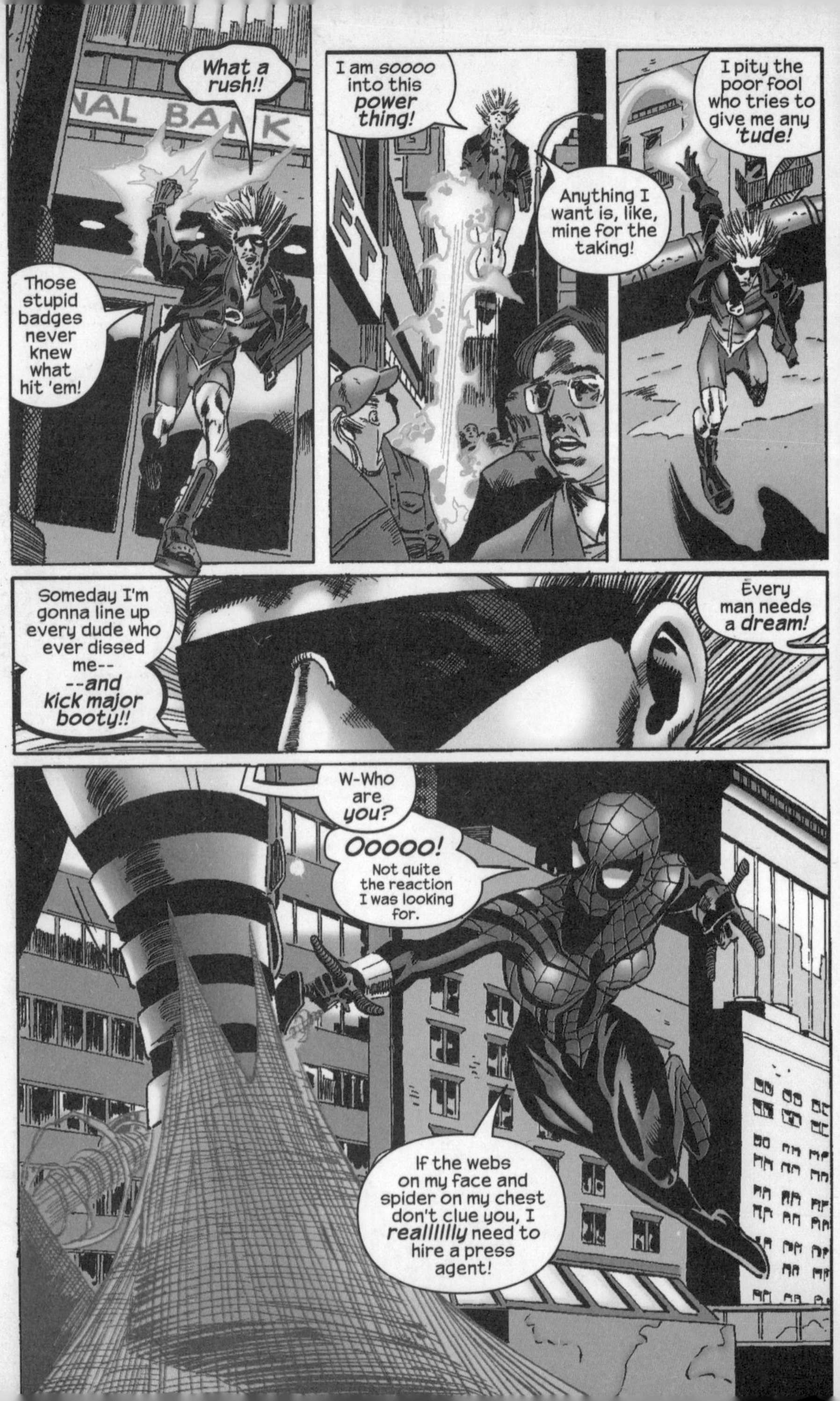

What a rush!!
Those stupid badges never knew what hit 'em!
NAL BANK
I am soooo into this power thing!
Anything I want is, like, mine for the taking!
I pity the poor fool who tries to give me any 'tude!
Someday I'm gonna line up every dude who ever dissed me--
--and kick major booty!!
Every man needs a dream!
W-Who are you?
Ooooo! Not quite the reaction I was looking for.
If the webs on my face and spider on my chest don't clue you, I reallllllly need to hire a press agent!

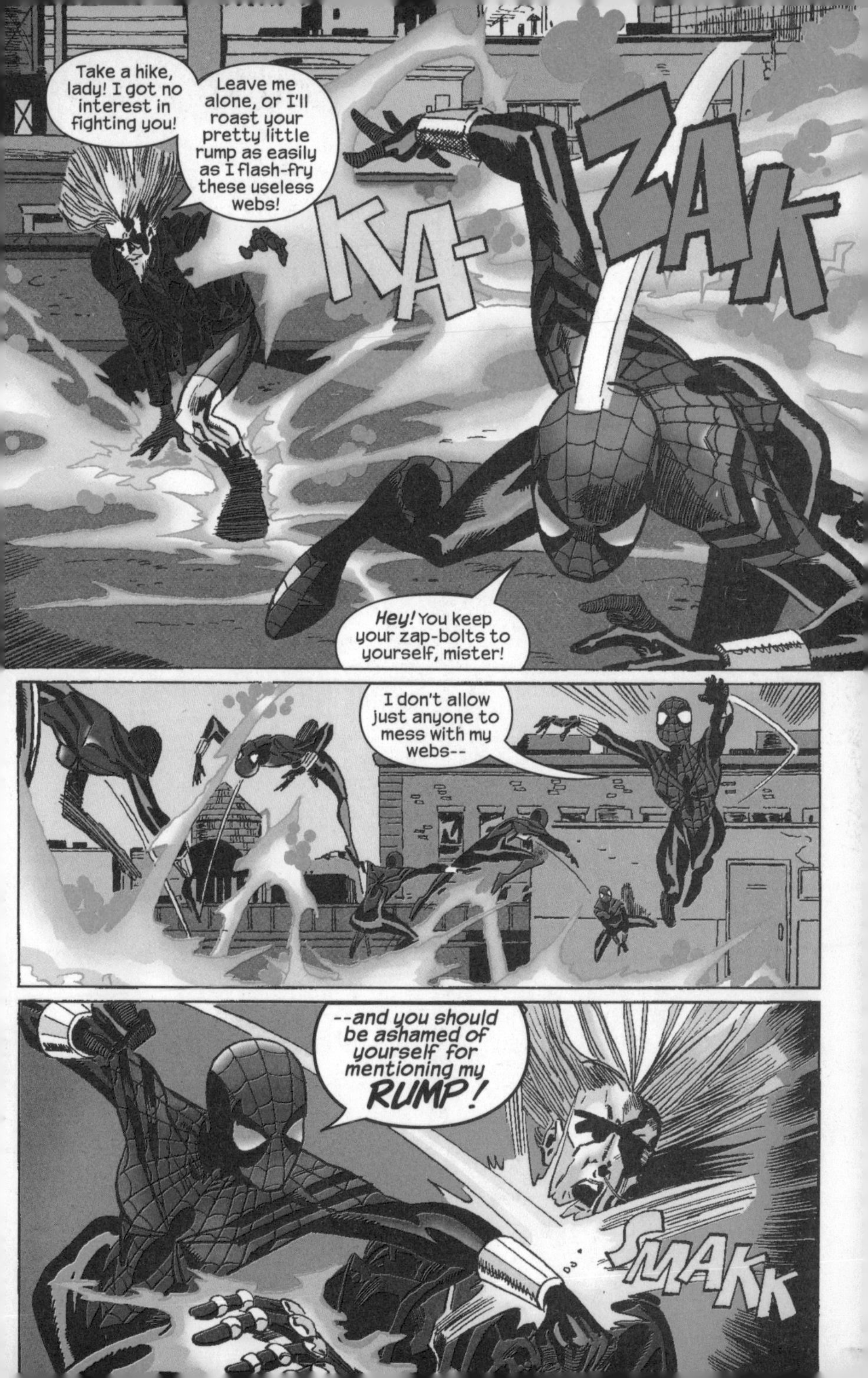

Take a hike, lady! I got no interest in fighting you!
Leave me alone, or I'll roast your pretty little rump as easily as I flash-fry these useless webs!
KA-ZAK
Hey! You keep your zap-bolts to yourself, mister!
I don't allow just anyone to mess with my webs--
--and you should be ashamed of yourself for mentioning my RUMP!
SMAKK

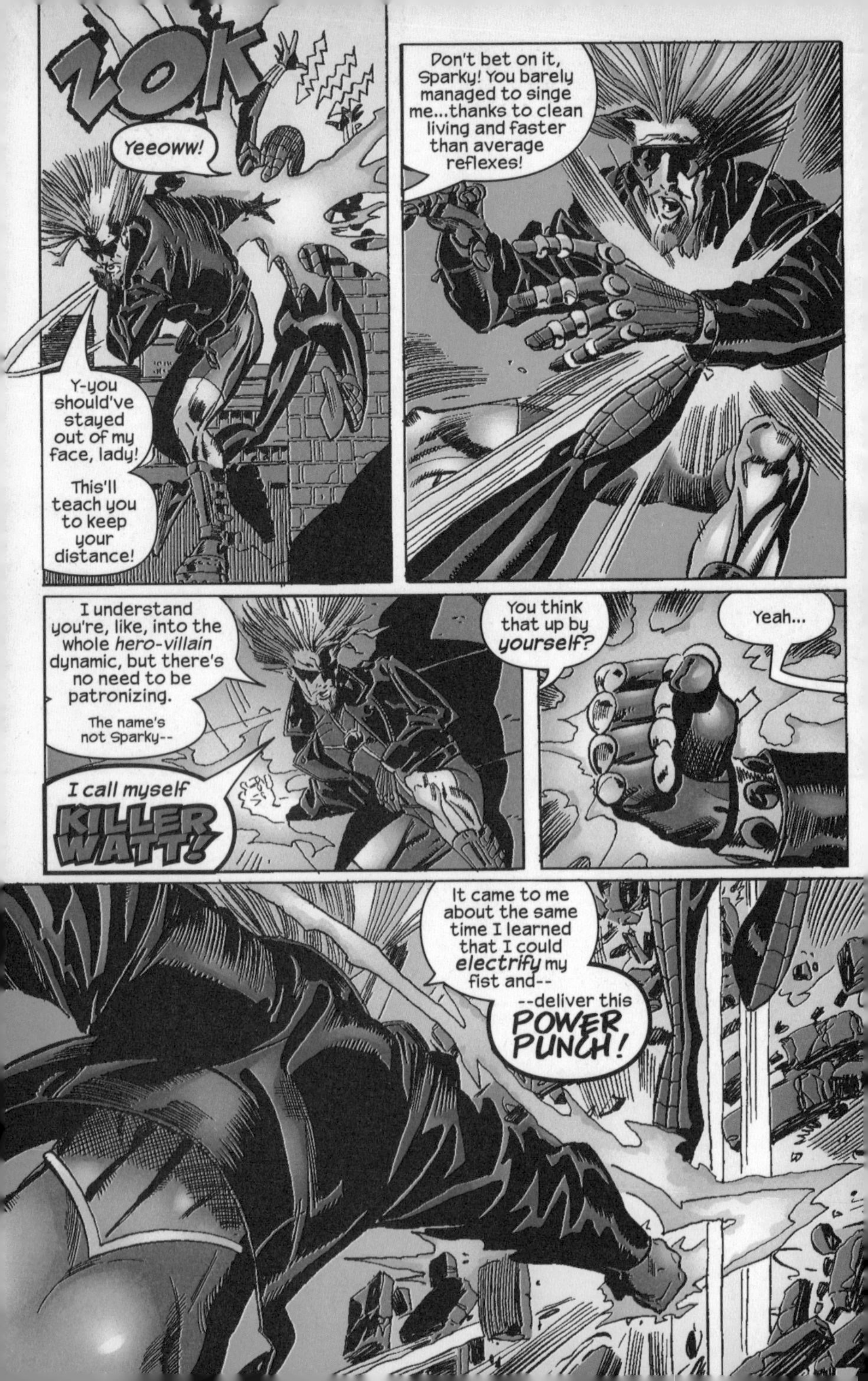
ZOK
Yeeoww!
Y-you should've stayed out of my face, lady!
This'll teach you to keep your distance!
Don't bet on it, Sparky! You barely managed to singe me...thanks to clean living and faster than average reflexes!
I understand you're, like, into the whole *hero-villain* dynamic, but there's no need to be patronizing.
The name's not Sparky--
I call myself
KILLER WATT!
You think that up by *yourself*?
Yeah...
It came to me about the same time I learned that I could *electrify* my fist and--
--deliver this
POWER PUNCH!

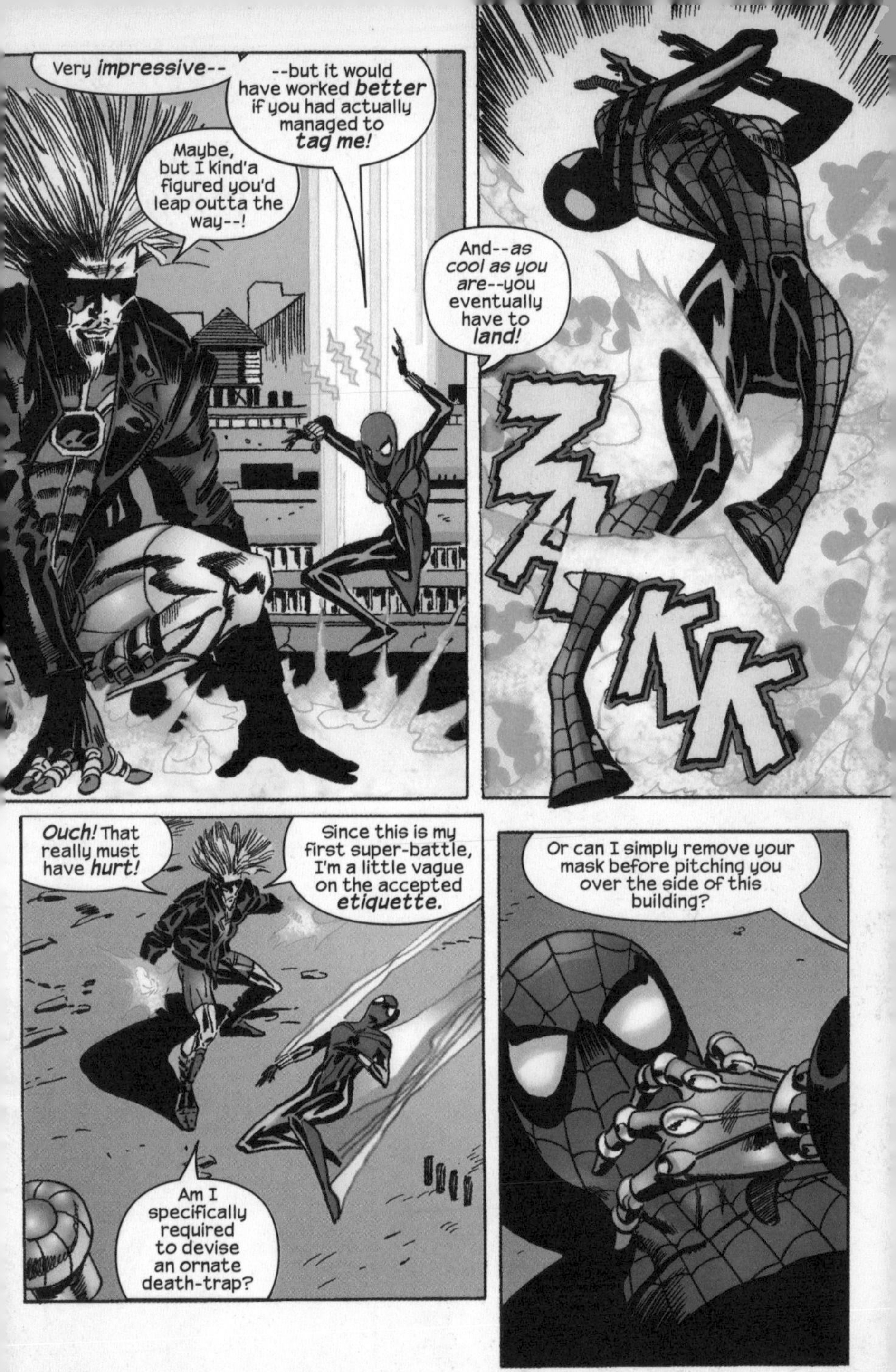

Very impressive--
--but it would have worked better if you had actually managed to tag me!
Maybe, but I kind'a figured you'd leap outta the way--!
And--as cool as you are--you eventually have to land!
ZAKKK
Ouch! That really must have hurt!
Since this is my first super-battle, I'm a little vague on the accepted etiquette.
Am I specifically required to devise an ornate death-trap?
Or can I simply remove your mask before pitching you over the side of this building?

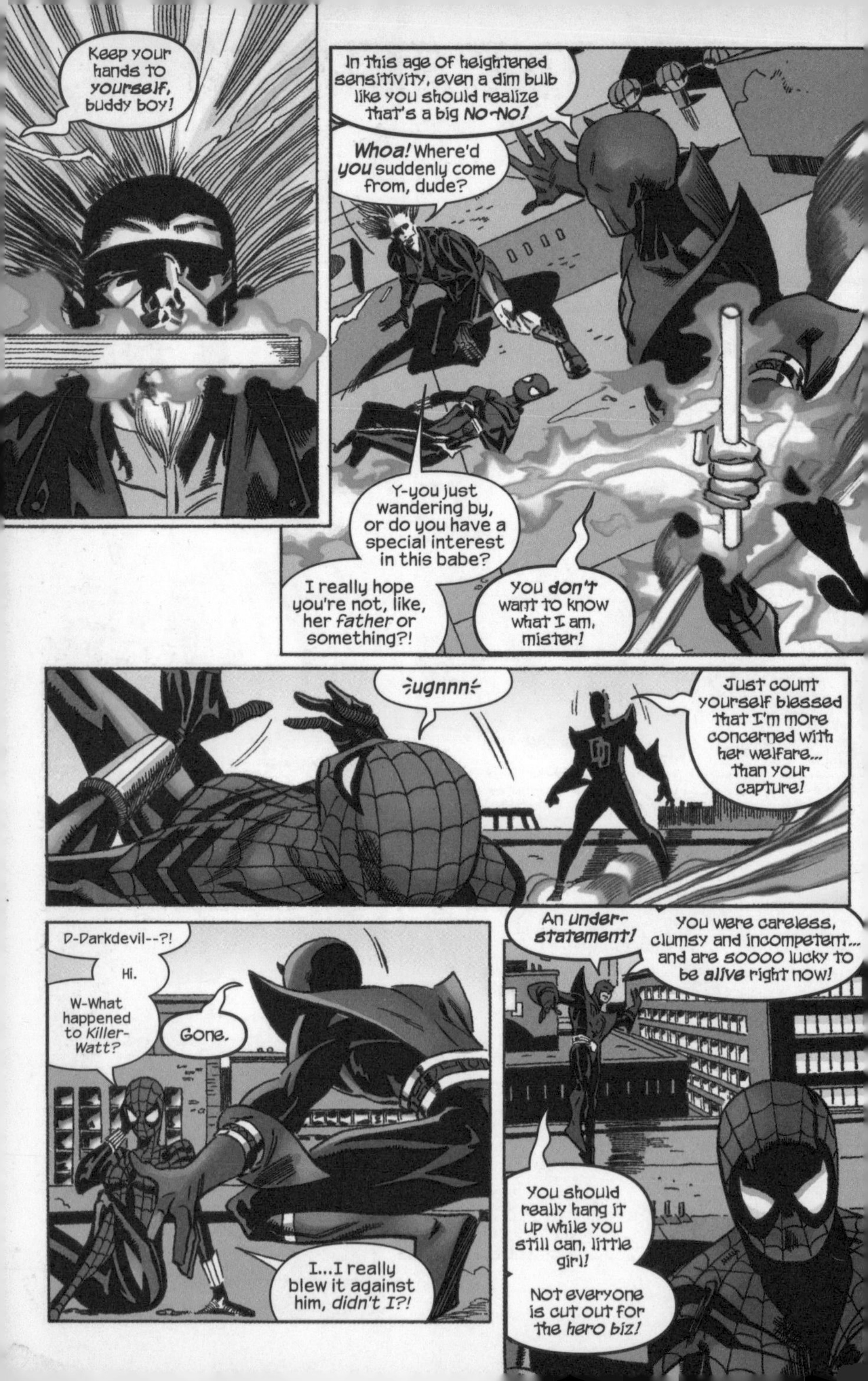
Keep your hands to yourself, buddy boy!
In this age of heightened sensitivity, even a dim bulb like you should realize that's a big NO-NO!
Whoa! Where'd you suddenly come from, dude?
Y-you just wandering by, or do you have a special interest in this babe?
I really hope you're not, like, her father or something?!
You don't want to know what I am, mister!
-ugnnn-
Just count yourself blessed that I'm more concerned with her welfare... than your capture!
D-Darkdevil--?!
Hi.
W-What happened to Killer-Watt?
Gone.
I...I really blew it against him, didn't I?!
An under-statement!
You were careless, clumsy and incompetent... and are SOOOO lucky to be alive right now!
You should really hang it up while you still can, little girl!
Not everyone is cut out for the hero biz!

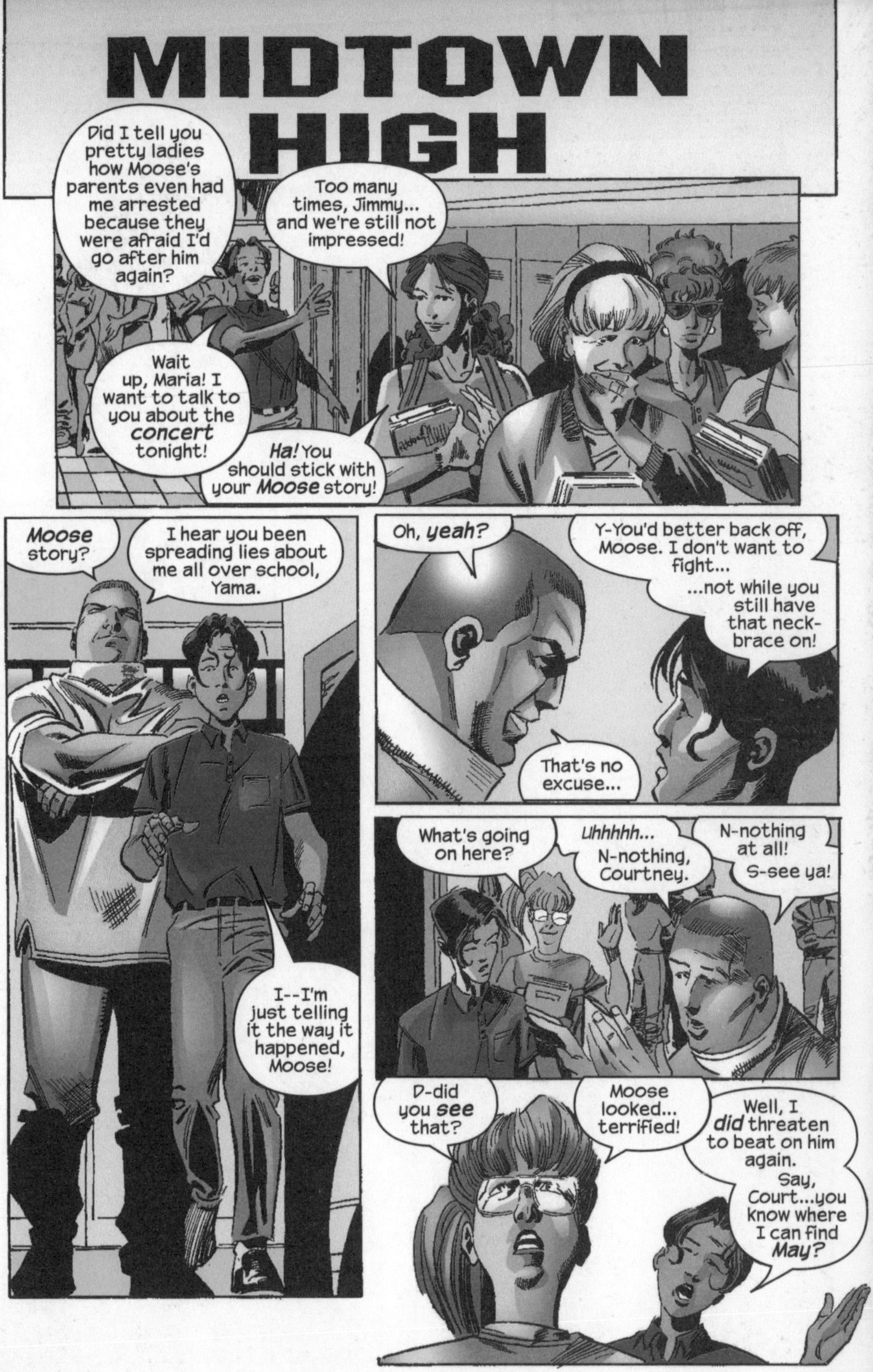
MIDTOWN HIGH
Did I tell you pretty ladies how Moose's parents even had me arrested because they were afraid I'd go after him again?
Too many times, Jimmy... and we're still not impressed!
Wait up, Maria! I want to talk to you about the concert tonight!
Ha! You should stick with your Moose story!
Moose story?
I hear you been spreading lies about me all over school, Yama.
I--I'm just telling it the way it happened, Moose!
Oh, yeah?
Y-You'd better back off, Moose. I don't want to fight...
...not while you still have that neck-brace on!
That's no excuse...
What's going on here?
Uhhhhh... N-nothing, Courtney.
N-nothing at all! S-see ya!
D-did you see that?
Moose looked... terrified!
Well, I did threaten to beat on him again.
Say, Court...you know where I can find May?

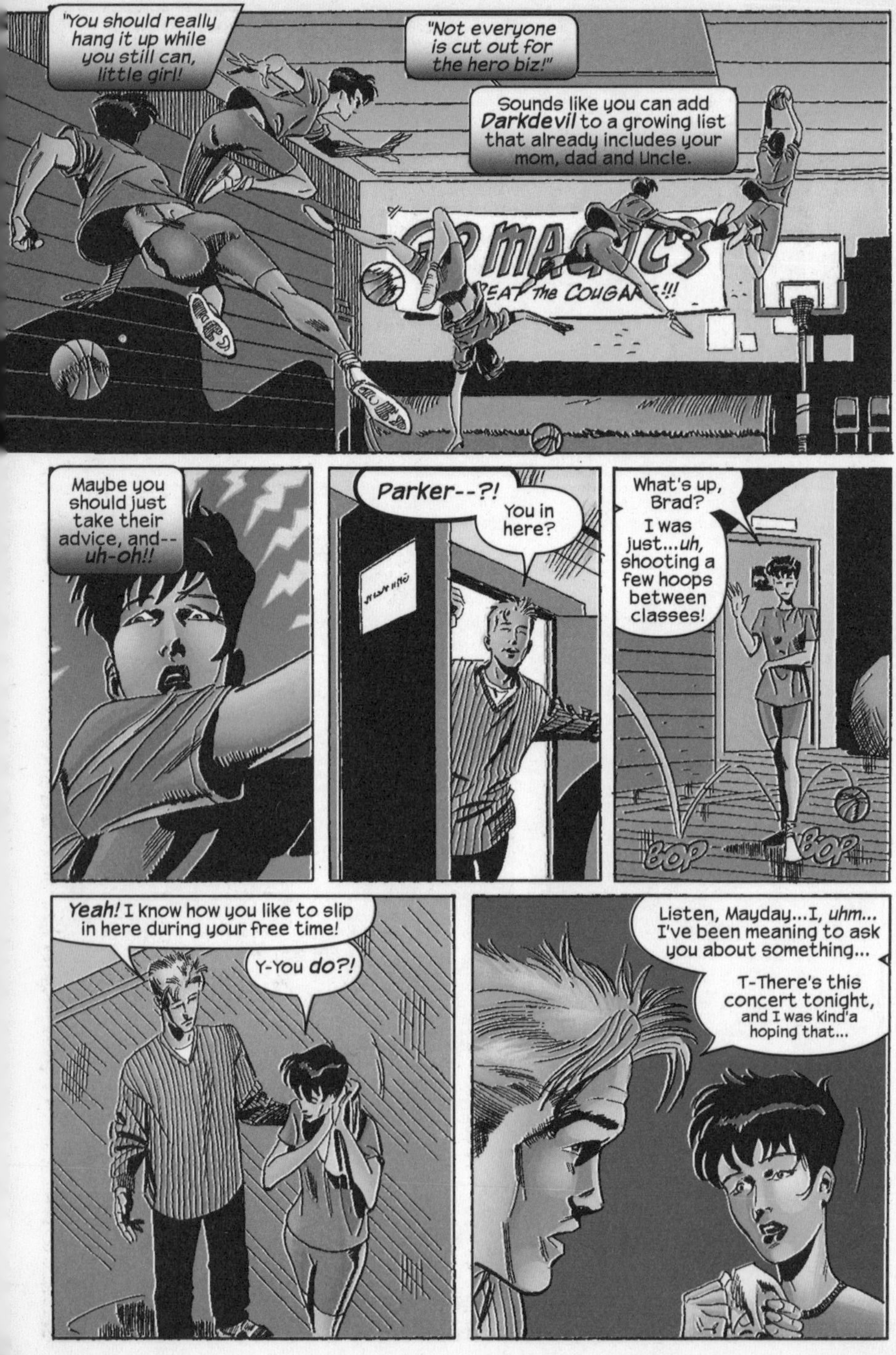
"You should really hang it up while you still can, little girl!"
"Not everyone is cut out for the hero biz!"
Sounds like you can add Darkdevil to a growing list that already includes your mom, dad and Uncle.
Maybe you should just take their advice, and-- uh-oh!!
Parker--?!
You in here?
What's up, Brad?
I was just...uh, shooting a few hoops between classes!
BOP
BOP
Yeah! I know how you like to slip in here during your free time!
Y-You do?!
Listen, Mayday...I, uhm... I've been meaning to ask you about something...
T-There's this concert tonight, and I was kind'a hoping that...

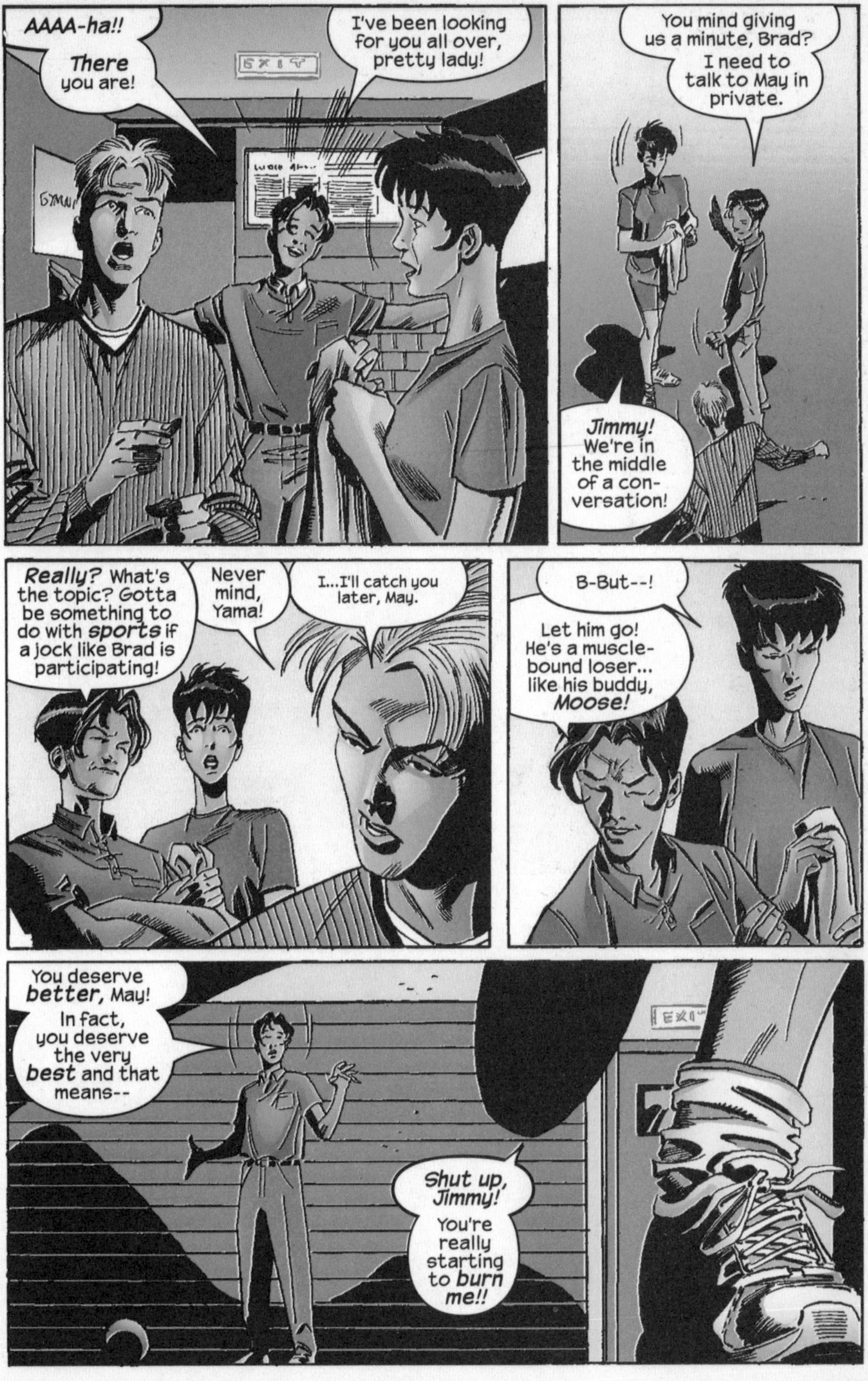
AAAA-ha!! There you are!
I've been looking for you all over, pretty lady!
EXIT
GYM
You mind giving us a minute, Brad? I need to talk to May in private.
Jimmy! We're in the middle of a conversation!
Really? What's the topic? Gotta be something to do with sports if a jock like Brad is participating!
Never mind, Yama!
I...I'll catch you later, May.
B-But--!
Let him go! He's a muscle-bound loser... like his buddy, Moose!
You deserve better, May! In fact, you deserve the very best and that means--
Shut up, Jimmy! You're really starting to burn me!!

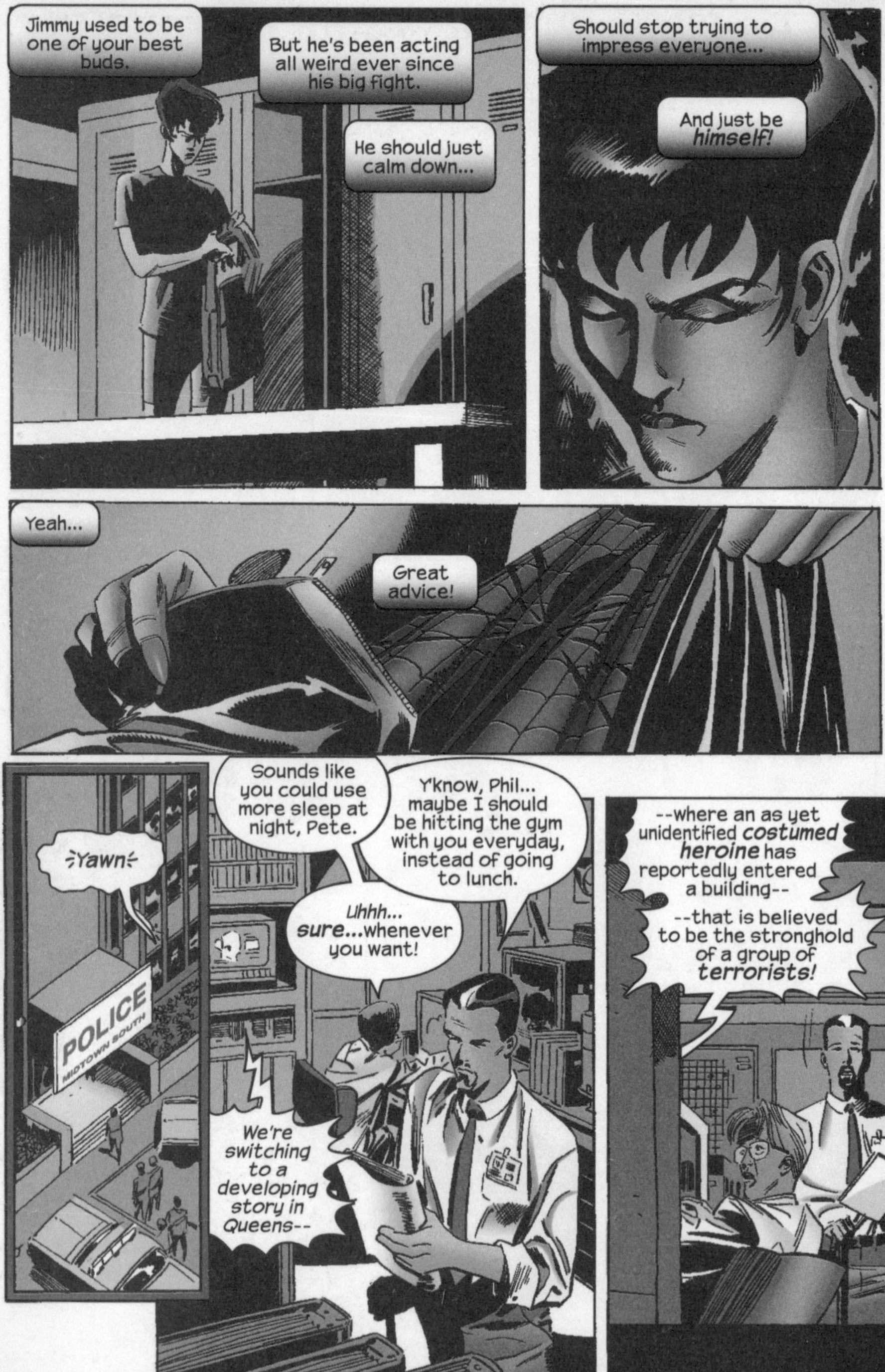

Jimmy used to be one of your best buds.
But he's been acting all weird ever since his big fight.
He should just calm down...
Should stop trying to impress everyone...
And just be *himself!*
Yeah...
Great advice!
Sounds like you could use more sleep at night, Pete.
Y'know, Phil... maybe I should be hitting the gym with you everyday, instead of going to lunch.
Yawn
Uhhh... **sure...**whenever you want!
POLICE
MIDTOWN SOUTH
We're switching to a developing story in Queens--
--where an as yet unidentified ***costumed heroine*** has reportedly entered a building--
--that is believed to be the stronghold of a group of ***terrorists!***

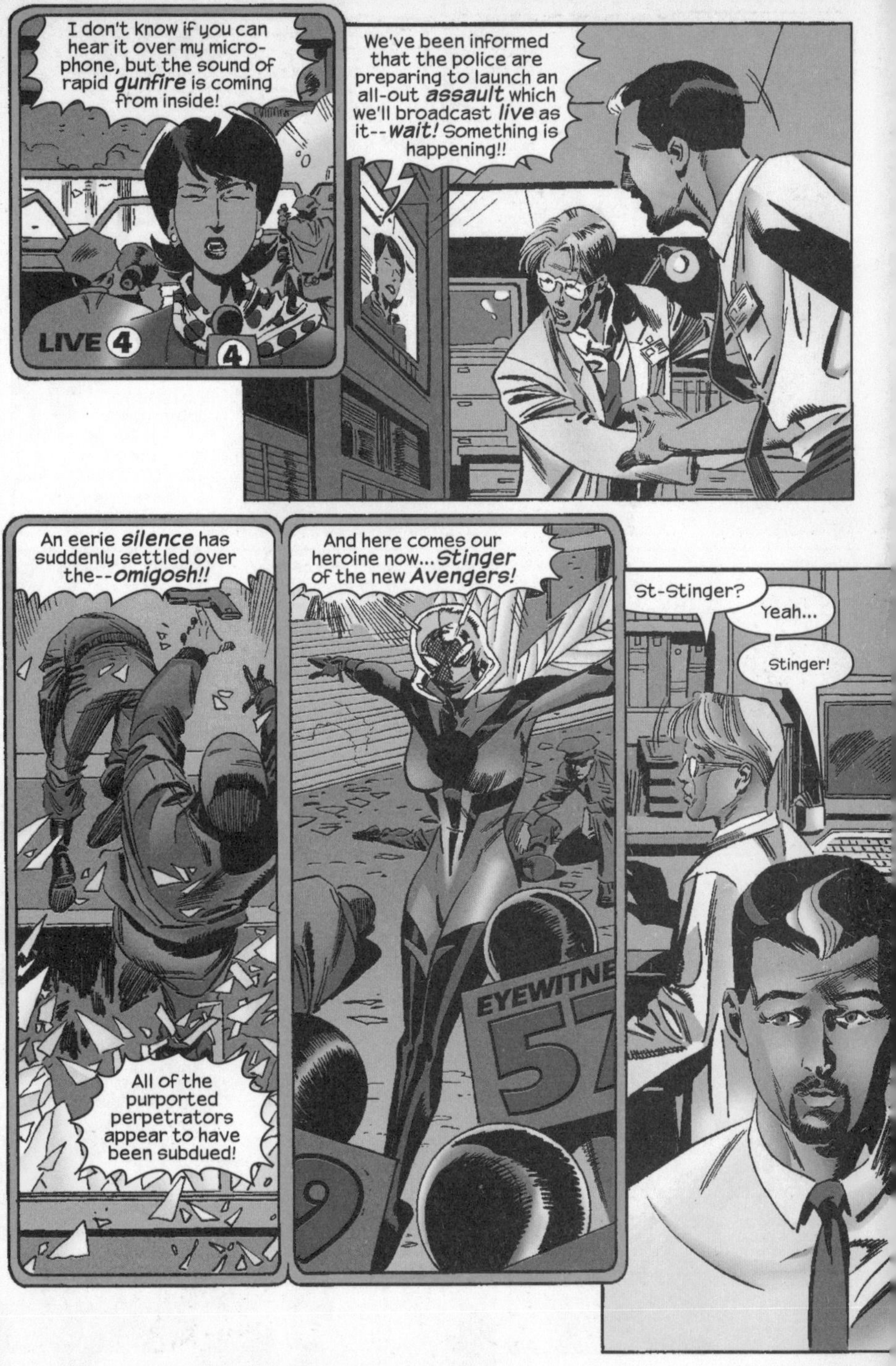
I don't know if you can hear it over my microphone, but the sound of rapid gunfire is coming from inside!
LIVE 4
4
We've been informed that the police are preparing to launch an all-out assault which we'll broadcast live as it--wait! Something is happening!!
An eerie silence has suddenly settled over the--omigosh!!
All of the purported perpetrators appear to have been subdued!
And here comes our heroine now...Stinger of the new Avengers!
EYEWITNE
57
9
St-Stinger?
Yeah...
Stinger!

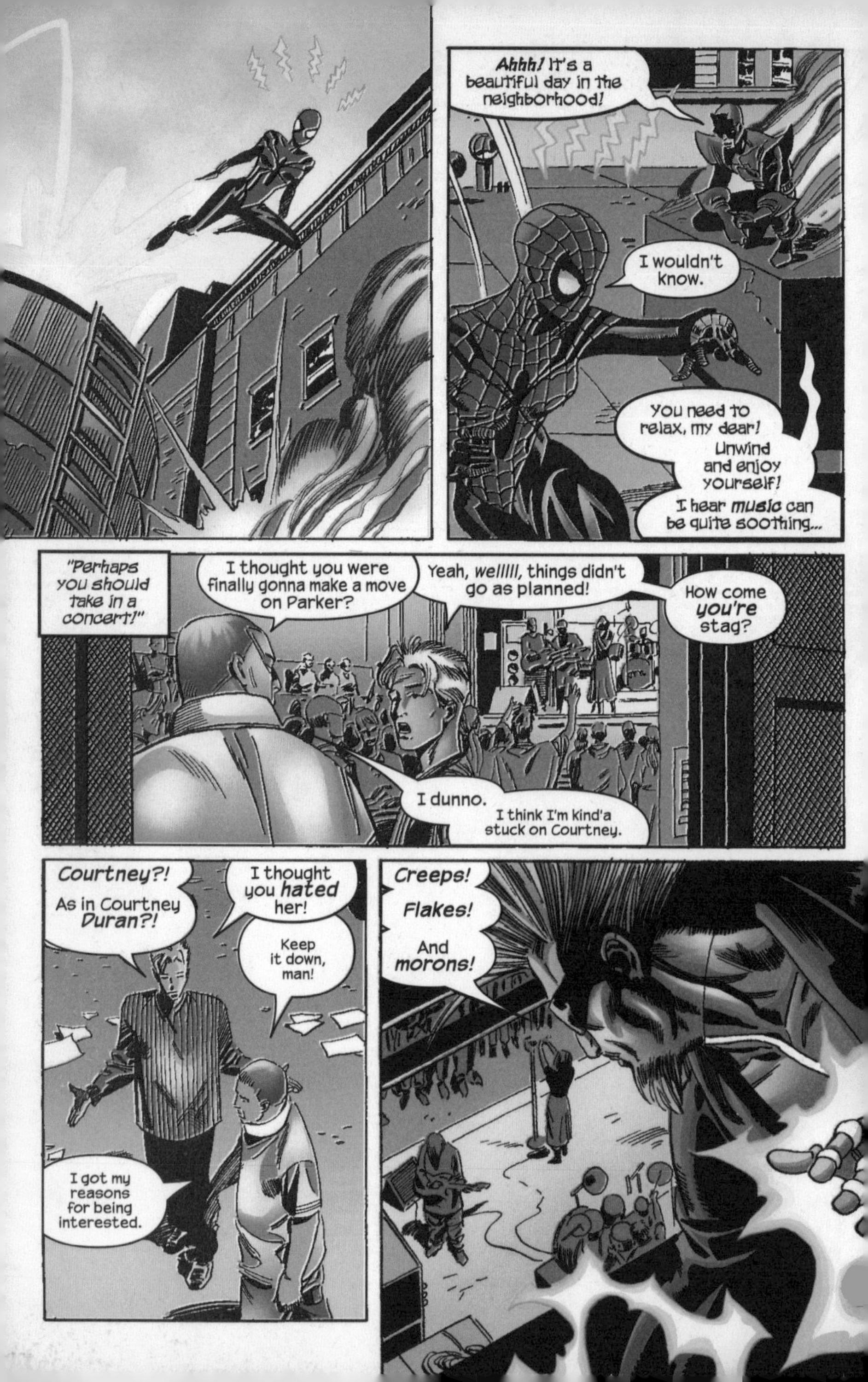

Ahhh! It's a beautiful day in the neighborhood!
I wouldn't know.
You need to relax, my dear!
Unwind and enjoy yourself!
I hear music can be quite soothing...
"Perhaps you should take in a concert!"
I thought you were finally gonna make a move on Parker?
Yeah, wellllll, things didn't go as planned!
How come you're stag?
I dunno.
I think I'm kind'a stuck on Courtney.
Courtney?!
As in Courtney Duran?!
I thought you hated her!
Keep it down, man!
I got my reasons for being interested.
Creeps!
Flakes!
And morons!

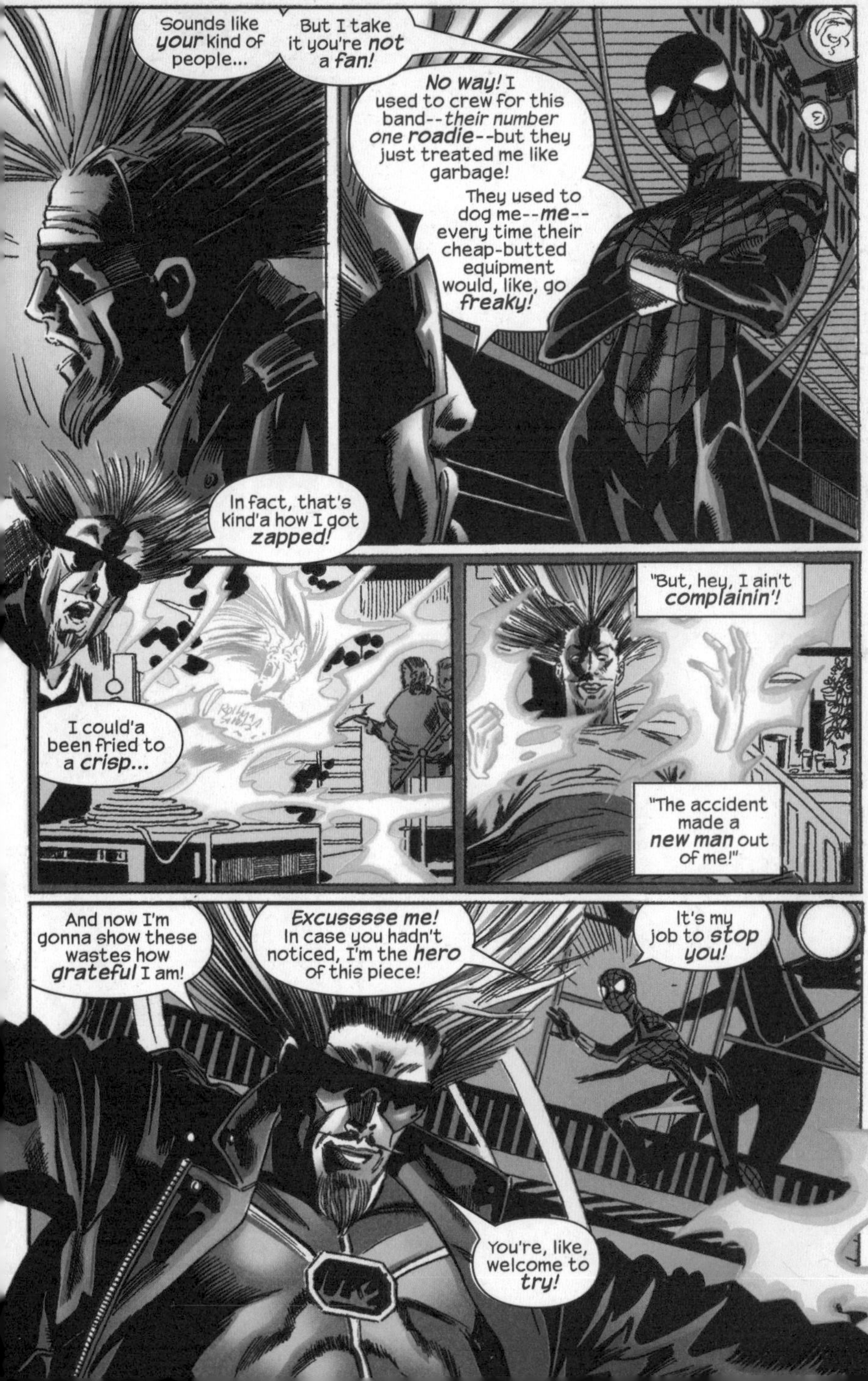
Sounds like your kind of people...
But I take it you're not a fan!
No way! I used to crew for this band--their number one roadie--but they just treated me like garbage!
They used to dog me--me--every time their cheap-butted equipment would, like, go freaky!
In fact, that's kind'a how I got zapped!
I could'a been fried to a crisp...
"But, hey, I ain't complainin'!
"The accident made a new man out of me!"
And now I'm gonna show these wastes how grateful I am!
Excusssse me! In case you hadn't noticed, I'm the hero of this piece!
It's my job to stop you!
You're, like, welcome to try!

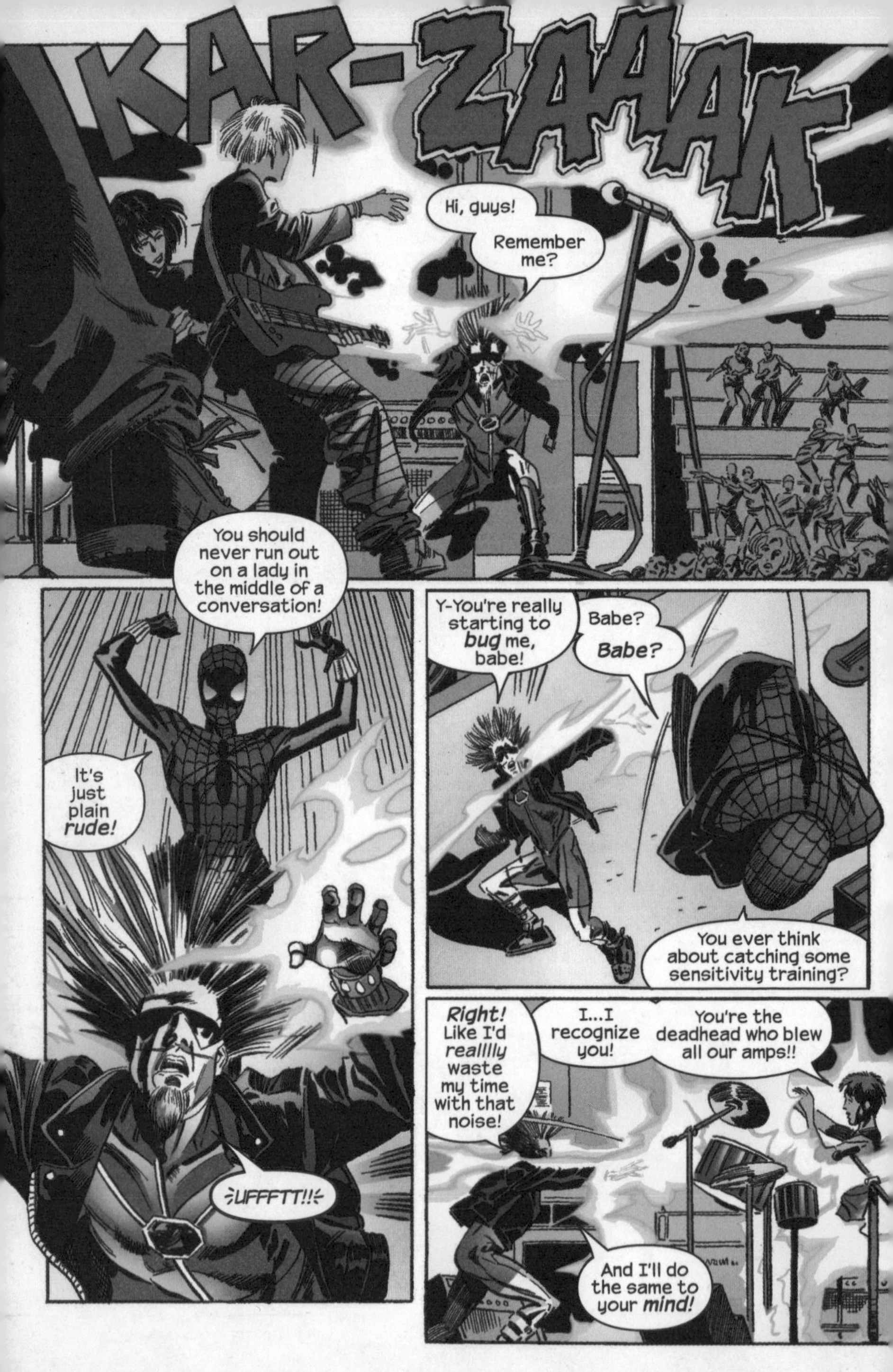
KAR-ZAAAK
Hi, guys!
Remember me?
You should never run out on a lady in the middle of a conversation!
It's just plain *rude!*
UFFFTT!!
Y-You're really starting to *bug* me, babe!
Babe?
Babe?
You ever think about catching some sensitivity training?
Right! Like I'd *realllly* waste my time with that noise!
I...I recognize you!
You're the deadhead who blew all our amps!!
And I'll do the same to your *mind!*

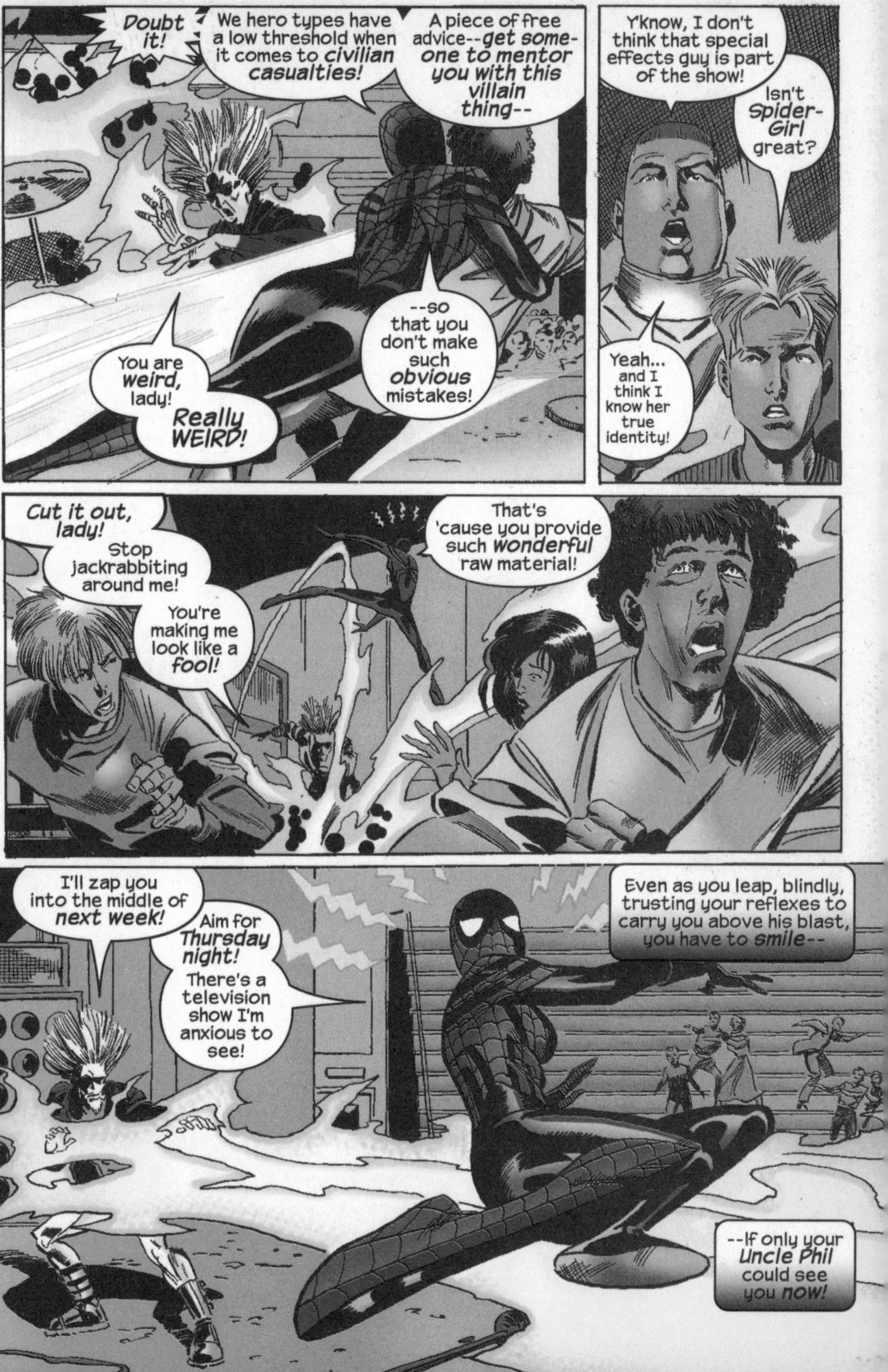
Doubt it!
We hero types have a low threshold when it comes to civilian casualties!
A piece of free advice--get someone to mentor you with this villain thing--
--so that you don't make such obvious mistakes!
You are weird, lady! Really WEIRD!
Y'know, I don't think that special effects guy is part of the show!
Isn't Spider-Girl great?
Yeah... and I think I know her true identity!
Cut it out, lady!
Stop jackrabbiting around me!
You're making me look like a fool!
That's 'cause you provide such wonderful raw material!
I'll zap you into the middle of next week!
Aim for Thursday night!
There's a television show I'm anxious to see!
Even as you leap, blindly, trusting your reflexes to carry you above his blast, you have to smile--
--If only your Uncle Phil could see you now!

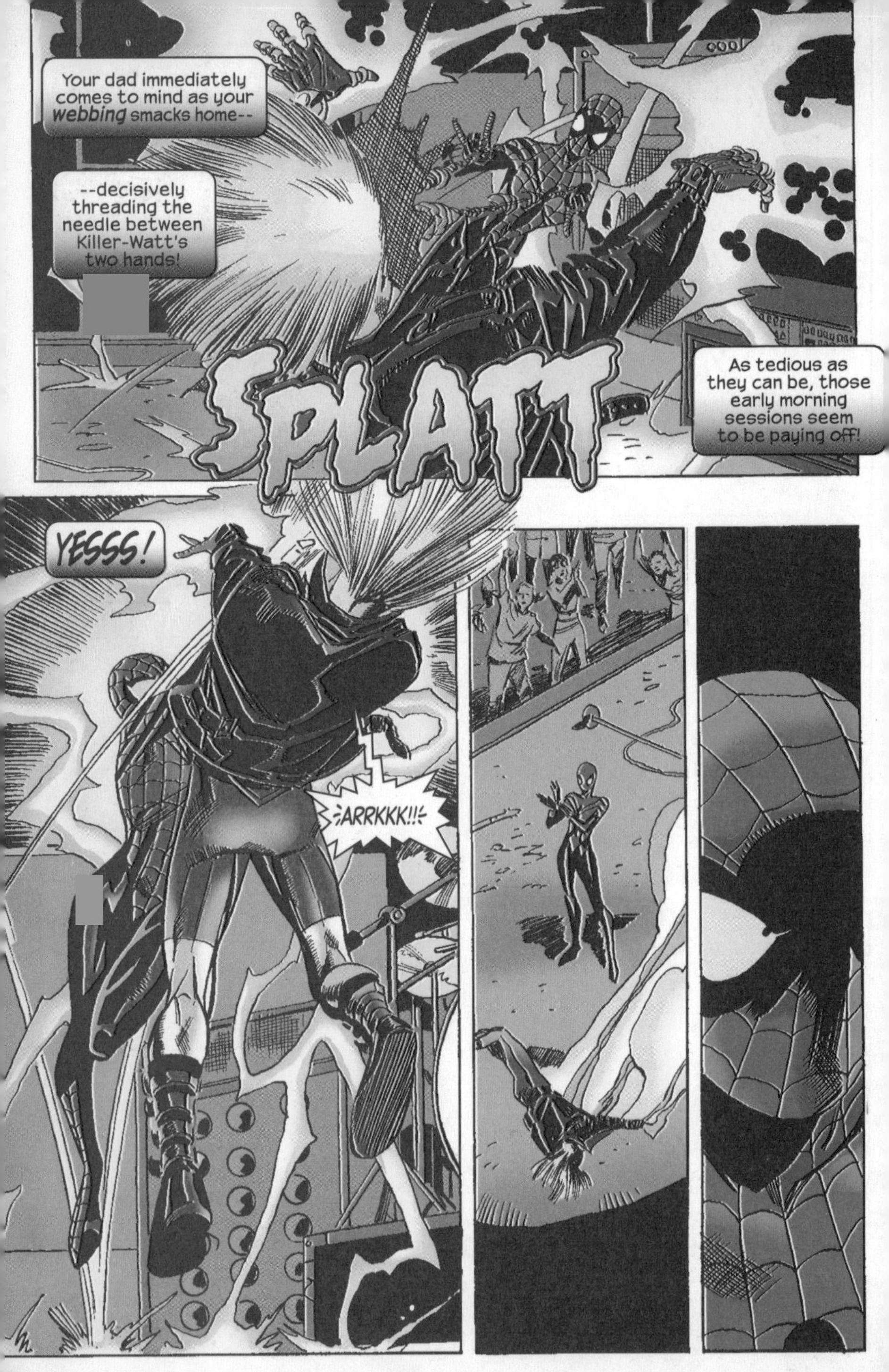

Your dad immediately comes to mind as your *webbing* smacks home--
--decisively threading the needle between Killer-Watt's two hands!
SPLATT
As tedious as they can be, those early morning sessions seem to be paying off!
YESSS!
ARRKKK!!

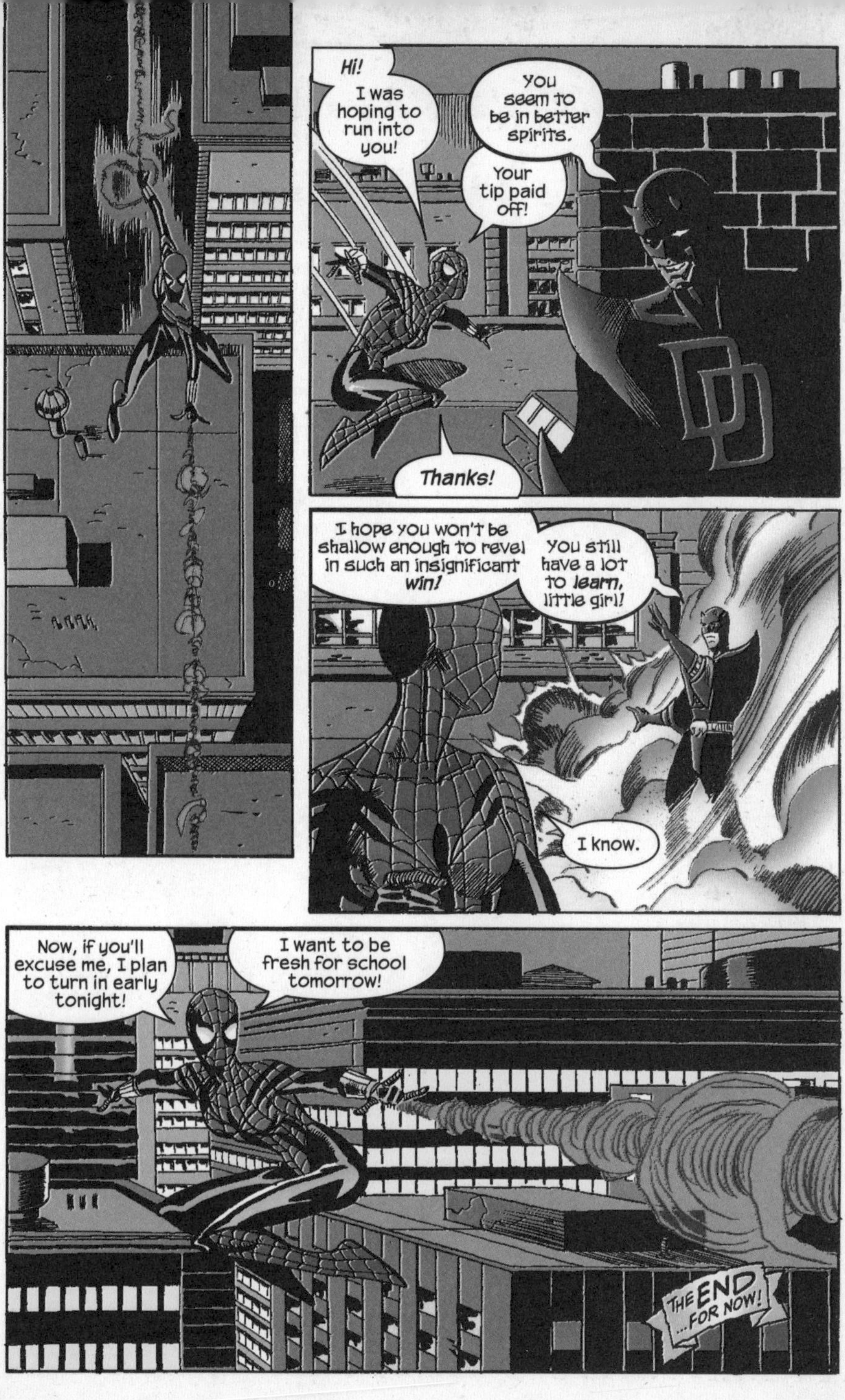
Hi!
I was hoping to run into you!
You seem to be in better spirits.
Your tip paid off!
Thanks!
I hope you won't be shallow enough to revel in such an insignificant win!
You still have a lot to learn, little girl!
I know.
Now, if you'll excuse me, I plan to turn in early tonight!
I want to be fresh for school tomorrow!
THE END ...FOR NOW!

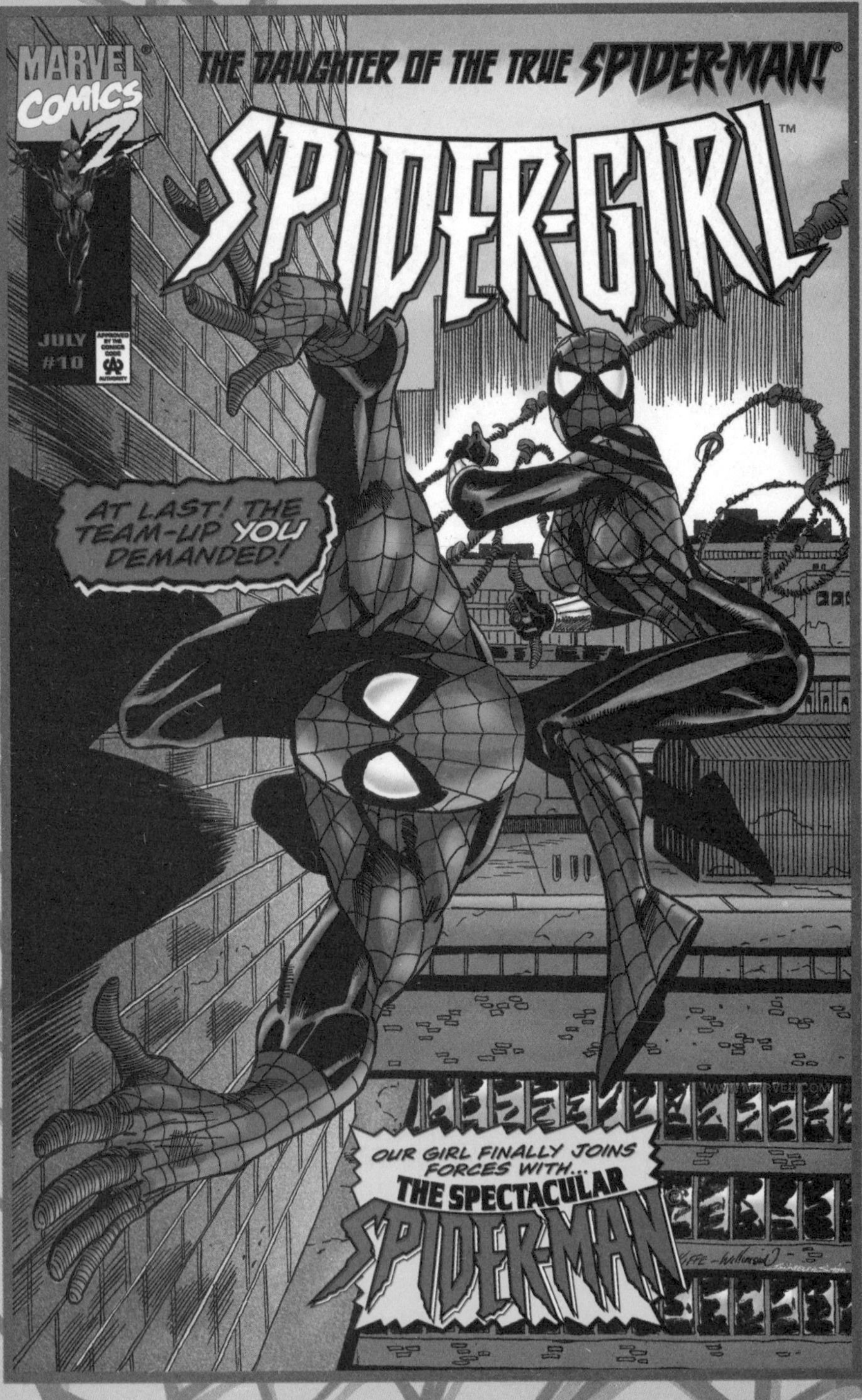
MARVEL COMICS 2
THE DAUGHTER OF THE TRUE SPIDER-MAN!
SPIDER-GIRL
JULY #10
AT LAST! THE TEAM-UP YOU DEMANDED!
OUR GIRL FINALLY JOINS FORCES WITH...
THE SPECTACULAR SPIDER-MAN

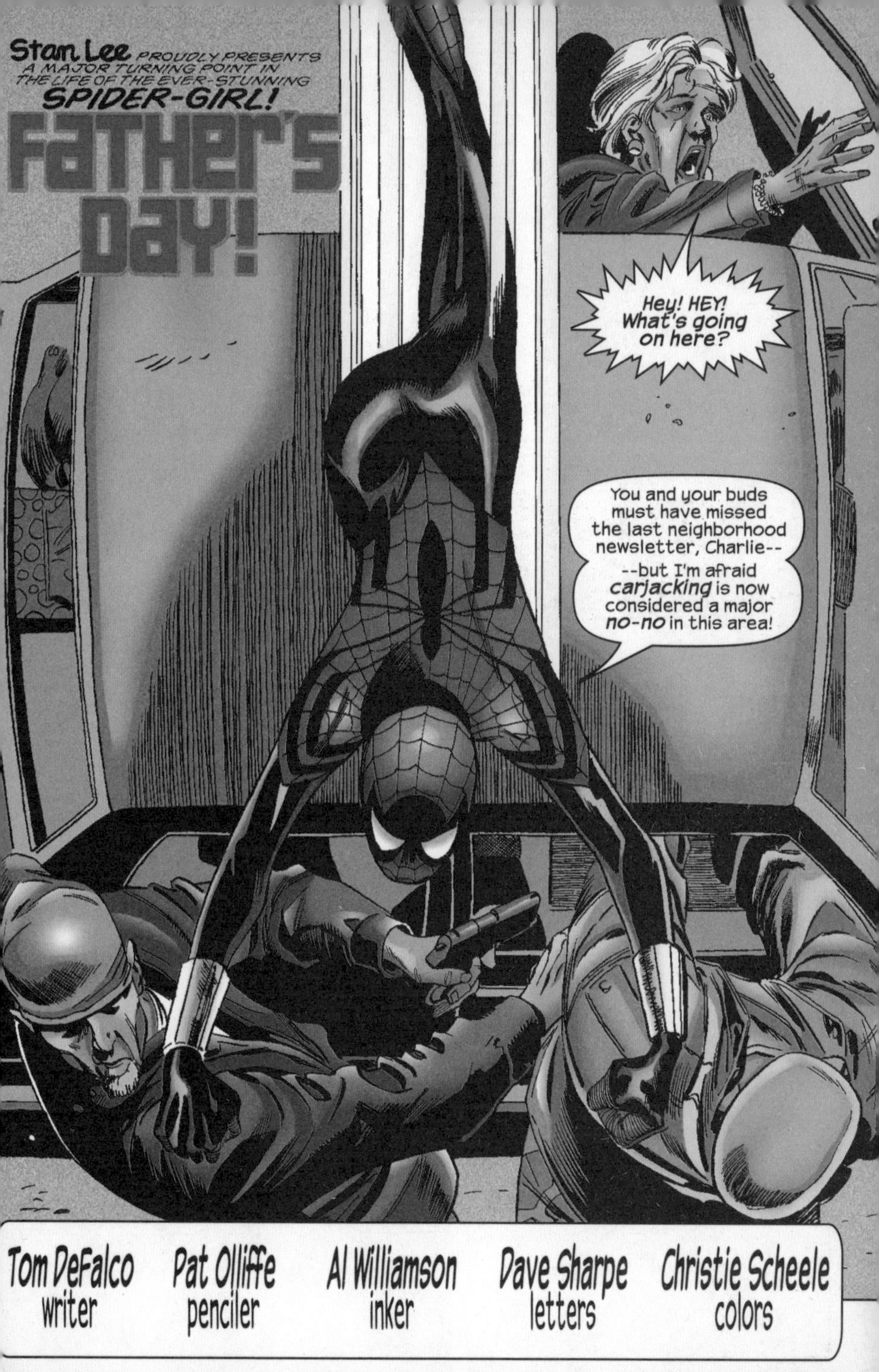

Stan Lee PROUDLY PRESENTS A MAJOR TURNING POINT IN THE LIFE OF THE EVER-STUNNING SPIDER-GIRL!
FATHER'S DAY!
Hey! HEY! What's going on here?
You and your buds must have missed the last neighborhood newsletter, Charlie--
--but I'm afraid carjacking is now considered a major no-no in this area!
Tom DeFalco writer
Pat Olliffe penciler
Al Williamson inker
Dave Sharpe letters
Christie Scheele colors

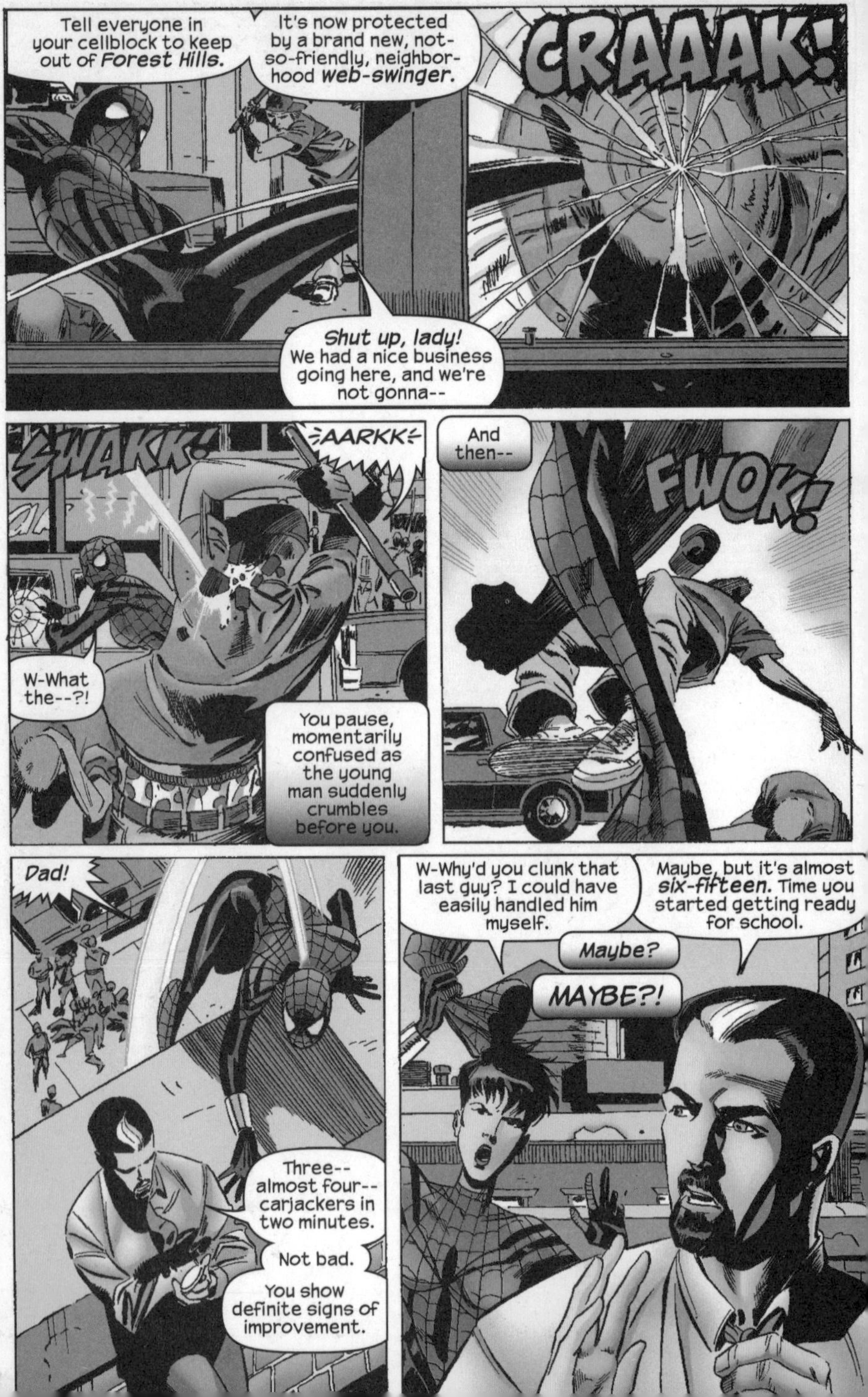

Tell everyone in your cellblock to keep out of *Forest Hills.*
It's now protected by a brand new, not-so-friendly, neighbor-hood ***web-swinger.***
CRAAAK!
Shut up, lady! We had a nice business going here, and we're not gonna--
SWAKK!
AARKK
W-What the--?!
You pause, momentarily confused as the young man suddenly crumbles before you.
And then--
FWOK!
Dad!
Three-- almost four-- carjackers in two minutes.
Not bad.
You show definite signs of improvement.
W-Why'd you clunk that last guy? I could have easily handled him myself.
Maybe, but it's almost ***six-fifteen.*** Time you started getting ready for school.
Maybe?
MAYBE?!

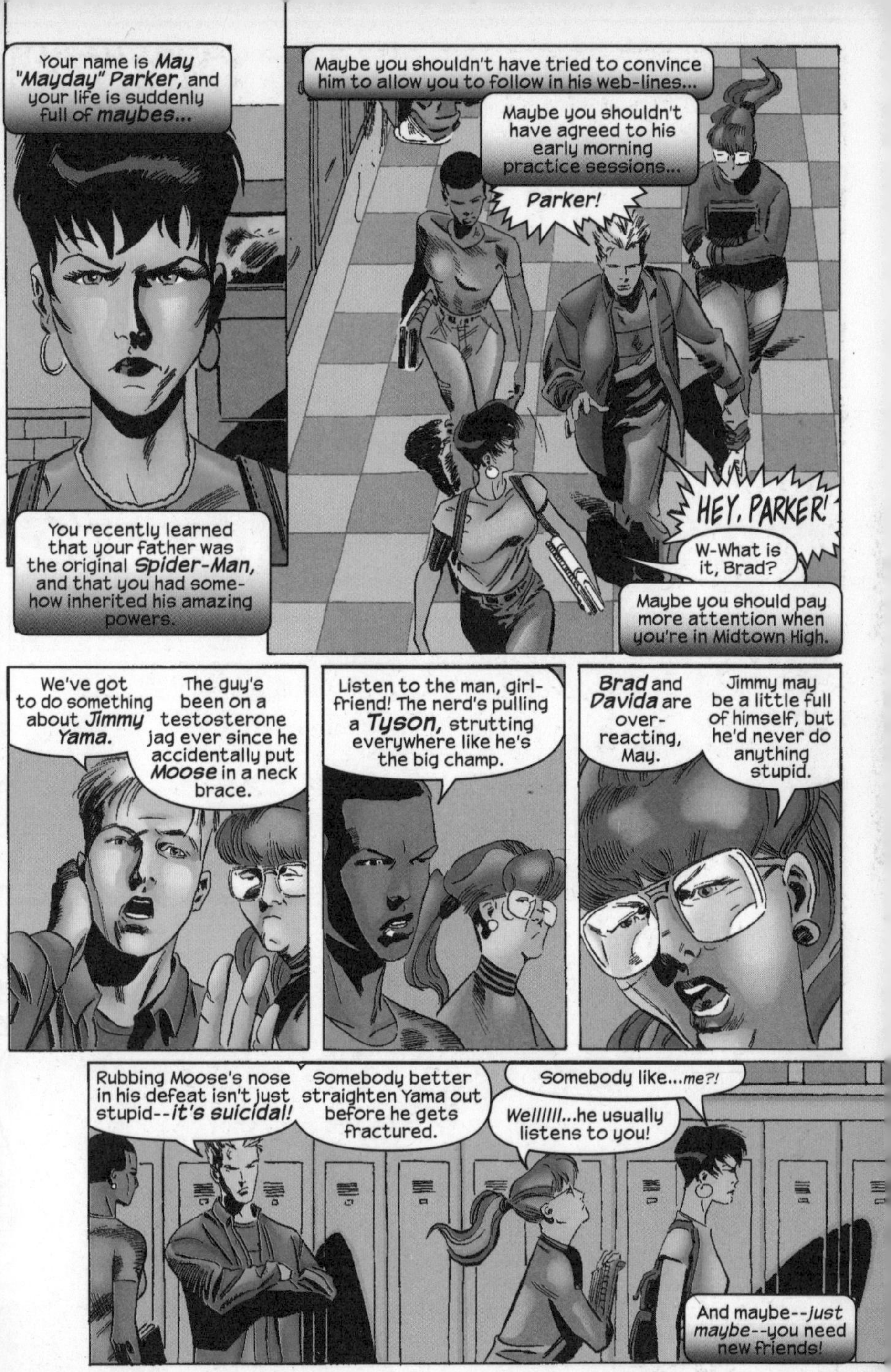

Your name is May "Mayday" Parker, and your life is suddenly full of maybes...
You recently learned that your father was the original Spider-Man, and that you had some-how inherited his amazing powers.
Maybe you shouldn't have tried to convince him to allow you to follow in his web-lines...
Maybe you shouldn't have agreed to his early morning practice sessions...
Parker!
HEY, PARKER!
W-What is it, Brad?
Maybe you should pay more attention when you're in Midtown High.
We've got to do something about Jimmy Yama.
The guy's been on a testosterone jag ever since he accidentally put Moose in a neck brace.
Listen to the man, girl-friend! The nerd's pulling a Tyson, strutting everywhere like he's the big champ.
Brad and Davida are over-reacting, May.
Jimmy may be a little full of himself, but he'd never do anything stupid.
Rubbing Moose's nose in his defeat isn't just stupid--it's suicidal!
Somebody better straighten Yama out before he gets fractured.
Somebody like...me?!
Wellllll...he usually listens to you!
And maybe--just maybe--you need new friends!

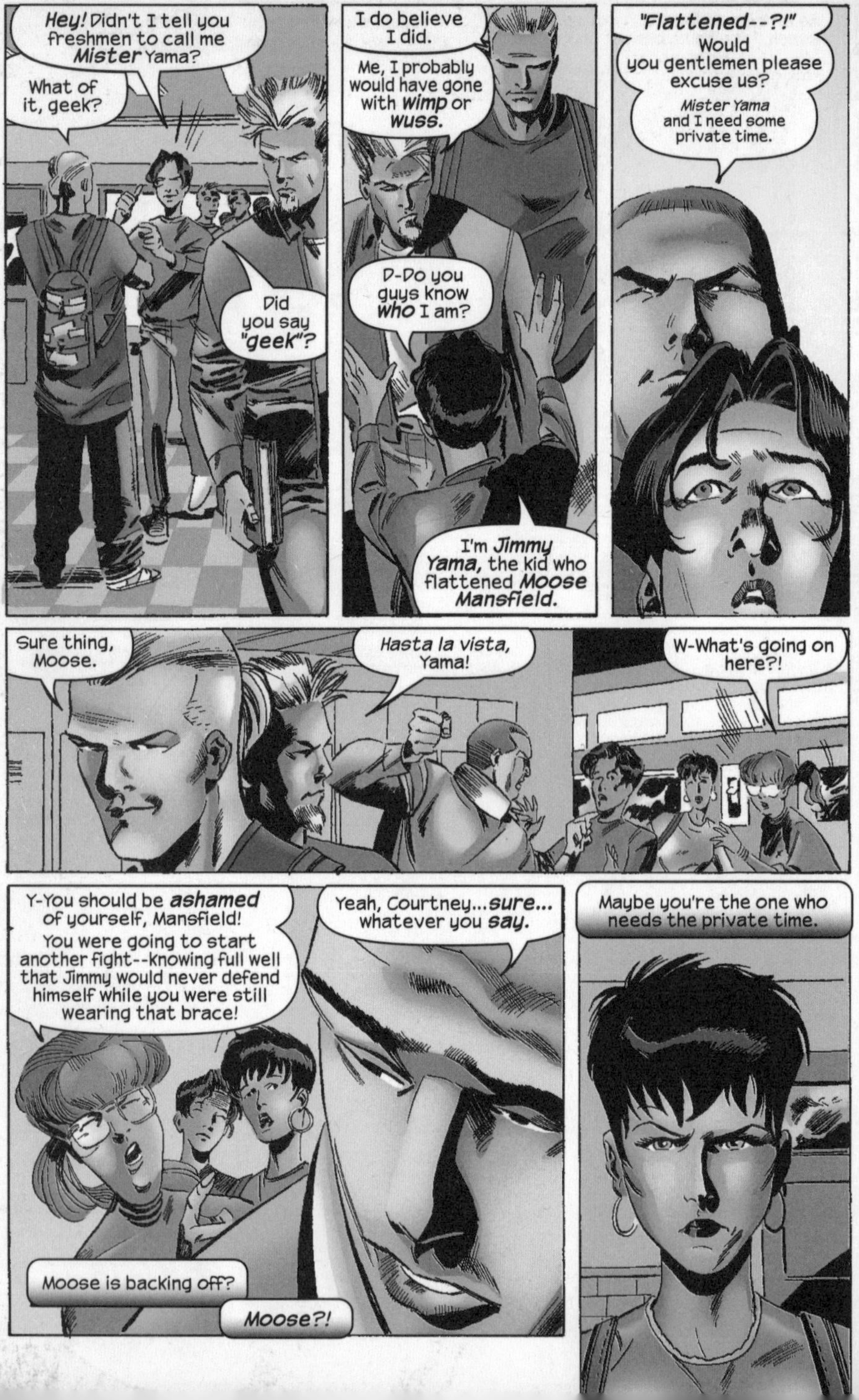
Hey! Didn't I tell you freshmen to call me Mister Yama?
What of it, geek?
Did you say "geek"?
I do believe I did.
Me, I probably would have gone with wimp or wuss.
D-Do you guys know who I am?
I'm Jimmy Yama, the kid who flattened Moose Mansfield.
"Flattened--?!" Would you gentlemen please excuse us?
Mister Yama and I need some private time.
Sure thing, Moose.
Hasta la vista, Yama!
W-What's going on here?!
Y-You should be ashamed of yourself, Mansfield!
You were going to start another fight--knowing full well that Jimmy would never defend himself while you were still wearing that brace!
Yeah, Courtney...sure... whatever you say.
Maybe you're the one who needs the private time.
Moose is backing off?
Moose?!

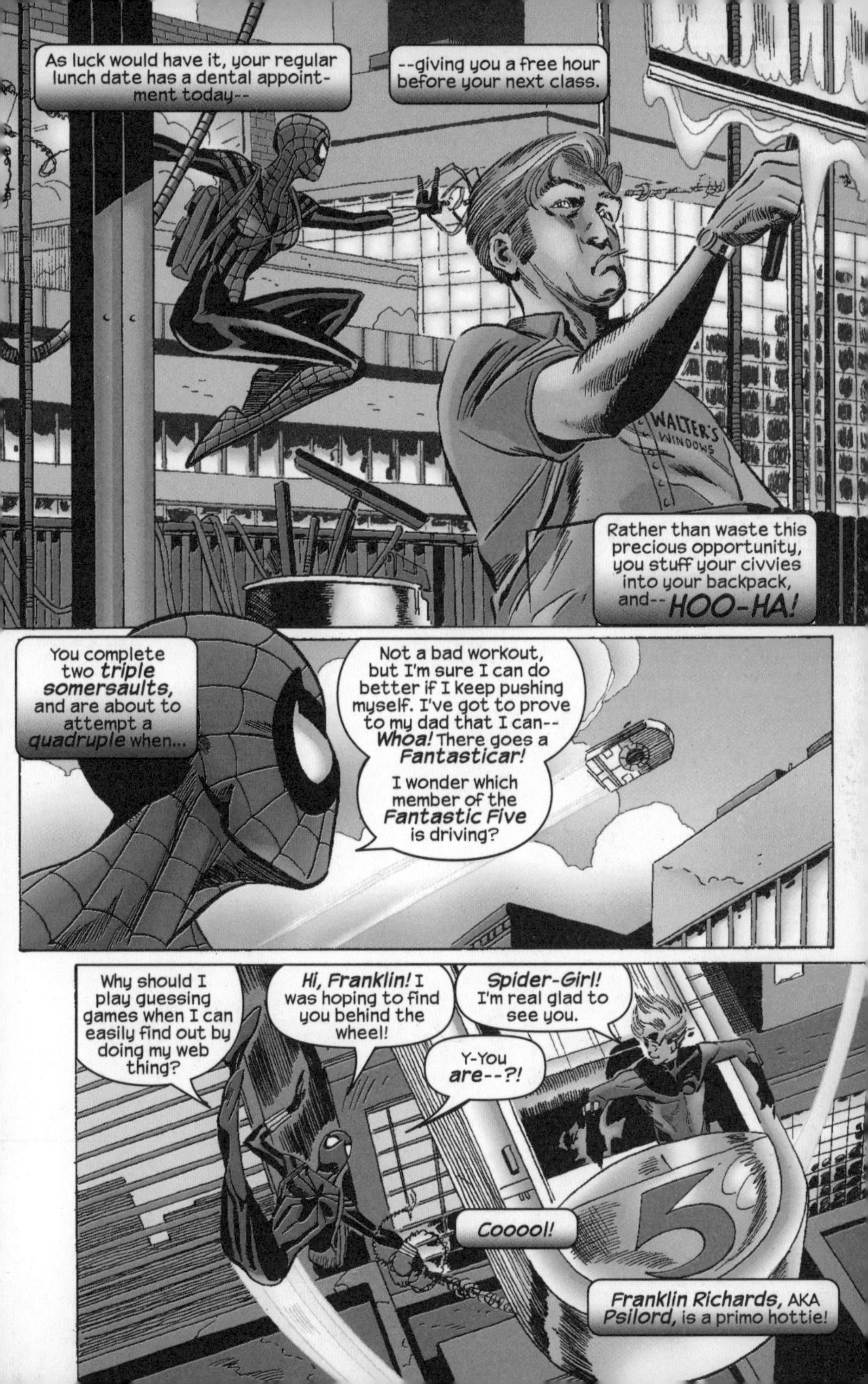
As luck would have it, your regular lunch date has a dental appointment today--
--giving you a free hour before your next class.
WALTER'S WINDOWS
Rather than waste this precious opportunity, you stuff your civvies into your backpack, and-- HOO-HA!
You complete two triple somersaults, and are about to attempt a quadruple when...
Not a bad workout, but I'm sure I can do better if I keep pushing myself. I've got to prove to my dad that I can-- Whoa! There goes a Fantasticar!
I wonder which member of the Fantastic Five is driving?
Why should I play guessing games when I can easily find out by doing my web thing?
Hi, Franklin! I was hoping to find you behind the wheel!
Spider-Girl! I'm real glad to see you.
Y-You are--?!
Cooool!
Franklin Richards, AKA Psilord, is a primo hottie!

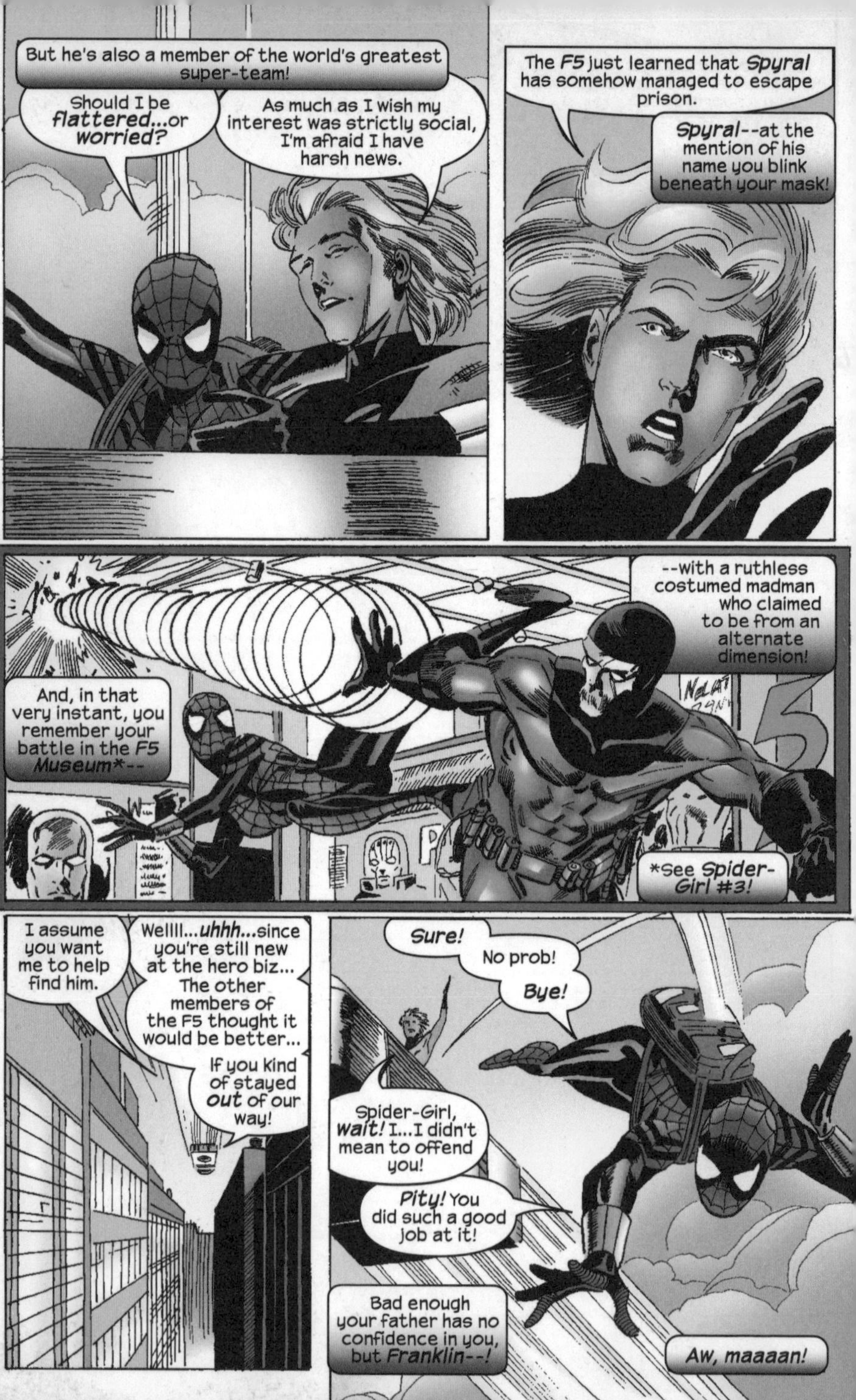

But he's also a member of the world's greatest super-team!
Should I be flattered...or worried?
As much as I wish my interest was strictly social, I'm afraid I have harsh news.
The F5 just learned that Spyral has somehow managed to escape prison.
Spyral--at the mention of his name you blink beneath your mask!
And, in that very instant, you remember your battle in the F5 Museum*--
--with a ruthless costumed madman who claimed to be from an alternate dimension!
*See Spider-Girl #3!
I assume you want me to help find him.
Wellll...uhhh...since you're still new at the hero biz... The other members of the F5 thought it would be better...
If you kind of stayed out of our way!
Sure!
No prob!
Bye!
Spider-Girl, wait! I...I didn't mean to offend you!
Pity! You did such a good job at it!
Bad enough your father has no confidence in you, but Franklin--!
Aw, maaaan!

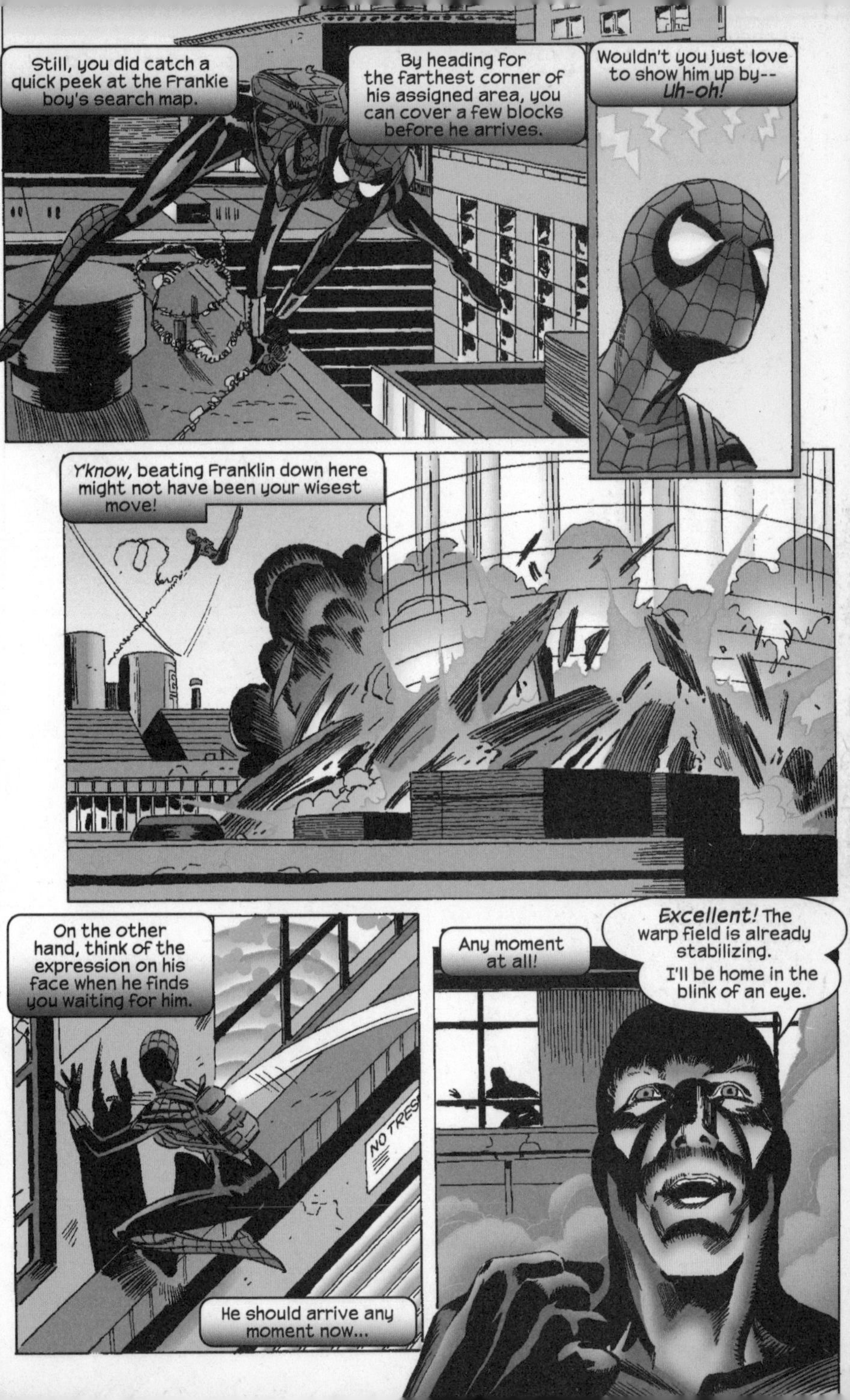
Still, you did catch a quick peek at the Frankie boy's search map.
By heading for the farthest corner of his assigned area, you can cover a few blocks before he arrives.
Wouldn't you just love to show him up by-- Uh-oh!
Y'know, beating Franklin down here might not have been your wisest move!
On the other hand, think of the expression on his face when he finds you waiting for him.
NO TRES
He should arrive any moment now...
Any moment at all!
Excellent! The warp field is already stabilizing.
I'll be home in the blink of an eye.

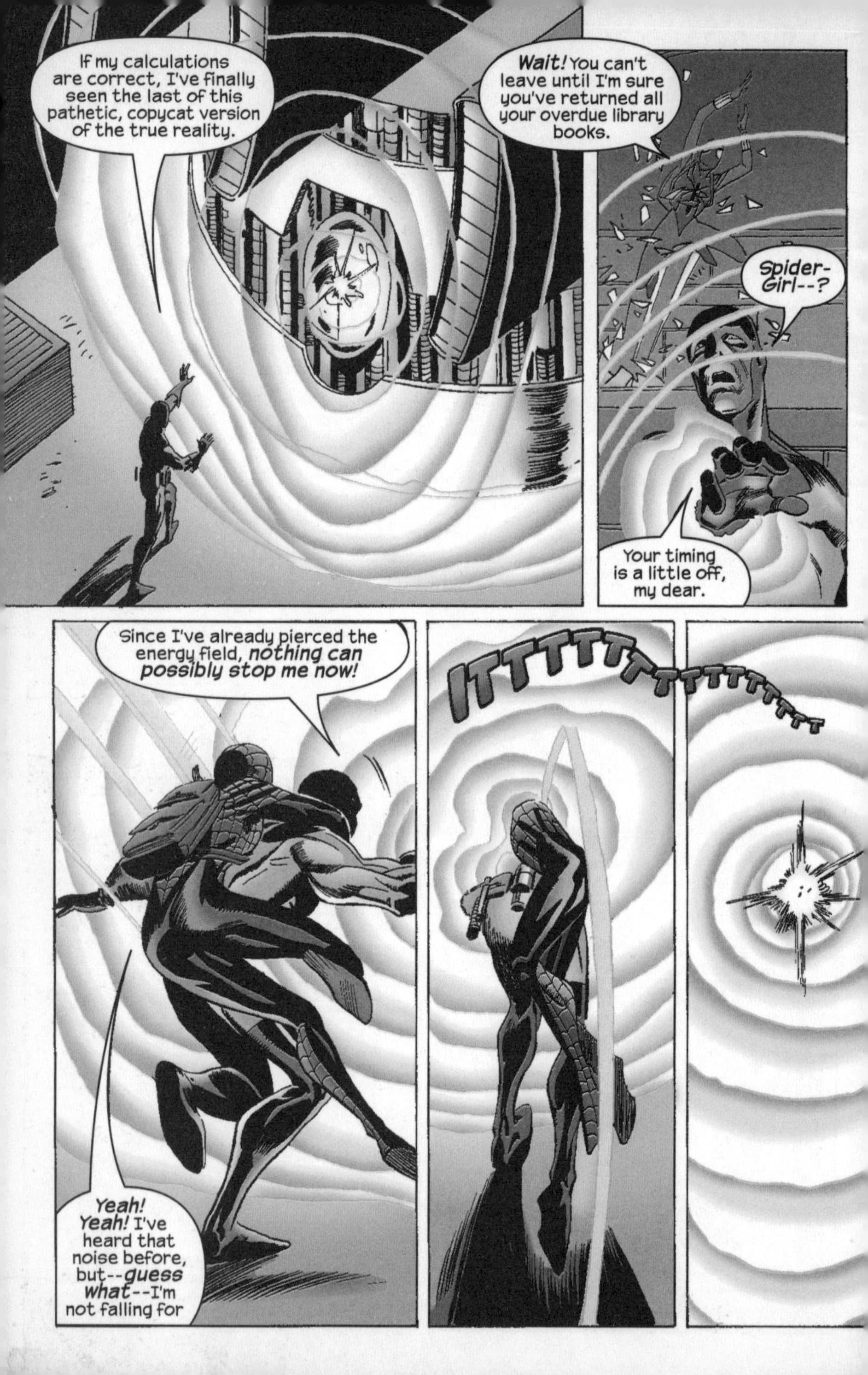
If my calculations are correct, I've finally seen the last of this pathetic, copycat version of the true reality.
Wait! You can't leave until I'm sure you've returned all your overdue library books.
Spider-Girl--?
Your timing is a little off, my dear.
Since I've already pierced the energy field, nothing can possibly stop me now!
Yeah! Yeah! I've heard that noise before, but--guess what--I'm not falling for
ITTTTTTTTTTTTTTTTTT

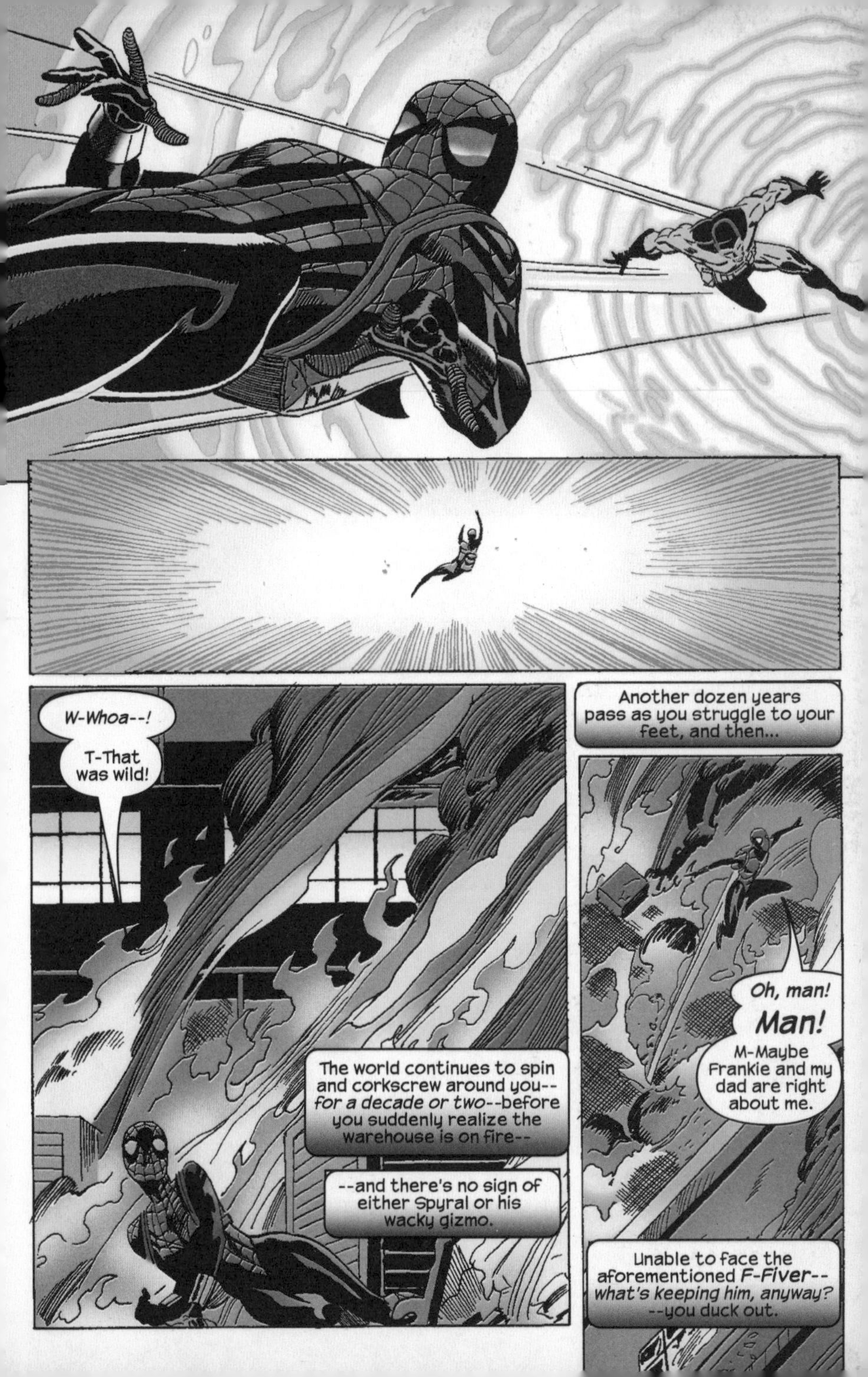
W-Whoa--!
T-That was wild!
The world continues to spin and corkscrew around you--for a decade or two--before you suddenly realize the warehouse is on fire--
--and there's no sign of either Spyral or his wacky gizmo.
Another dozen years pass as you struggle to your feet, and then...
Oh, man! Man! M-Maybe Frankie and my dad are right about me.
Unable to face the aforementioned F-Fiver--what's keeping him, anyway?--you duck out.

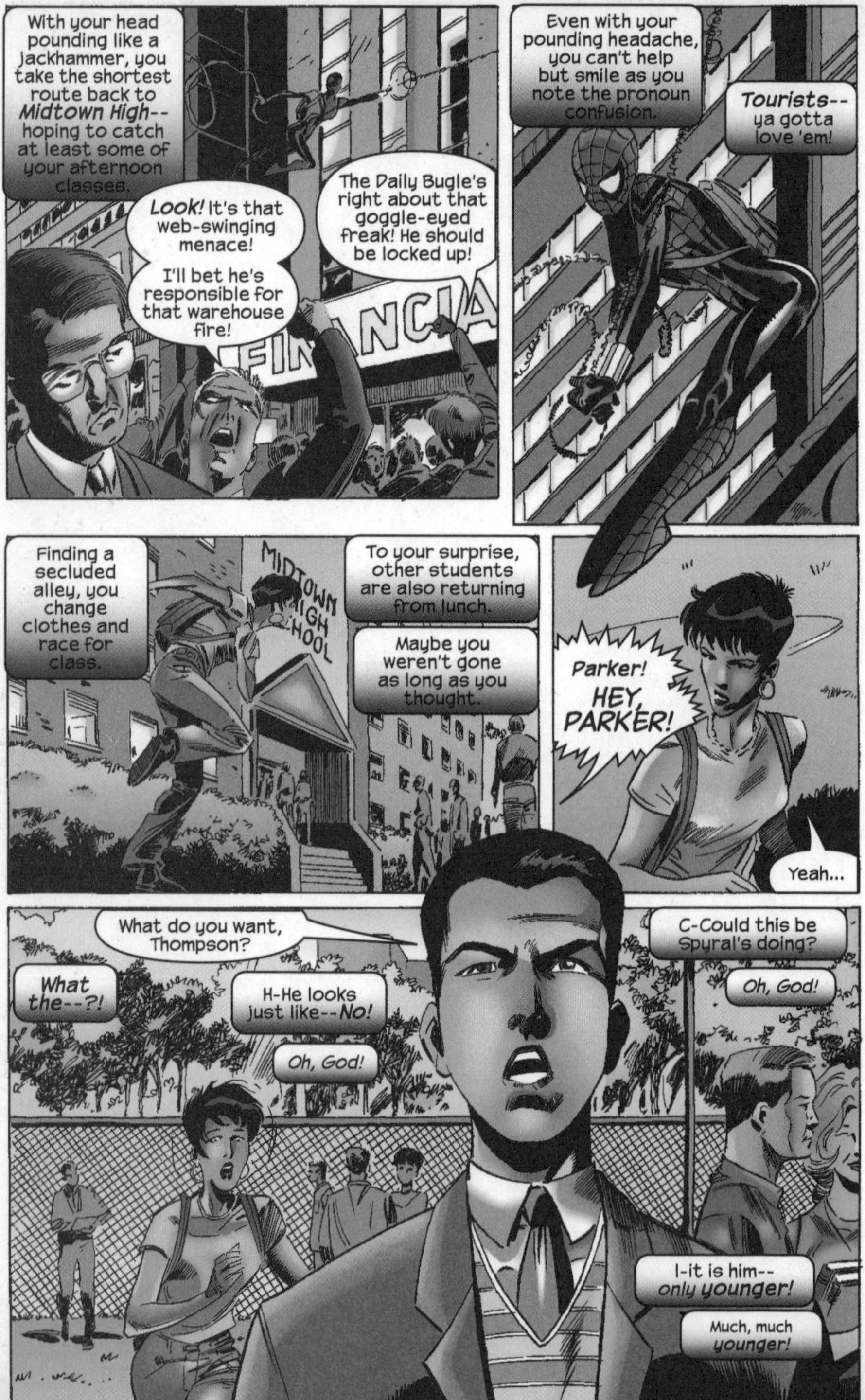
With your head pounding like a jackhammer, you take the shortest route back to *Midtown High*--hoping to catch at least some of your afternoon classes.
Look! It's that web-swinging menace!
I'll bet he's responsible for that warehouse fire!
The Daily Bugle's right about that goggle-eyed freak! He should be locked up!
FINANCIA
Even with your pounding headache, you can't help but smile as you note the pronoun confusion.
Tourists--ya gotta love 'em!
Finding a secluded alley, you change clothes and race for class.
MIDTOWN HIGH SCHOOL
To your surprise, other students are also returning from lunch.
Maybe you weren't gone as long as you thought.
Parker! HEY, PARKER!
Yeah...
What do you want, Thompson?
What the--?!
H-He looks just like--*No!*
Oh, God!
C-Could this be Spyral's doing?
Oh, God!
I-it is him--only *younger!*
Much, much *younger!*

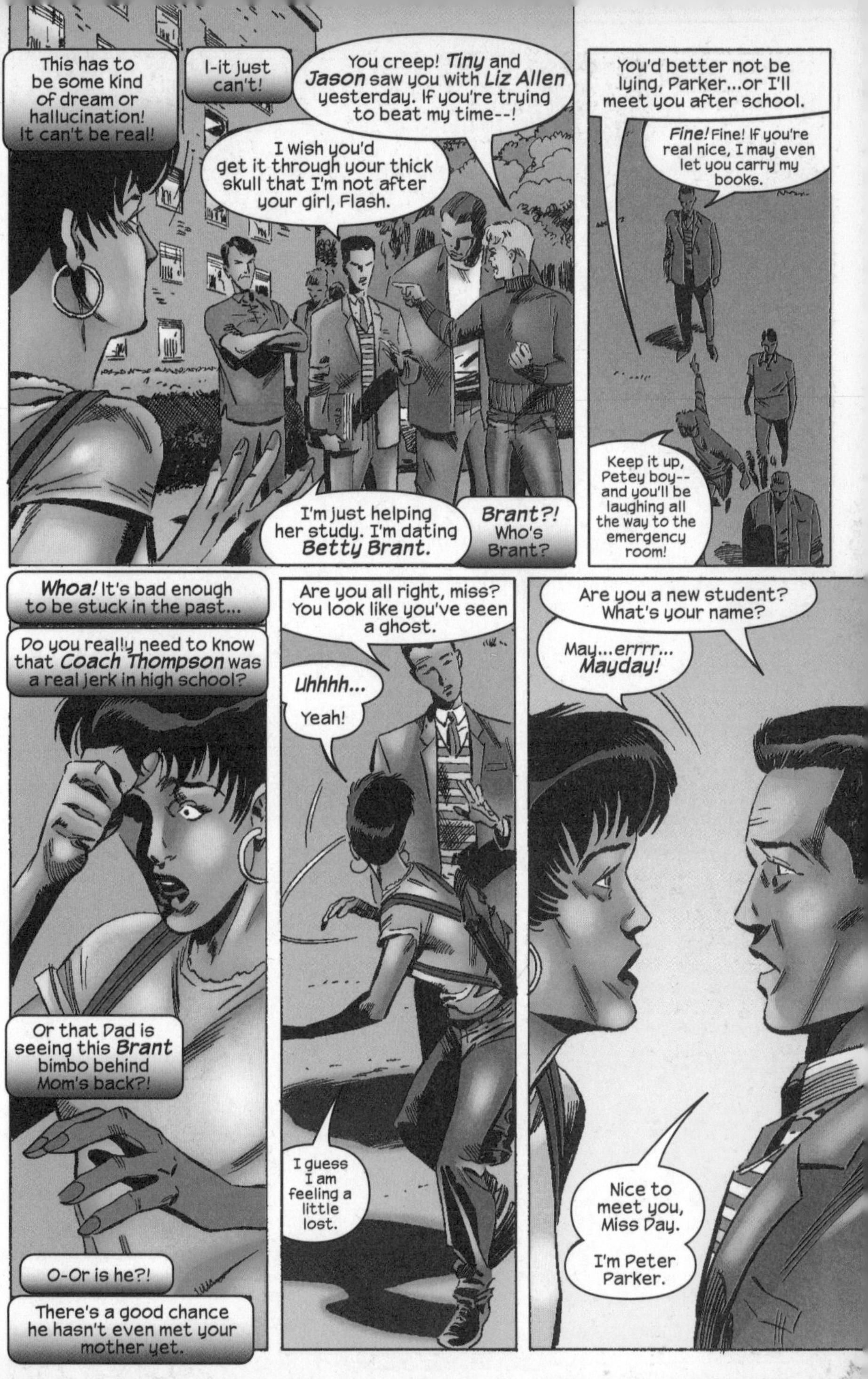

This has to be some kind of dream or hallucination! It can't be real!
I-it just can't!
You creep! Tiny and Jason saw you with Liz Allen yesterday. If you're trying to beat my time--!
I wish you'd get it through your thick skull that I'm not after your girl, Flash.
I'm just helping her study. I'm dating Betty Brant.
Brant?! Who's Brant?
You'd better not be lying, Parker...or I'll meet you after school.
Fine! Fine! If you're real nice, I may even let you carry my books.
Keep it up, Petey boy--and you'll be laughing all the way to the emergency room!
Whoa! It's bad enough to be stuck in the past...
Do you really need to know that Coach Thompson was a real jerk in high school?
Or that Dad is seeing this Brant bimbo behind Mom's back?!
O-Or is he?!
There's a good chance he hasn't even met your mother yet.
Are you all right, miss? You look like you've seen a ghost.
Uhhhh...
Yeah!
I guess I am feeling a little lost.
Are you a new student? What's your name?
May...errrr... Mayday!
Nice to meet you, Miss Day.
I'm Peter Parker.

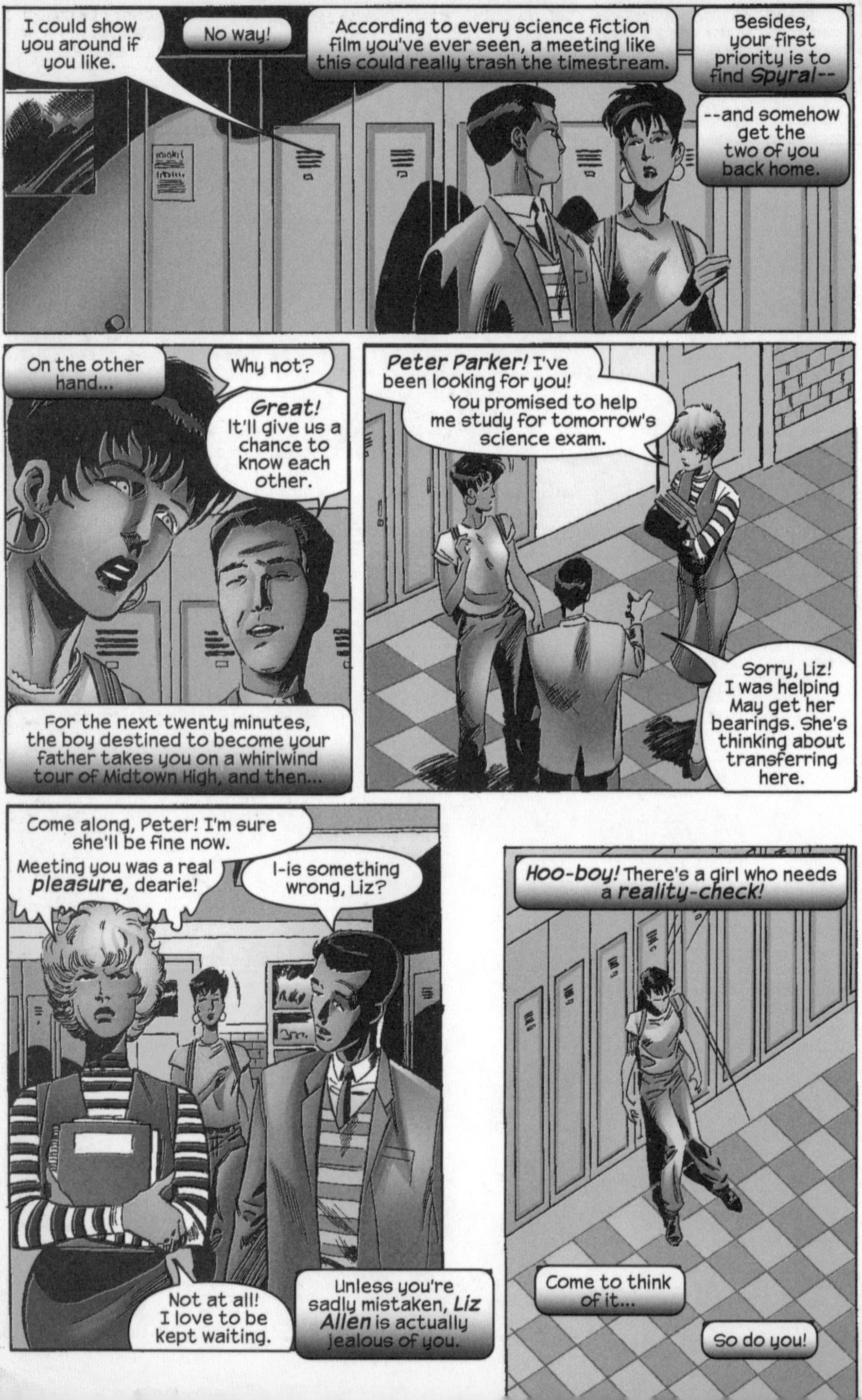
I could show you around if you like.
No way!
According to every science fiction film you've ever seen, a meeting like this could really trash the timestream.
Besides, your first priority is to find *Spyral*--
--and somehow get the two of you back home.
On the other hand...
Why not?
Great! It'll give us a chance to know each other.
For the next twenty minutes, the boy destined to become your father takes you on a whirlwind tour of Midtown High, and then...
Peter Parker! I've been looking for you! You promised to help me study for tomorrow's science exam.
Sorry, Liz! I was helping May get her bearings. She's thinking about transferring here.
Come along, Peter! I'm sure she'll be fine now.
Meeting you was a real *pleasure,* dearie!
I-is something wrong, Liz?
Not at all! I love to be kept waiting.
Unless you're sadly mistaken, *Liz Allen* is actually jealous of you.
Hoo-boy! There's a girl who needs a *reality-check!*
Come to think of it...
So do you!

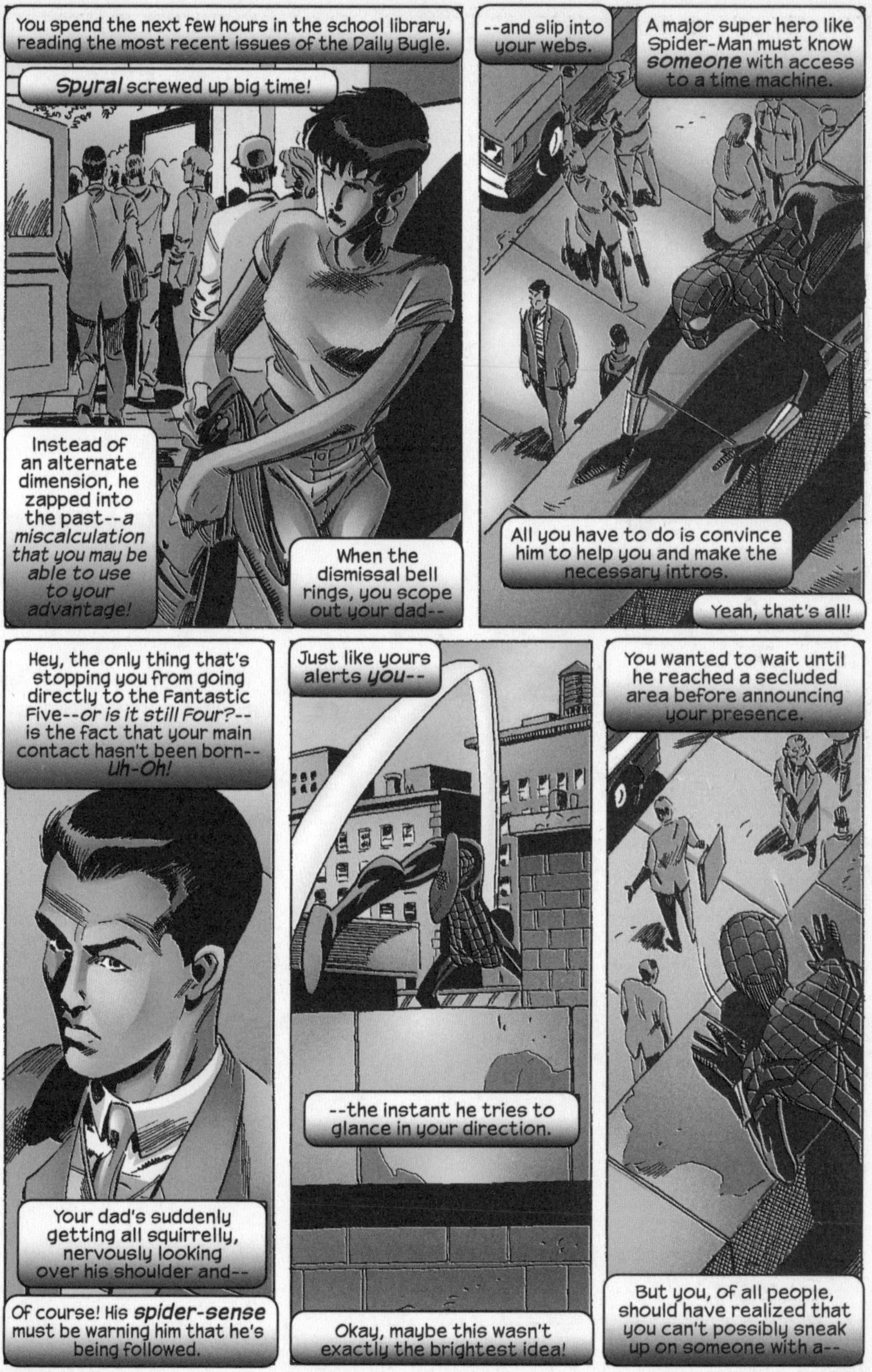
You spend the next few hours in the school library, reading the most recent issues of the Daily Bugle.
Spyral screwed up big time!
Instead of an alternate dimension, he zapped into the past--a miscalculation that you may be able to use to your advantage!
When the dismissal bell rings, you scope out your dad--
--and slip into your webs.
A major super hero like Spider-Man must know someone with access to a time machine.
All you have to do is convince him to help you and make the necessary intros.
Yeah, that's all!
Hey, the only thing that's stopping you from going directly to the Fantastic Five--or is it still Four?--is the fact that your main contact hasn't been born--Uh-Oh!
Your dad's suddenly getting all squirrelly, nervously looking over his shoulder and--
Of course! His spider-sense must be warning him that he's being followed.
Just like yours alerts you--
--the instant he tries to glance in your direction.
Okay, maybe this wasn't exactly the brightest idea!
You wanted to wait until he reached a secluded area before announcing your presence.
But you, of all people, should have realized that you can't possibly sneak up on someone with a--

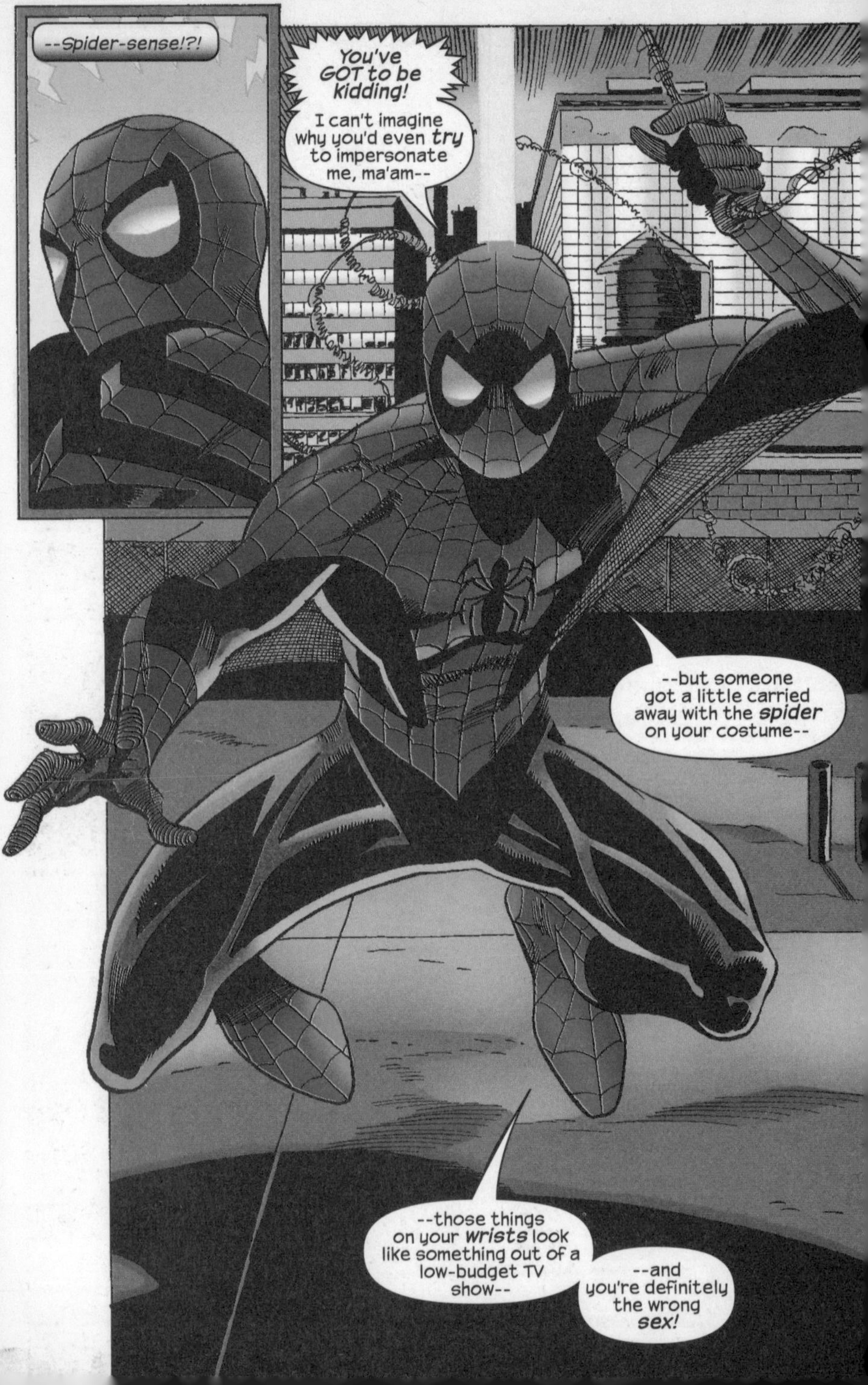
--Spider-sense!?!
You've GOT to be kidding!
I can't imagine why you'd even try to impersonate me, ma'am--
--but someone got a little carried away with the spider on your costume--
--those things on your wrists look like something out of a low-budget TV show--
--and you're definitely the wrong sex!

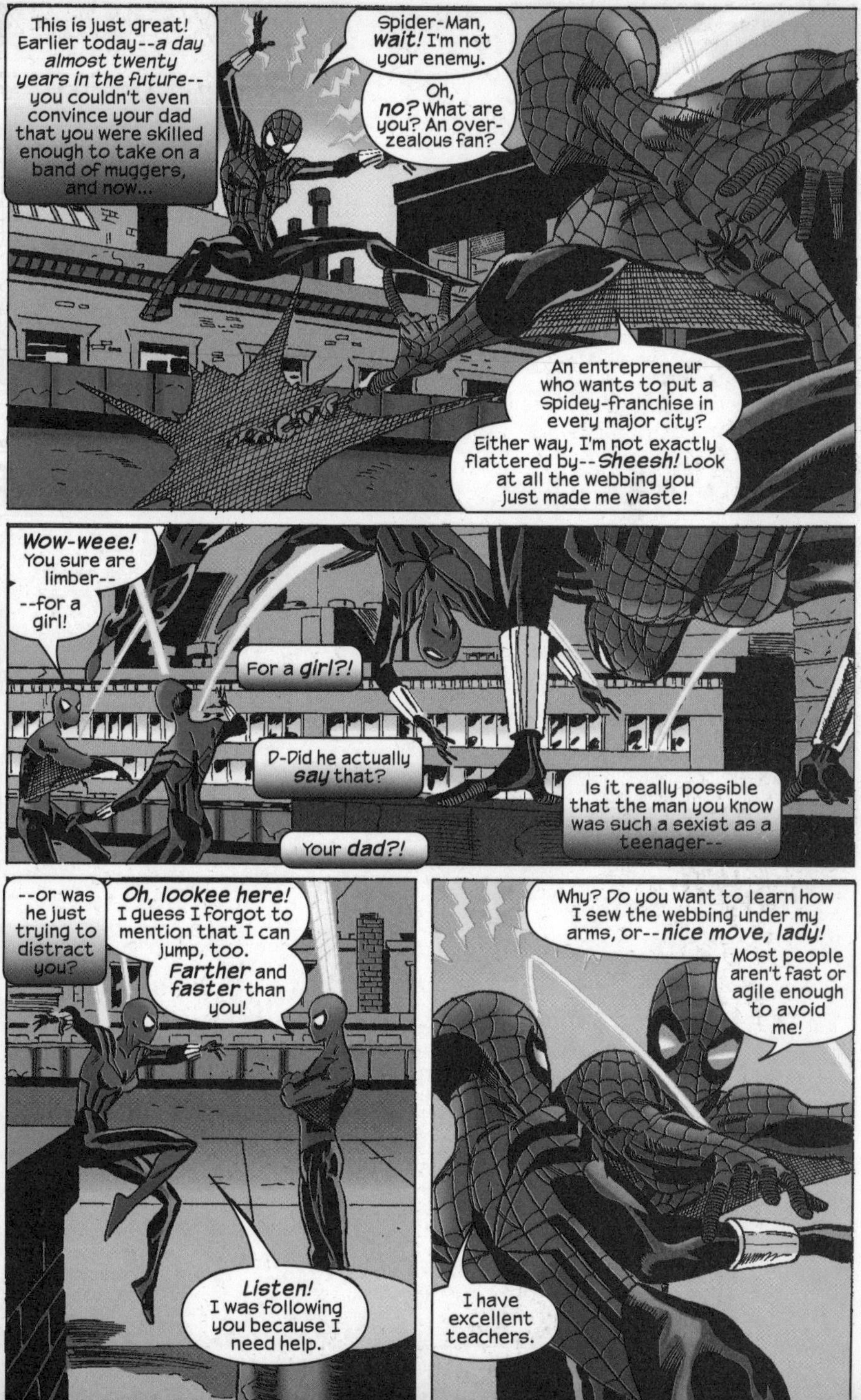

This is just great! Earlier today--a day almost twenty years in the future--you couldn't even convince your dad that you were skilled enough to take on a band of muggers, and now...
Spider-Man, wait! I'm not your enemy.
Oh, no? What are you? An over-zealous fan?
An entrepreneur who wants to put a Spidey-franchise in every major city?
Either way, I'm not exactly flattered by--Sheesh! Look at all the webbing you just made me waste!
Wow-weee! You sure are limber--
--for a girl!
For a girl?!
D-Did he actually say that?
Your dad?!
Is it really possible that the man you know was such a sexist as a teenager--
--or was he just trying to distract you?
Oh, lookee here! I guess I forgot to mention that I can jump, too. Farther and faster than you!
Listen! I was following you because I need help.
Why? Do you want to learn how I sew the webbing under my arms, or--nice move, lady!
Most people aren't fast or agile enough to avoid me!
I have excellent teachers.

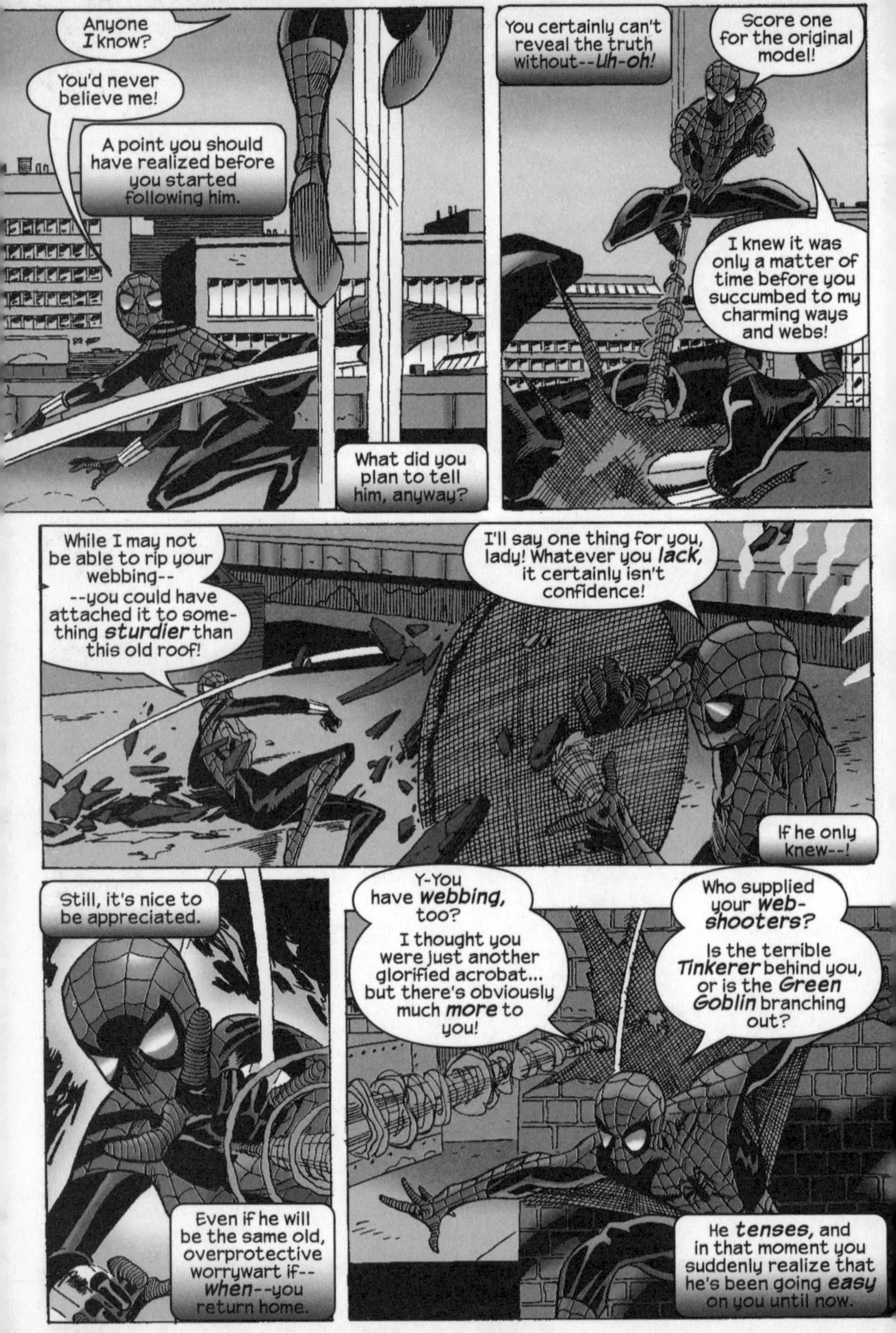
Anyone I know?
You'd never believe me!
A point you should have realized before you started following him.
What did you plan to tell him, anyway?
You certainly can't reveal the truth without--Uh-oh!
Score one for the original model!
I knew it was only a matter of time before you succumbed to my charming ways and webs!
While I may not be able to rip your webbing--
--you could have attached it to some-thing sturdier than this old roof!
I'll say one thing for you, lady! Whatever you lack, it certainly isn't confidence!
If he only knew--!
Still, it's nice to be appreciated.
Even if he will be the same old, overprotective worrywart if--when--you return home.
Y-You have webbing, too?
I thought you were just another glorified acrobat... but there's obviously much more to you!
Who supplied your web-shooters?
Is the terrible Tinkerer behind you, or is the Green Goblin branching out?
He tenses, and in that moment you suddenly realize that he's been going easy on you until now.

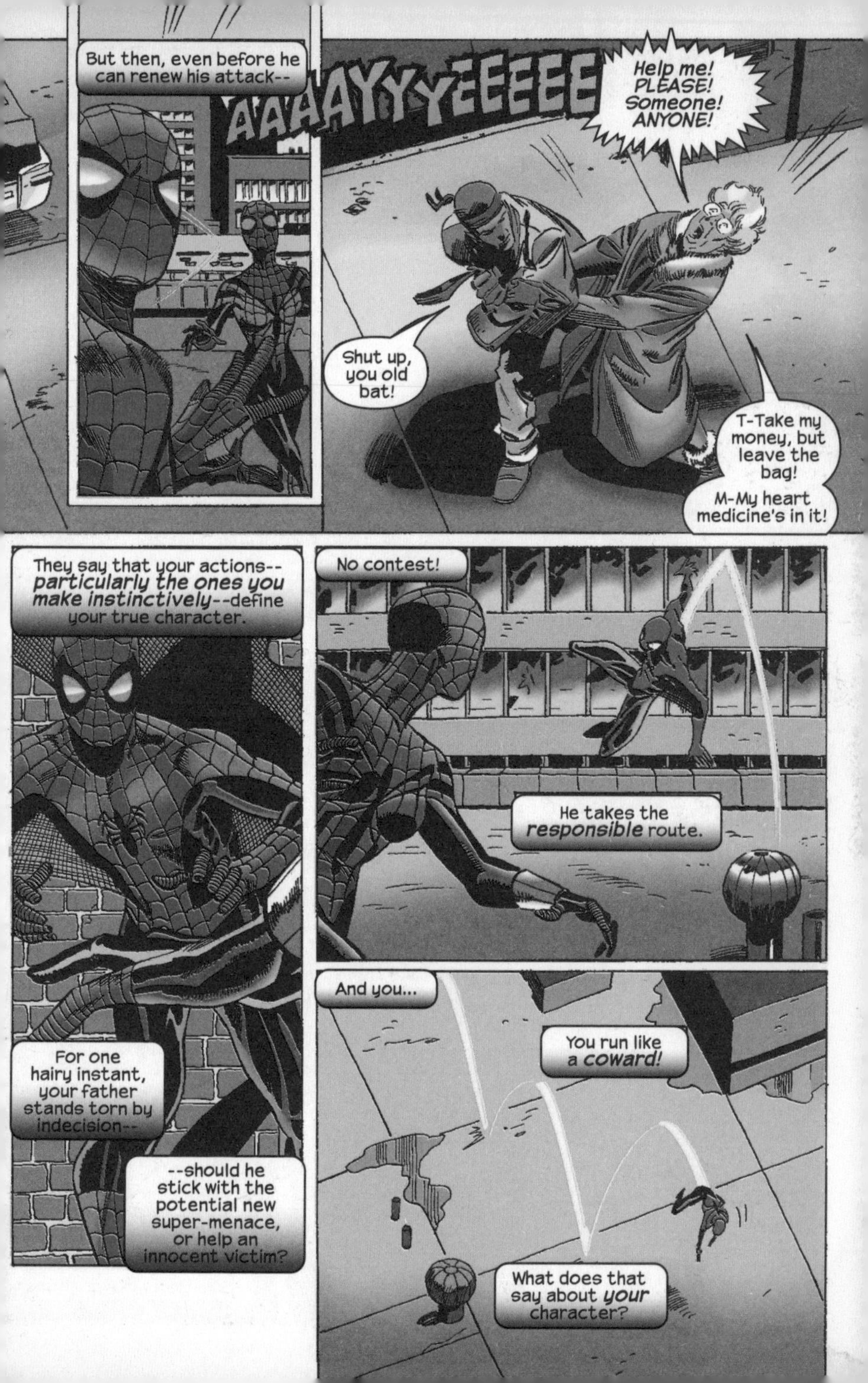

But then, even before he can renew his attack--
AAAAYYYEEEEE
Help me! PLEASE! Someone! ANYONE!
Shut up, you old bat!
T-Take my money, but leave the bag!
M-My heart medicine's in it!
They say that your actions--particularly the ones you make instinctively--define your true character.
For one hairy instant, your father stands torn by indecision--
--should he stick with the potential new super-menace, or help an innocent victim?
No contest!
He takes the responsible route.
And you...
You run like a coward!
What does that say about your character?

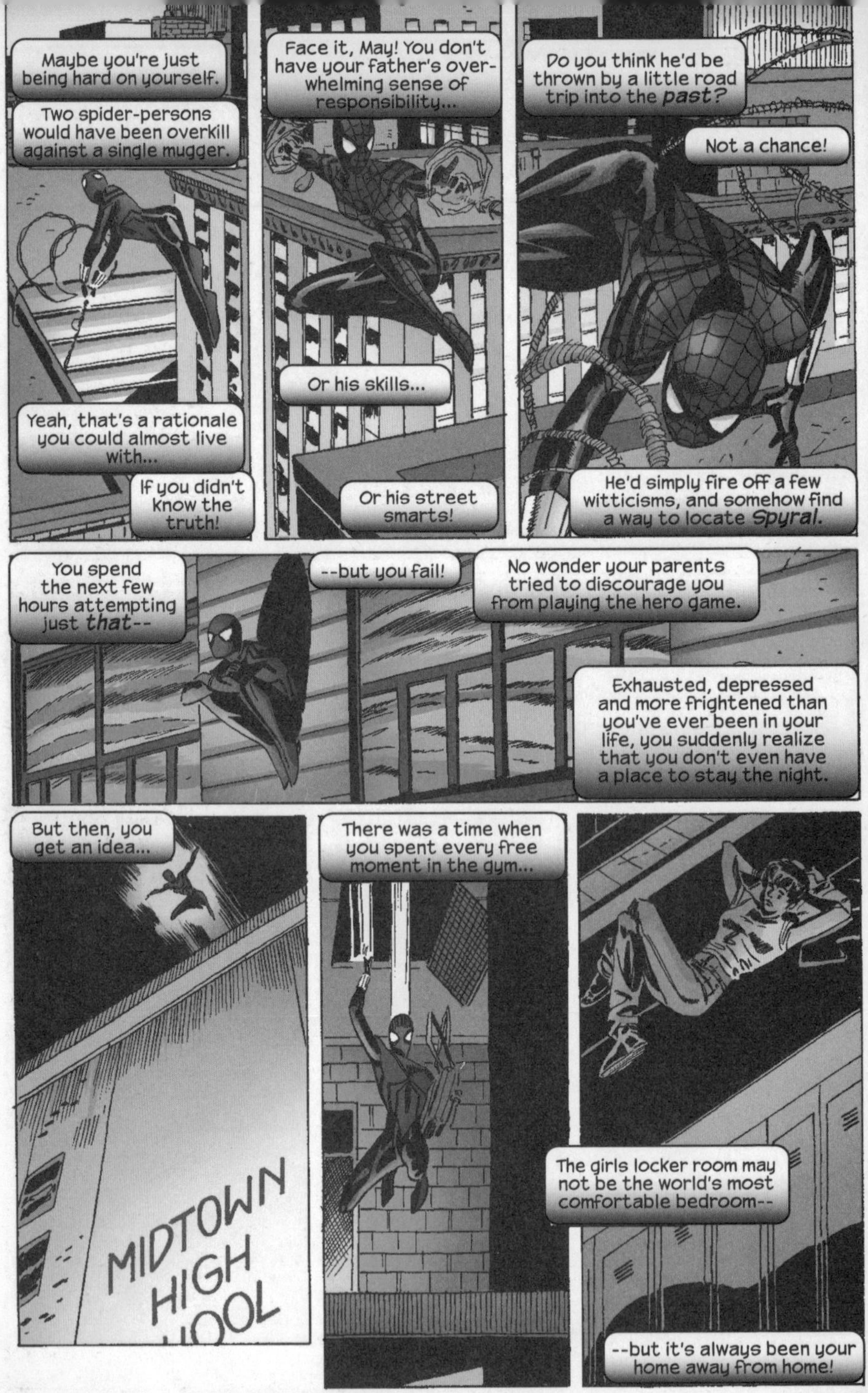
Maybe you're just being hard on yourself.
Two spider-persons would have been overkill against a single mugger.
Yeah, that's a rationale you could almost live with...
If you didn't know the truth!
Face it, May! You don't have your father's over-whelming sense of responsibility...
Or his skills...
Or his street smarts!
Do you think he'd be thrown by a little road trip into the *past?*
Not a chance!
He'd simply fire off a few witticisms, and somehow find a way to locate *Spyral.*
You spend the next few hours attempting just *that*--
--but you fail!
No wonder your parents tried to discourage you from playing the hero game.
Exhausted, depressed and more frightened than you've ever been in your life, you suddenly realize that you don't even have a place to stay the night.
But then, you get an idea...
MIDTOWN HIGH HOOL
There was a time when you spent every free moment in the gym...
The girls locker room may not be the world's most comfortable bedroom--
--but it's always been your home away from home!

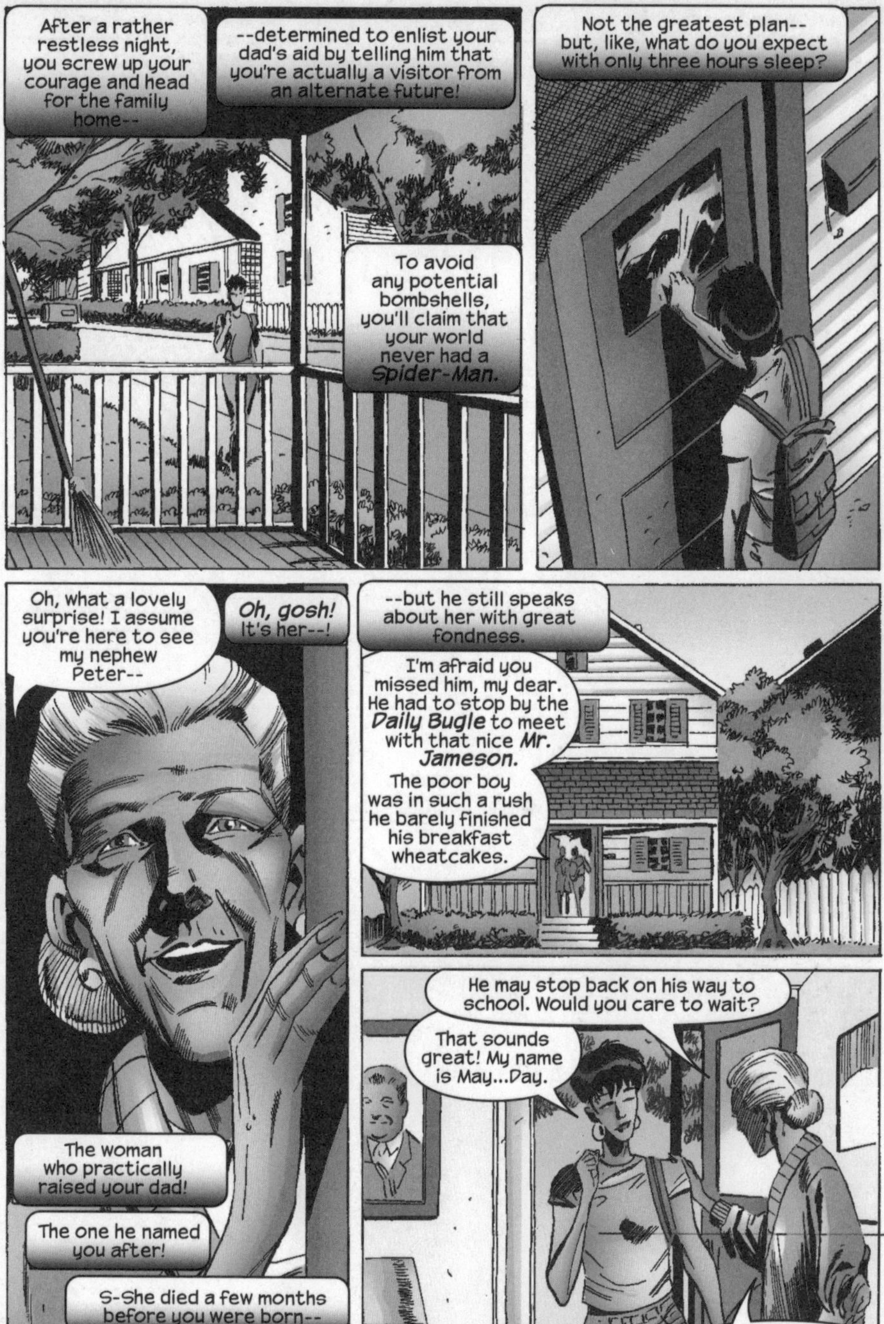
After a rather restless night, you screw up your courage and head for the family home--
--determined to enlist your dad's aid by telling him that you're actually a visitor from an alternate future!
To avoid any potential bombshells, you'll claim that your world never had a Spider-Man.
Not the greatest plan--but, like, what do you expect with only three hours sleep?
Oh, what a lovely surprise! I assume you're here to see my nephew Peter--
Oh, gosh! It's her--!
The woman who practically raised your dad!
The one he named you after!
S-She died a few months before you were born--
--but he still speaks about her with great fondness.
I'm afraid you missed him, my dear. He had to stop by the Daily Bugle to meet with that nice Mr. Jameson.
The poor boy was in such a rush he barely finished his breakfast wheatcakes.
He may stop back on his way to school. Would you care to wait?
That sounds great! My name is May...Day.
What a coincidence! My first name is also May.

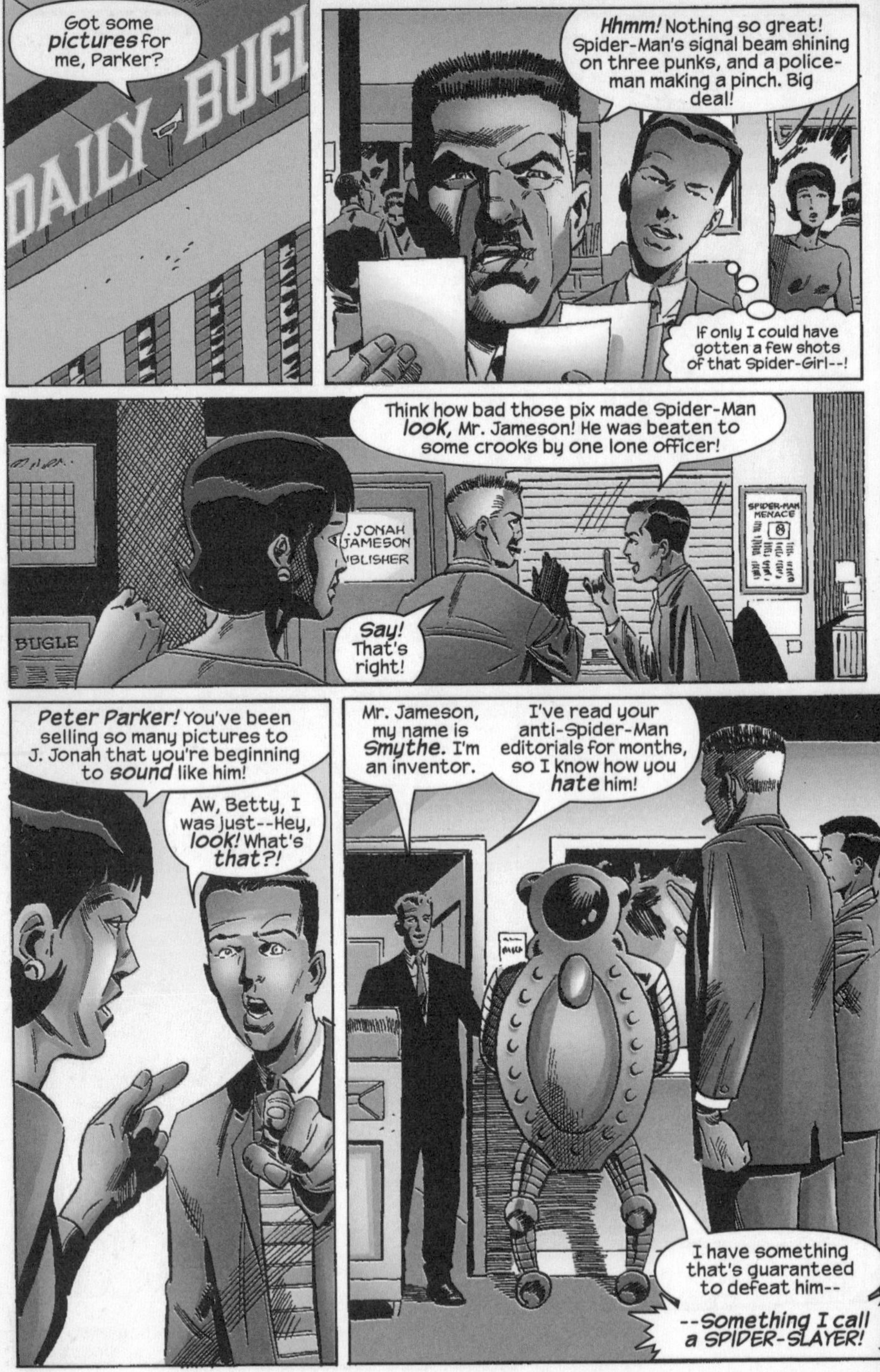
Got some pictures for me, Parker?
DAILY BUGL
Hhmm! Nothing so great! Spider-Man's signal beam shining on three punks, and a policeman making a pinch. Big deal!
If only I could have gotten a few shots of that Spider-Girl--!
Think how bad those pix made Spider-Man look, Mr. Jameson! He was beaten to some crooks by one lone officer!
. JONAH JAMESON UBLISHER
SPIDER-MAN MENACE
BUGLE
Say! That's right!
Peter Parker! You've been selling so many pictures to J. Jonah that you're beginning to sound like him!
Aw, Betty, I was just--Hey, look! What's that?!
Mr. Jameson, my name is Smythe. I'm an inventor.
I've read your anti-Spider-Man editorials for months, so I know how you hate him!
I have something that's guaranteed to defeat him--
--Something I call a SPIDER-SLAYER!

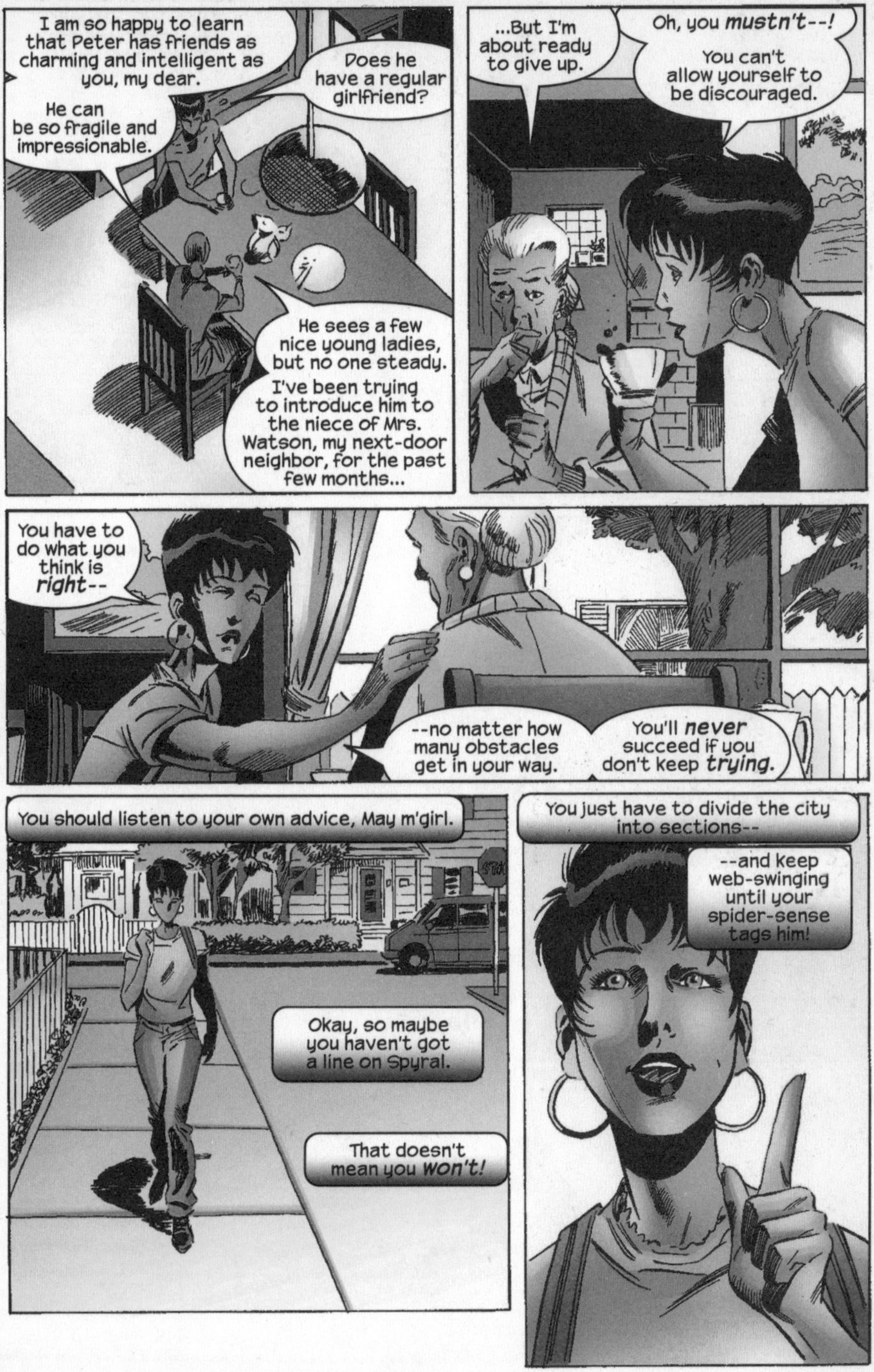
I am so happy to learn that Peter has friends as charming and intelligent as you, my dear.
He can be so fragile and impressionable.
Does he have a regular girlfriend?
He sees a few nice young ladies, but no one steady.
I've been trying to introduce him to the niece of Mrs. Watson, my next-door neighbor, for the past few months...
...But I'm about ready to give up.
Oh, you mustn't--!
You can't allow yourself to be discouraged.
You have to do what you think is right--
--no matter how many obstacles get in your way.
You'll never succeed if you don't keep trying.
You should listen to your own advice, May m'girl.
Okay, so maybe you haven't got a line on Spyral.
That doesn't mean you won't!
You just have to divide the city into sections--
--and keep web-swinging until your spider-sense tags him!

Okay, so it may take a while...a *lonnnnnng* while!

Big deal! Since you'll be traveling through time anyway, you just aim your return for a few minutes after you left.

Simple, no?

You just have to keep a positive attitude, and-- *now WHAT?!*

Look, Mr. Jameson! My spider-slayer is already zeroing in on Spider-Man!

Let me take over the controls, Smythe!

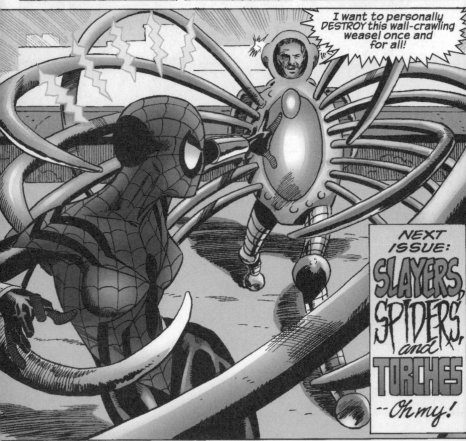

I want to personally *DESTROY* this wall-crawling weasel once and for all!

NEXT ISSUE:
SLAYERS,
SPIDERS,
and
TORCHES
--Oh my!

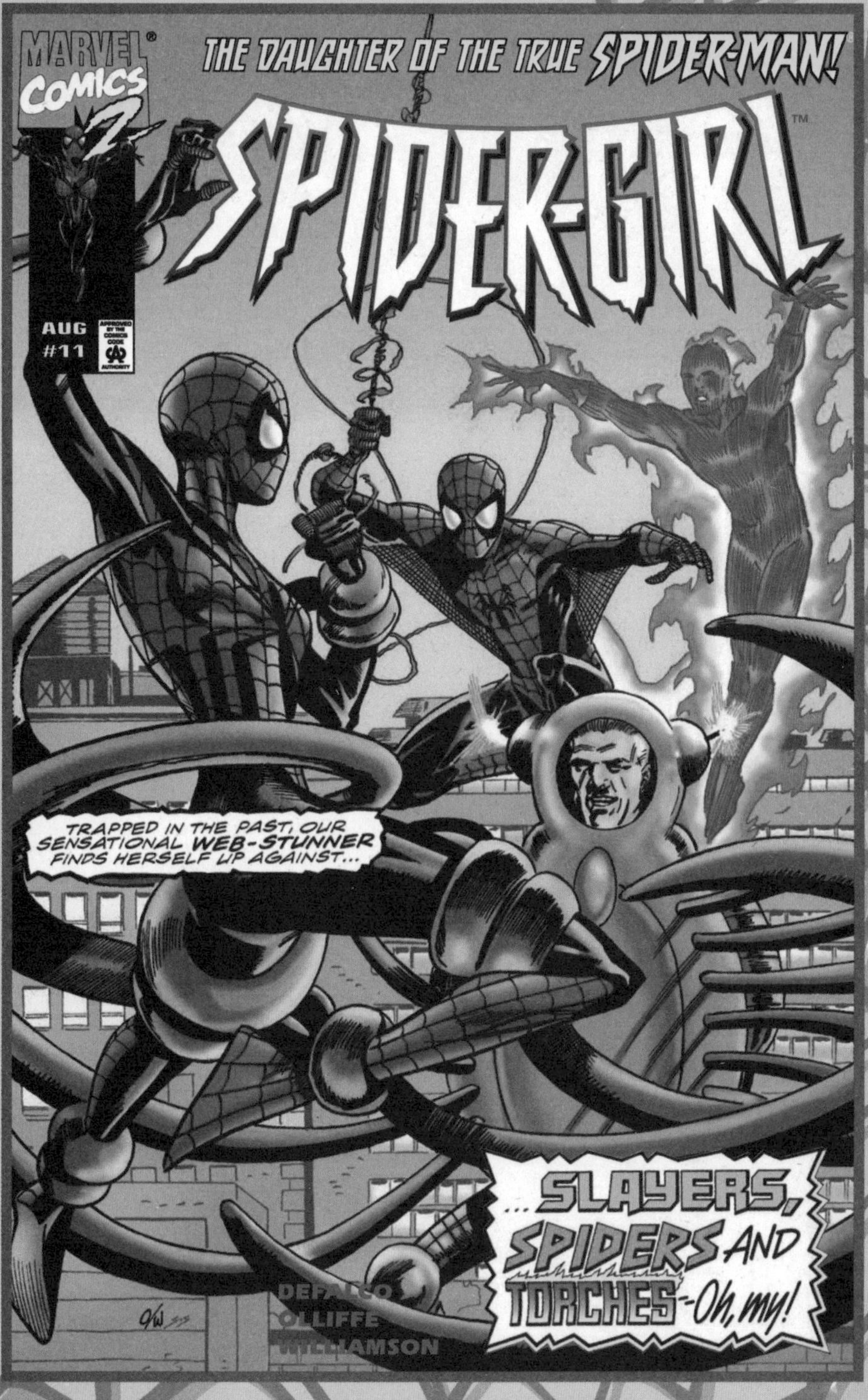
MARVEL COMICS
THE DAUGHTER OF THE TRUE SPIDER-MAN!
SPIDER-GIRL
AUG
#11
TRAPPED IN THE PAST, OUR SENSATIONAL WEB-STUNNER FINDS HERSELF UP AGAINST...
...SLAYERS, SPIDERS AND TORCHES-Oh, my!
DEFALCO
OLLIFFE
WILLIAMSON

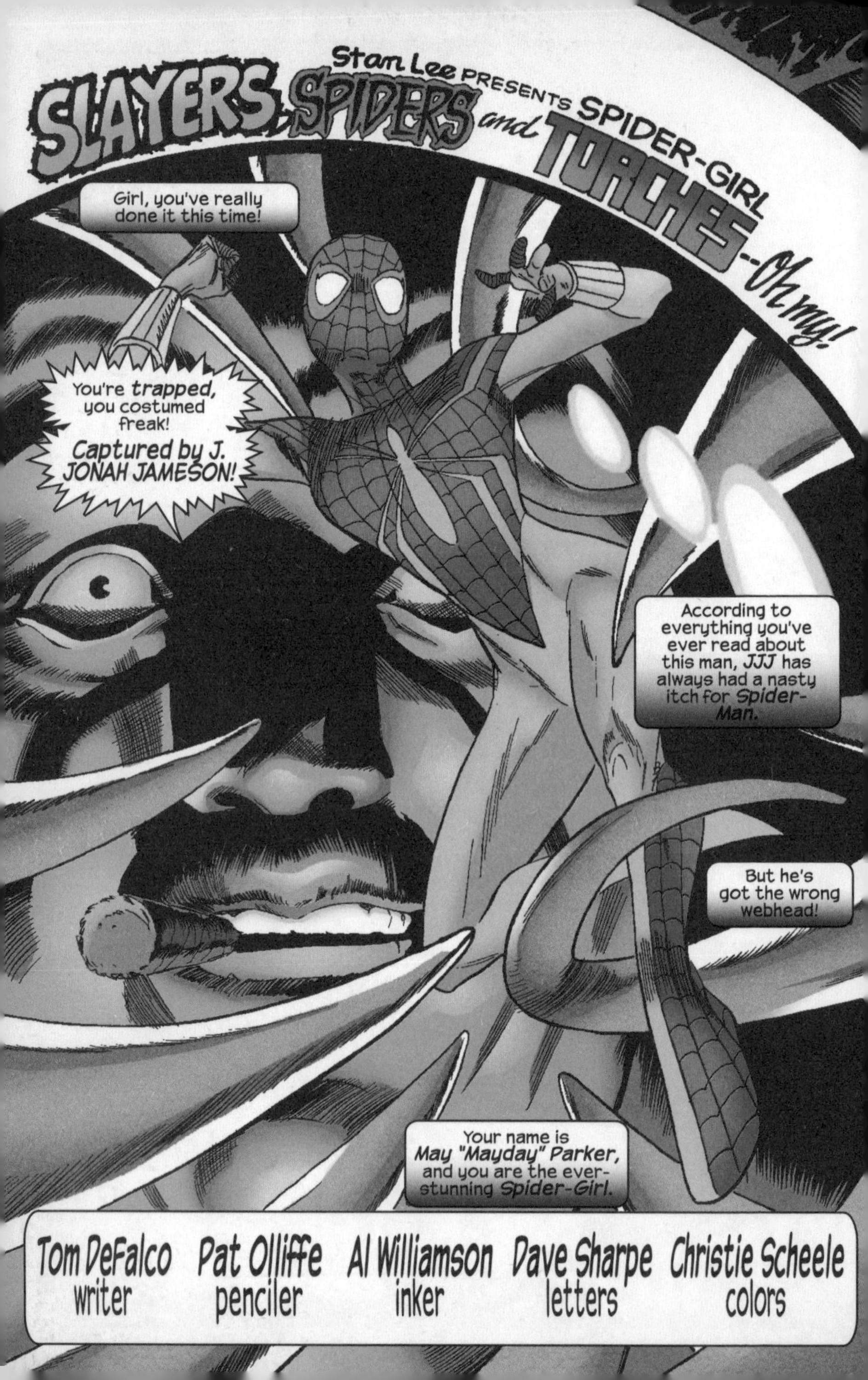
Stan Lee PRESENTS SPIDER-GIRL
SLAYERS, SPIDERS and TORCHES--Oh my!
Girl, you've really done it this time!
You're trapped, you costumed freak! Captured by J. JONAH JAMESON!
According to everything you've ever read about this man, JJJ has always had a nasty itch for Spider-Man.
But he's got the wrong webhead!
Your name is May "Mayday" Parker, and you are the ever-stunning Spider-Girl.
Tom DeFalco writer
Pat Olliffe penciler
Al Williamson inker
Dave Sharpe letters
Christie Scheele colors

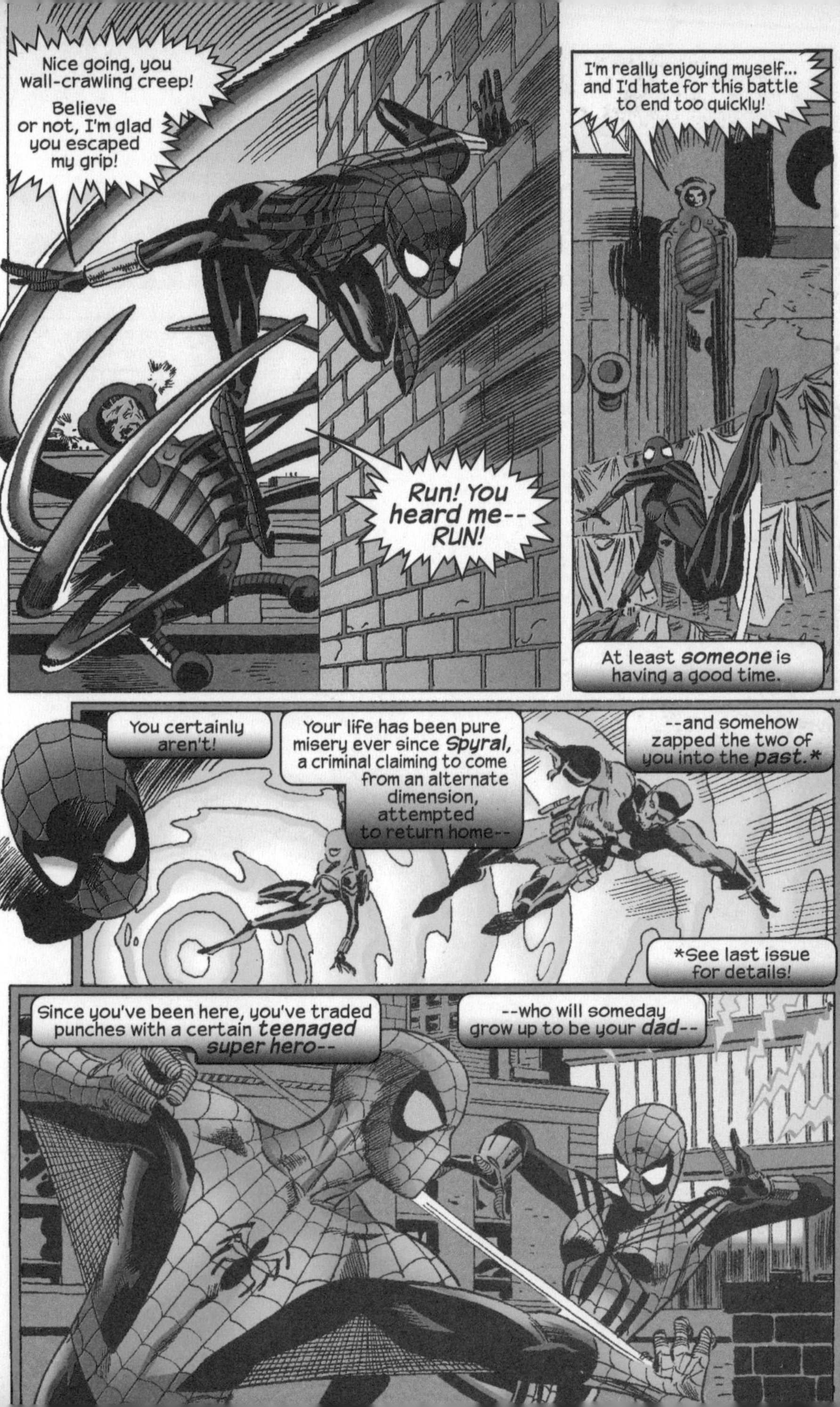

Nice going, you wall-crawling creep!
Believe or not, I'm glad you escaped my grip!
Run! You heard me-- RUN!
I'm really enjoying myself... and I'd hate for this battle to end too quickly!
At least someone is having a good time.
You certainly aren't!
Your life has been pure misery ever since Spyral, a criminal claiming to come from an alternate dimension, attempted to return home--
--and somehow zapped the two of you into the past.*
*See last issue for details!
Since you've been here, you've traded punches with a certain teenaged super hero--
--who will someday grow up to be your dad--

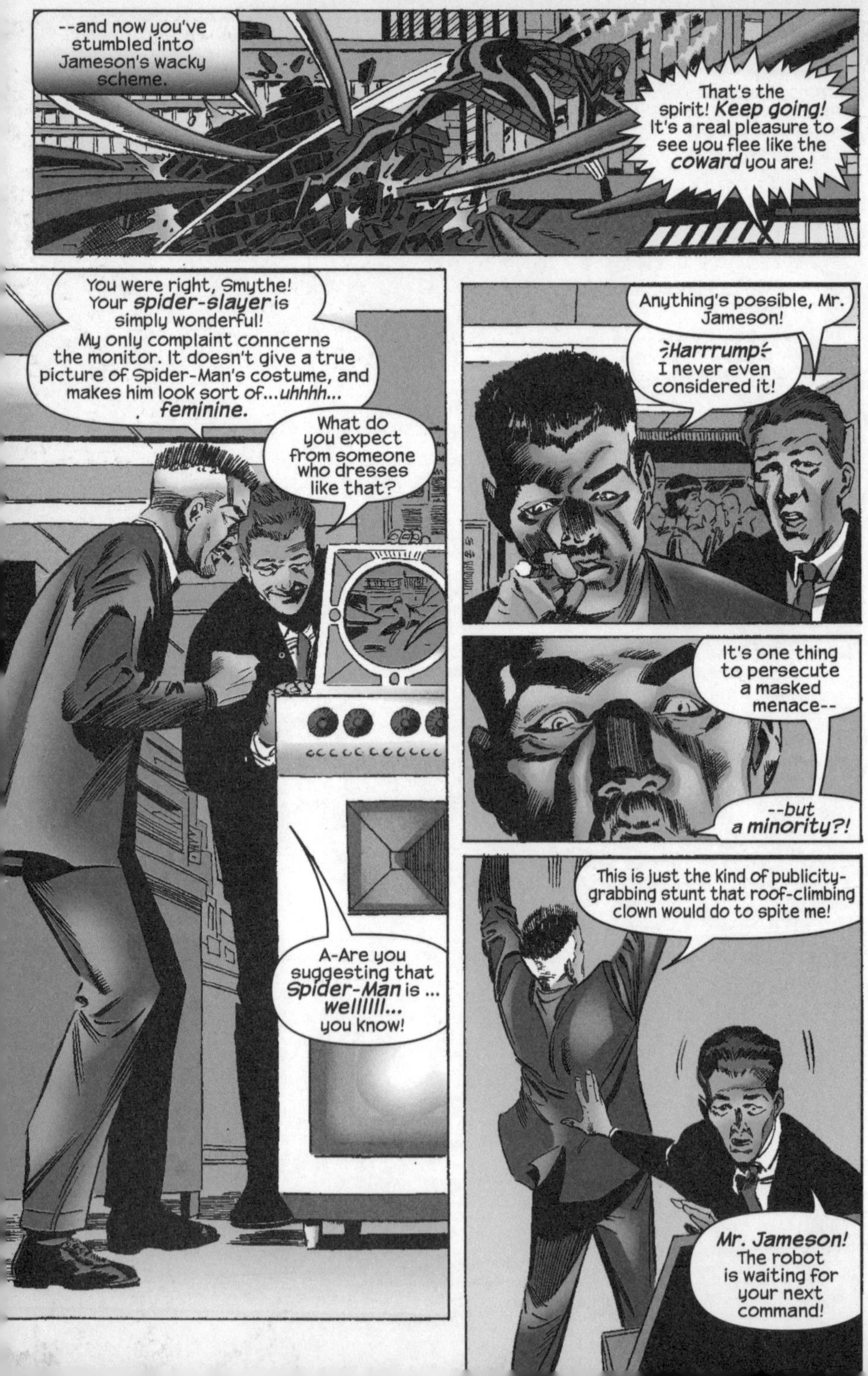
--and now you've stumbled into Jameson's wacky scheme.
That's the spirit! Keep going! It's a real pleasure to see you flee like the coward you are!
You were right, Smythe! Your spider-slayer is simply wonderful! My only complaint conncerns the monitor. It doesn't give a true picture of Spider-Man's costume, and makes him look sort of...uhhhh... feminine.
What do you expect from someone who dresses like that?
A-Are you suggesting that Spider-Man is ... wellllll... you know!
Anything's possible, Mr. Jameson!
Harrrump I never even considered it!
It's one thing to persecute a masked menace--
--but a minority?!
This is just the kind of publicity-grabbing stunt that roof-climbing clown would do to spite me!
Mr. Jameson! The robot is waiting for your next command!

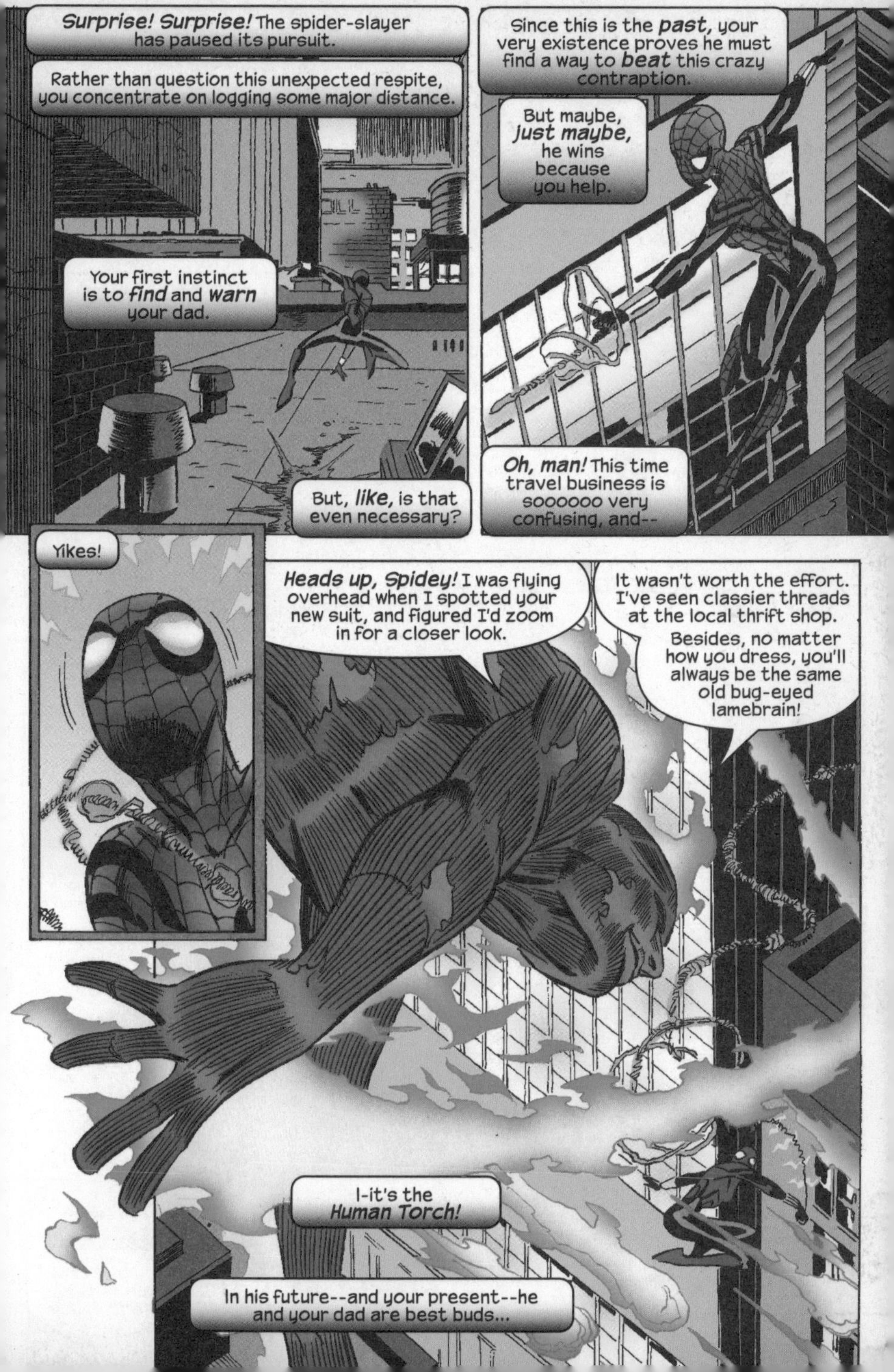

Surprise! Surprise! The spider-slayer has paused its pursuit.
Rather than question this unexpected respite, you concentrate on logging some major distance.
Your first instinct is to *find* and *warn* your dad.
But, *like,* is that even necessary?
Since this is the *past,* your very existence proves he must find a way to *beat* this crazy contraption.
But maybe, *just maybe,* he wins because you help.
Oh, man! This time travel business is soooooo very confusing, and--
Yikes!
Heads up, Spidey! I was flying overhead when I spotted your new suit, and figured I'd zoom in for a closer look.
It wasn't worth the effort. I've seen classier threads at the local thrift shop.
Besides, no matter how you dress, you'll always be the same old bug-eyed lamebrain!
I-it's the *Human Torch!*
In his future--and your present--he and your dad are best buds...

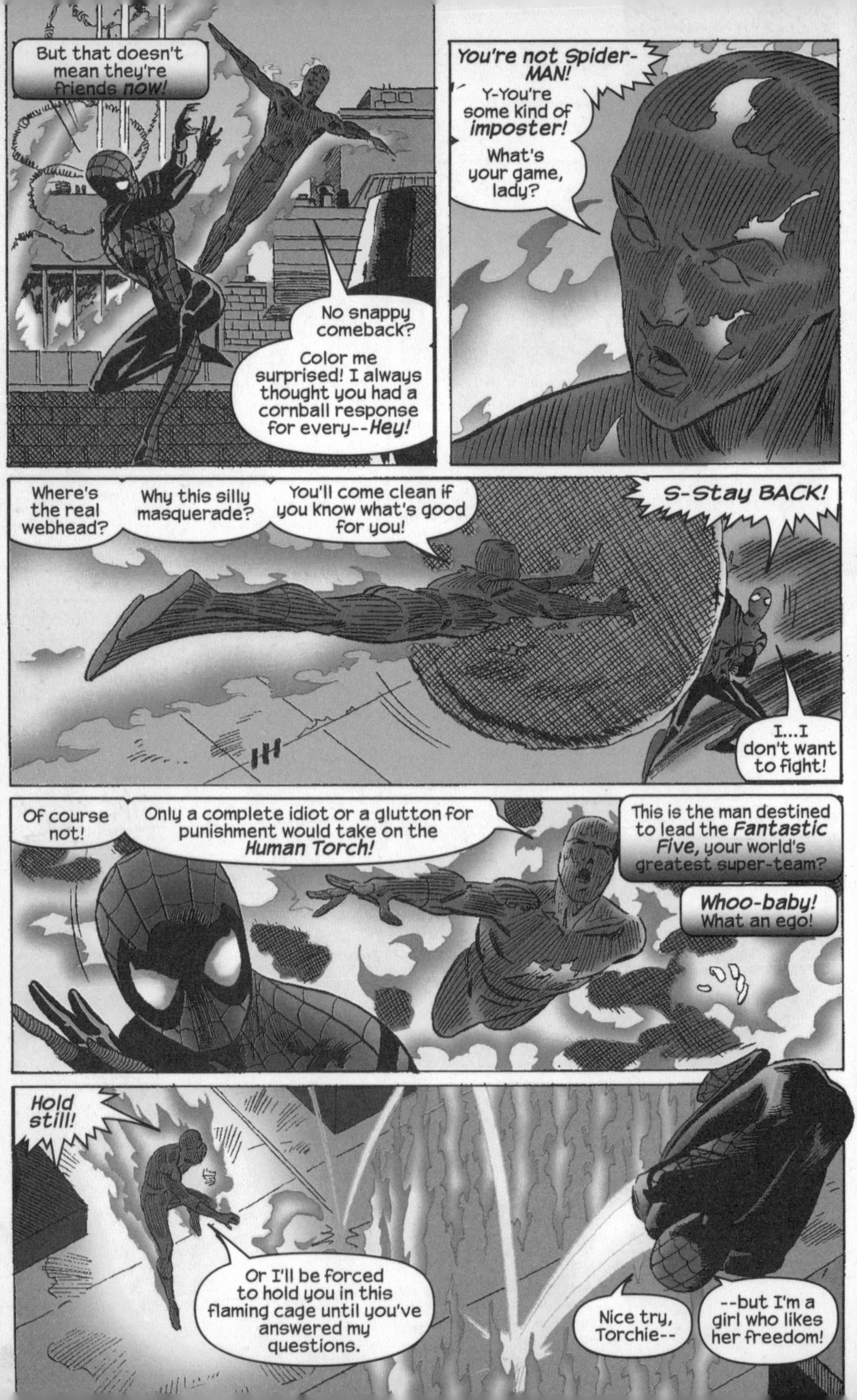

But that doesn't mean they're friends *now!*
No snappy comeback?
Color me surprised! I always thought you had a cornball response for every--*Hey!*
You're not Spider-MAN!
Y-You're some kind of *imposter!*
What's your game, lady?
Where's the real webhead?
Why this silly masquerade?
You'll come clean if you know what's good for you!
S-Stay BACK!
I...I don't want to fight!
Of course not!
Only a complete idiot or a glutton for punishment would take on the *Human Torch!*
This is the man destined to lead the *Fantastic Five,* your world's greatest super-team?
Whoo-baby! What an ego!
Hold still!
Or I'll be forced to hold you in this flaming cage until you've answered my questions.
Nice try, Torchie--
--but I'm a girl who likes her freedom!

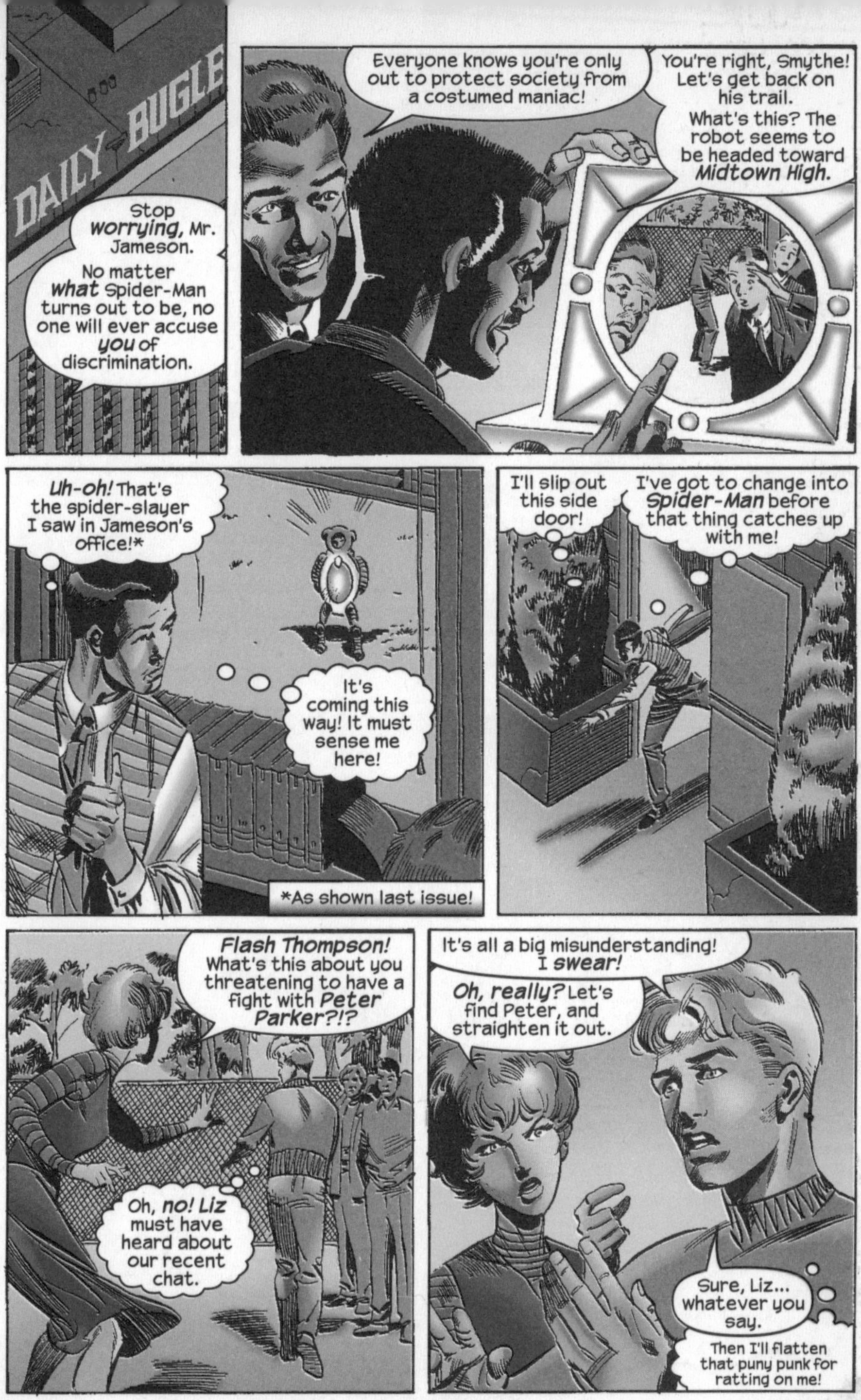
DAILY BUGLE
Stop worrying, Mr. Jameson.
No matter what Spider-Man turns out to be, no one will ever accuse you of discrimination.
Everyone knows you're only out to protect society from a costumed maniac!
You're right, Smythe! Let's get back on his trail.
What's this? The robot seems to be headed toward Midtown High.
Uh-oh! That's the spider-slayer I saw in Jameson's office!*
It's coming this way! It must sense me here!
*As shown last issue!
I'll slip out this side door!
I've got to change into Spider-Man before that thing catches up with me!
Flash Thompson! What's this about you threatening to have a fight with Peter Parker?!?
Oh, no! Liz must have heard about our recent chat.
It's all a big misunderstanding! I swear!
Oh, really? Let's find Peter, and straighten it out.
Sure, Liz... whatever you say.
Then I'll flatten that puny punk for ratting on me!

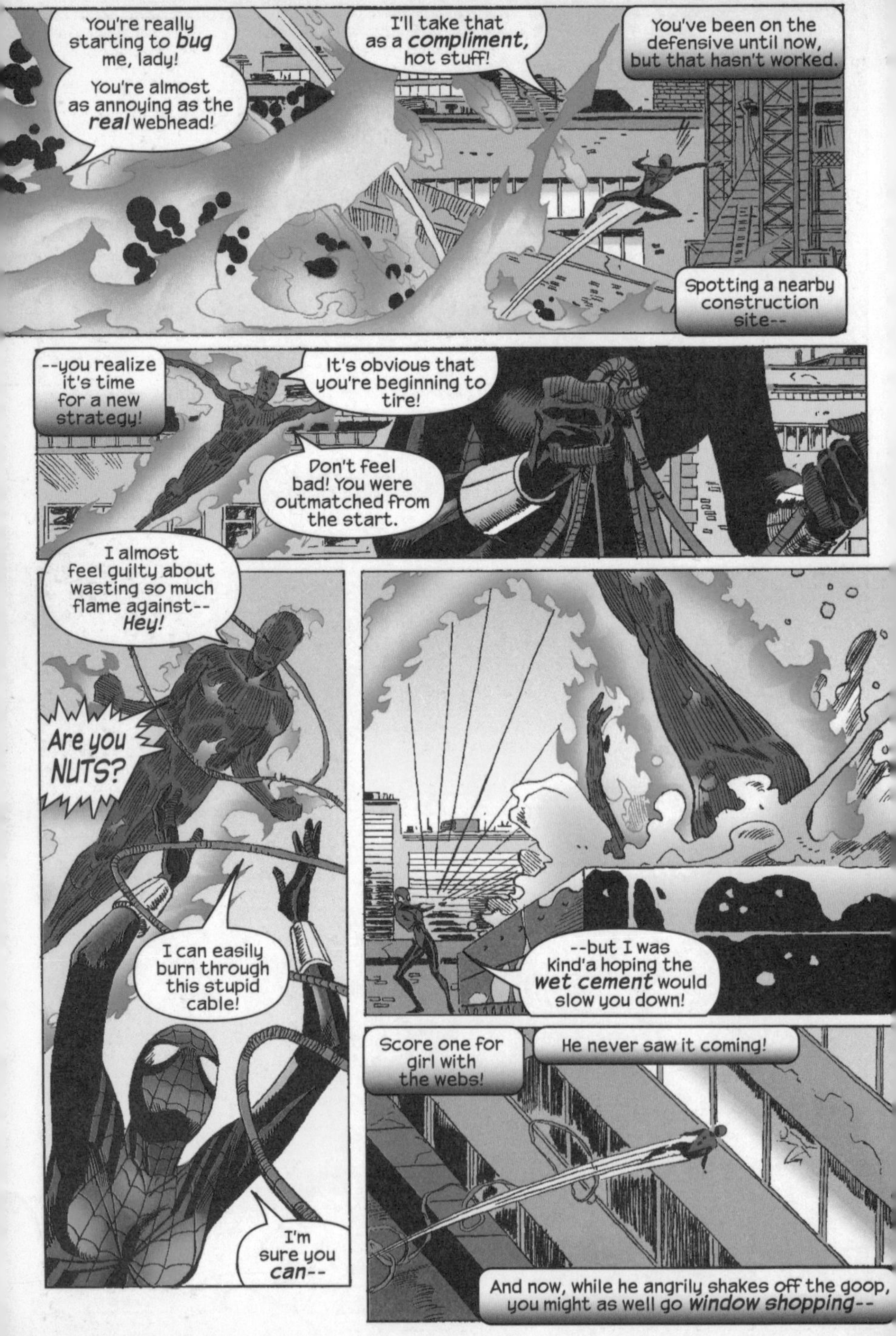
You're really starting to *bug* me, lady!
You're almost as annoying as the *real* webhead!
I'll take that as a *compliment,* hot stuff!
You've been on the defensive until now, but that hasn't worked.
Spotting a nearby construction site--
--you realize it's time for a new strategy!
It's obvious that you're beginning to tire!
Don't feel bad! You were outmatched from the start.
I almost feel guilty about wasting so much flame against-- *Hey!*
Are you NUTS?
I can easily burn through this stupid cable!
I'm sure you *can*--
--but I was kind'a hoping the *wet cement* would slow you down!
Score one for girl with the webs!
He never saw it coming!
And now, while he angrily shakes off the goop, you might as well go *window shopping*--

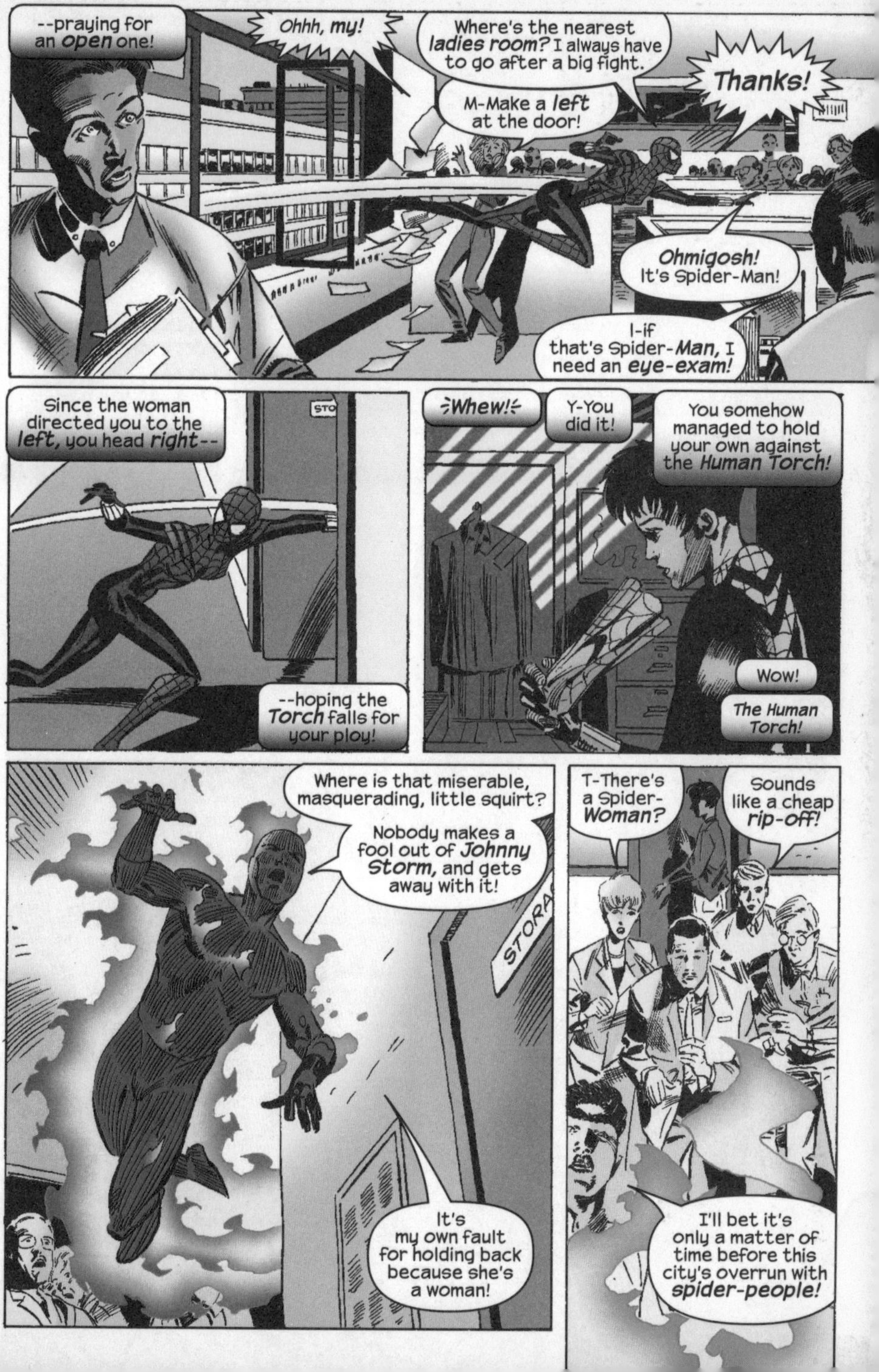
--praying for an open one!
Ohhh, my!
Where's the nearest ladies room? I always have to go after a big fight.
M-Make a left at the door!
Thanks!
Ohmigosh! It's Spider-Man!
I-if that's Spider-Man, I need an eye-exam!
Since the woman directed you to the left, you head right--
--hoping the Torch falls for your ploy!
Whew!
Y-You did it!
You somehow managed to hold your own against the Human Torch!
Wow!
The Human Torch!
Where is that miserable, masquerading, little squirt?
Nobody makes a fool out of Johnny Storm, and gets away with it!
It's my own fault for holding back because she's a woman!
T-There's a Spider-Woman?
Sounds like a cheap rip-off!
I'll bet it's only a matter of time before this city's overrun with spider-people!

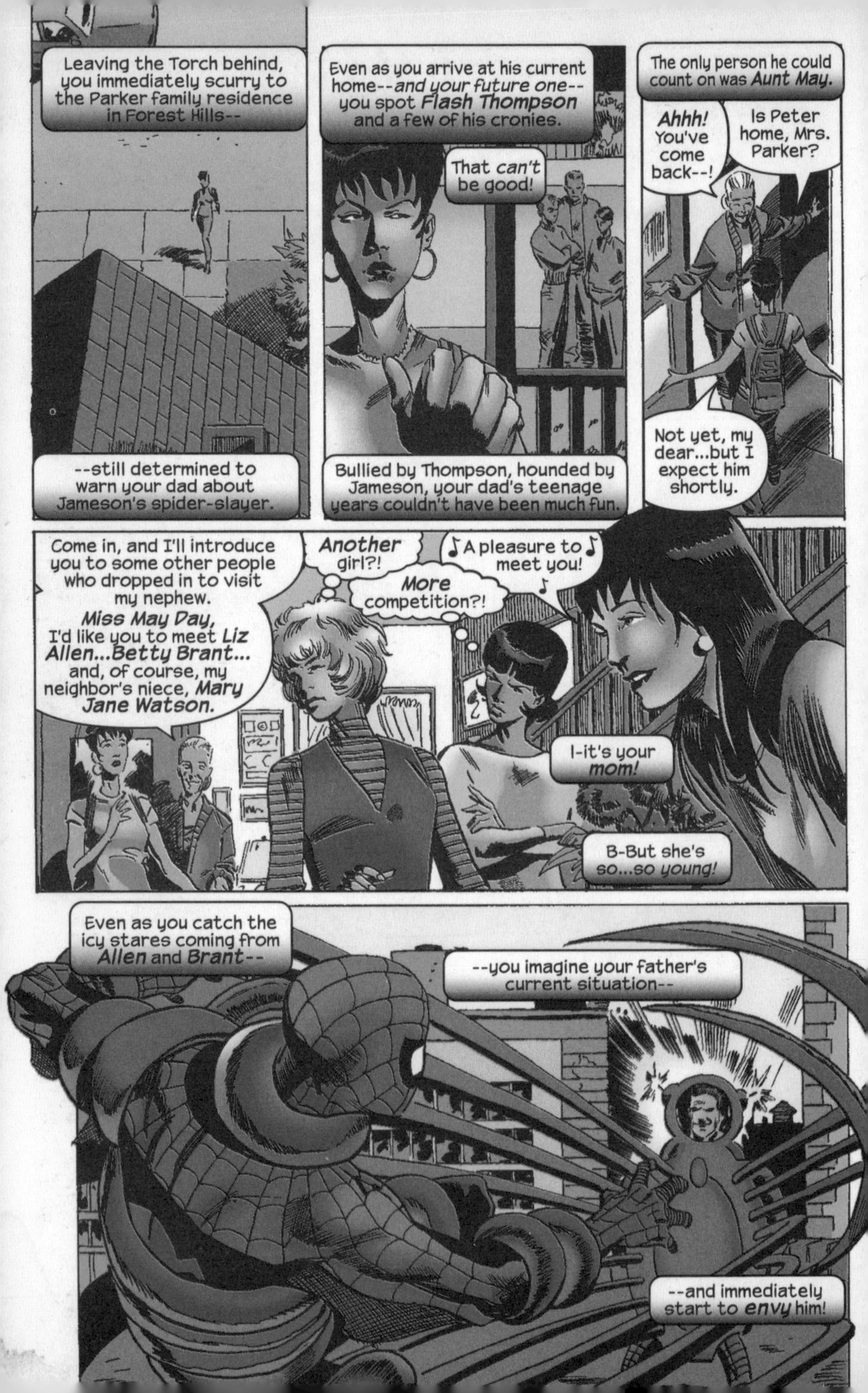

Leaving the Torch behind, you immediately scurry to the Parker family residence in Forest Hills--
--still determined to warn your dad about Jameson's spider-slayer.
Even as you arrive at his current home--and your future one--you spot Flash Thompson and a few of his cronies.
That can't be good!
Bullied by Thompson, hounded by Jameson, your dad's teenage years couldn't have been much fun.
The only person he could count on was Aunt May.
Is Peter home, Mrs. Parker?
Ahhh! You've come back--!
Not yet, my dear...but I expect him shortly.
Come in, and I'll introduce you to some other people who dropped in to visit my nephew. Miss May Day, I'd like you to meet Liz Allen...Betty Brant... and, of course, my neighbor's niece, Mary Jane Watson.
Another girl?!
More competition?!
♪A pleasure to♪ meet you! ♪
I-it's your mom!
B-But she's so...so young!
Even as you catch the icy stares coming from Allen and Brant--
--you imagine your father's current situation--
--and immediately start to envy him!

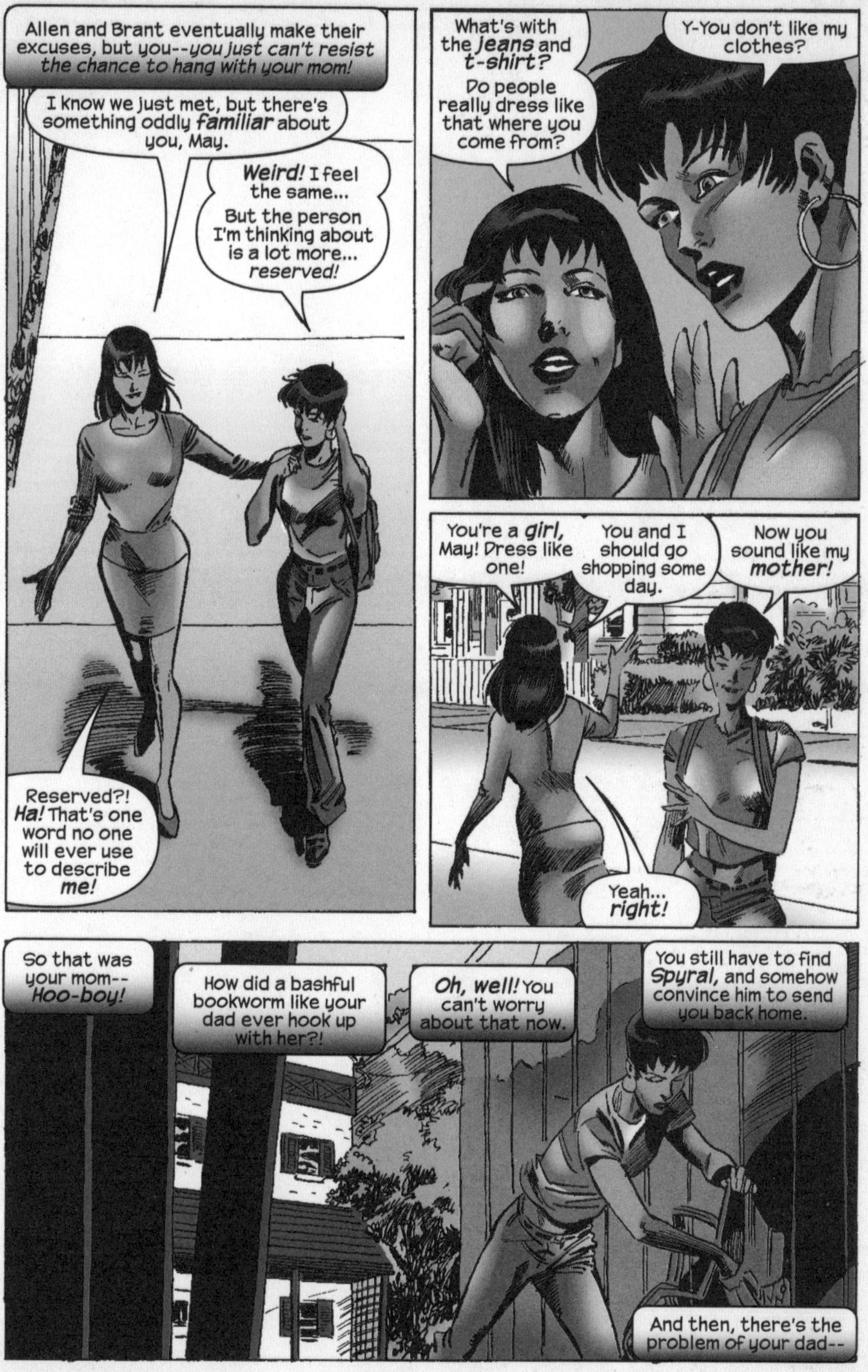
Allen and Brant eventually make their excuses, but you--you just can't resist the chance to hang with your mom!
I know we just met, but there's something oddly familiar about you, May.
Weird! I feel the same... But the person I'm thinking about is a lot more... reserved!
Reserved?! Ha! That's one word no one will ever use to describe me!
What's with the jeans and t-shirt? Do people really dress like that where you come from?
Y-You don't like my clothes?
You're a girl, May! Dress like one!
You and I should go shopping some day.
Now you sound like my mother!
Yeah... right!
So that was your mom-- Hoo-boy!
How did a bashful bookworm like your dad ever hook up with her?!
Oh, well! You can't worry about that now.
You still have to find Spyral, and somehow convince him to send you back home.
And then, there's the problem of your dad--

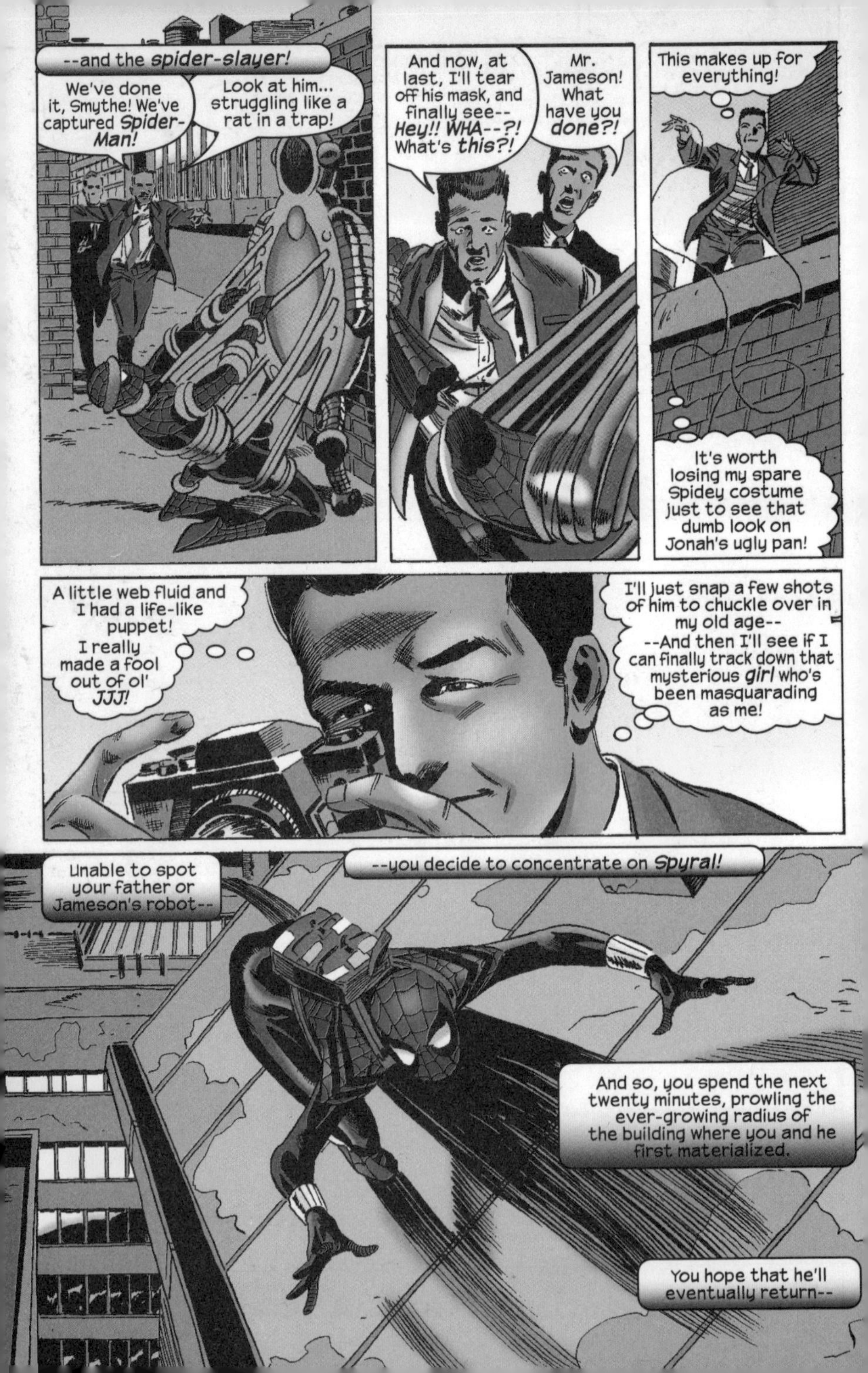
--and the spider-slayer!
We've done it, Smythe! We've captured Spider-Man!
Look at him... struggling like a rat in a trap!
And now, at last, I'll tear off his mask, and finally see-- Hey!! WHA--?! What's this?!
Mr. Jameson! What have you done?!
This makes up for everything!
It's worth losing my spare Spidey costume just to see that dumb look on Jonah's ugly pan!
A little web fluid and I had a life-like puppet!
I really made a fool out of ol' JJJ!
I'll just snap a few shots of him to chuckle over in my old age--
--And then I'll see if I can finally track down that mysterious girl who's been masquarading as me!
Unable to spot your father or Jameson's robot--
--you decide to concentrate on Spyral!
And so, you spend the next twenty minutes, prowling the ever-growing radius of the building where you and he first materialized.
You hope that he'll eventually return--

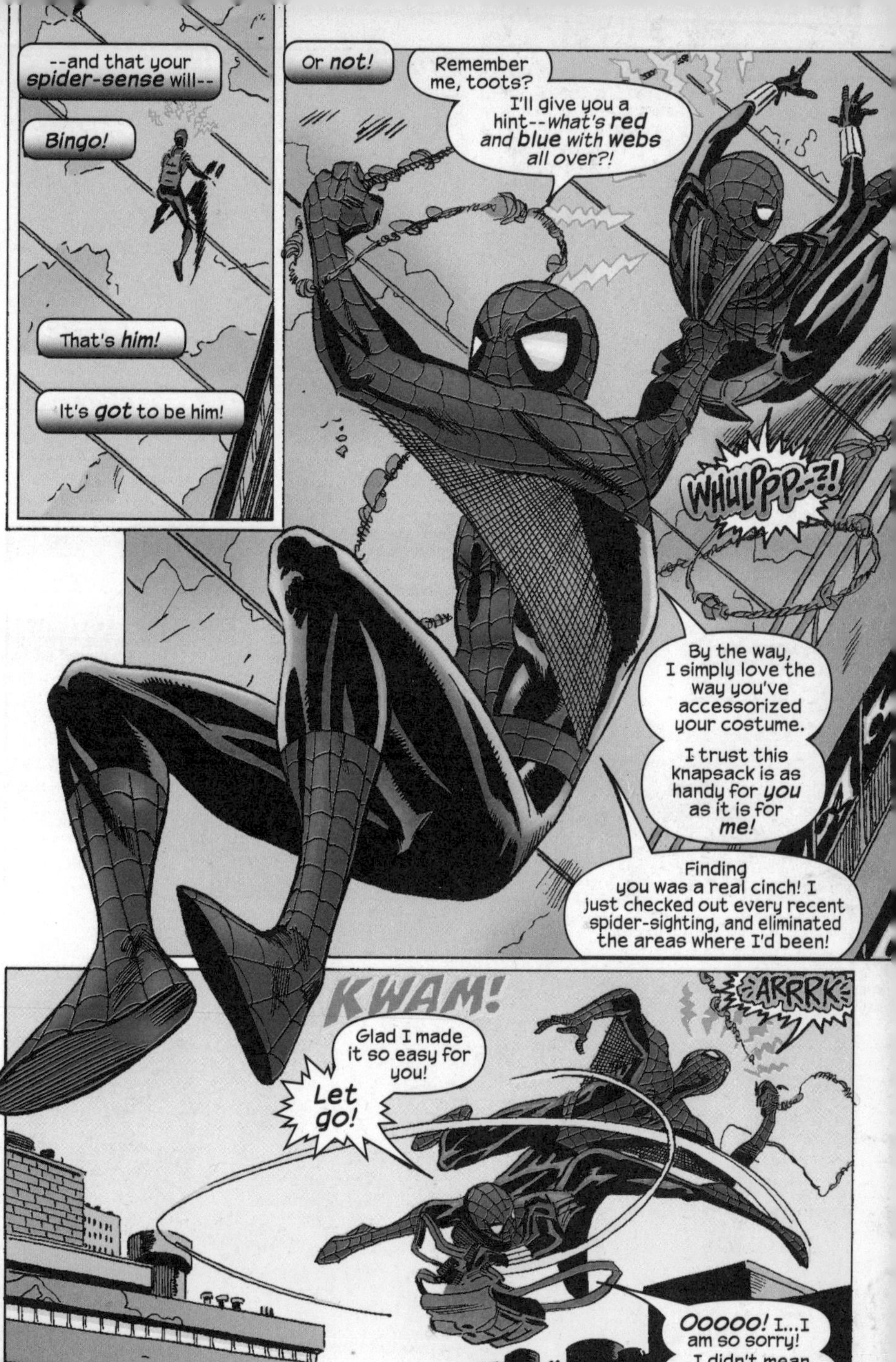
--and that your spider-sense will--
Bingo!
That's him!
It's got to be him!
Or not!
Remember me, toots?
I'll give you a hint--what's red and blue with webs all over?!
WHULPPP--?!
By the way, I simply love the way you've accessorized your costume.
I trust this knapsack is as handy for you as it is for me!
Finding you was a real cinch! I just checked out every recent spider-sighting, and eliminated the areas where I'd been!
KWAM!
ARRRK
Glad I made it so easy for you!
Let go!
Ooooo! I...I am so sorry! I didn't mean to kick so hard!

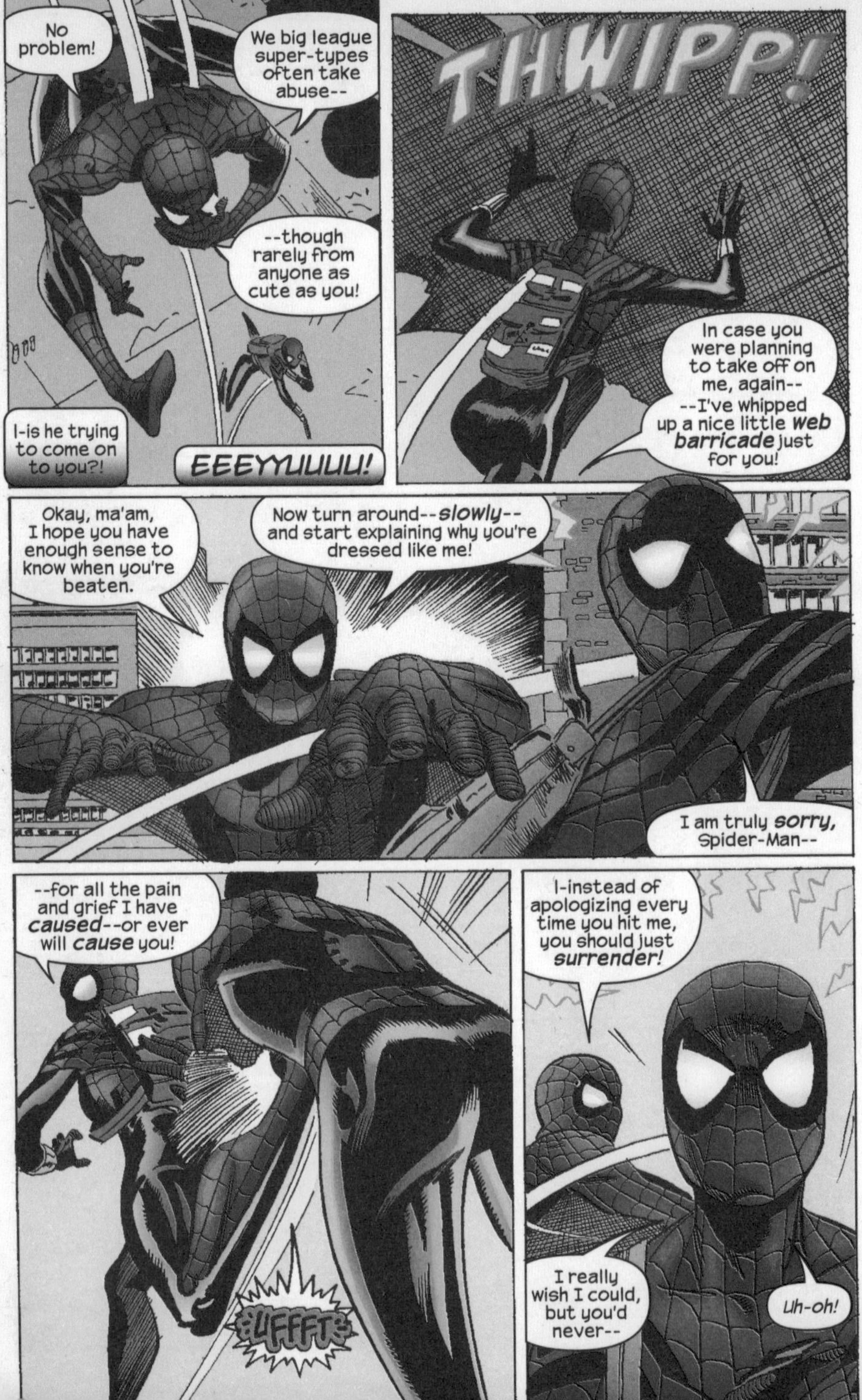
No problem!
We big league super-types often take abuse--
--though rarely from anyone as cute as you!
I-is he trying to come on to you?!
EEEYYUUUUU!
THWIPP!
In case you were planning to take off on me, again--
--I've whipped up a nice little web barricade just for you!
Okay, ma'am, I hope you have enough sense to know when you're beaten.
Now turn around--slowly--and start explaining why you're dressed like me!
I am truly sorry, Spider-Man--
--for all the pain and grief I have caused--or ever will cause you!
UFFFT
I-instead of apologizing every time you hit me, you should just surrender!
I really wish I could, but you'd never--
Uh-oh!

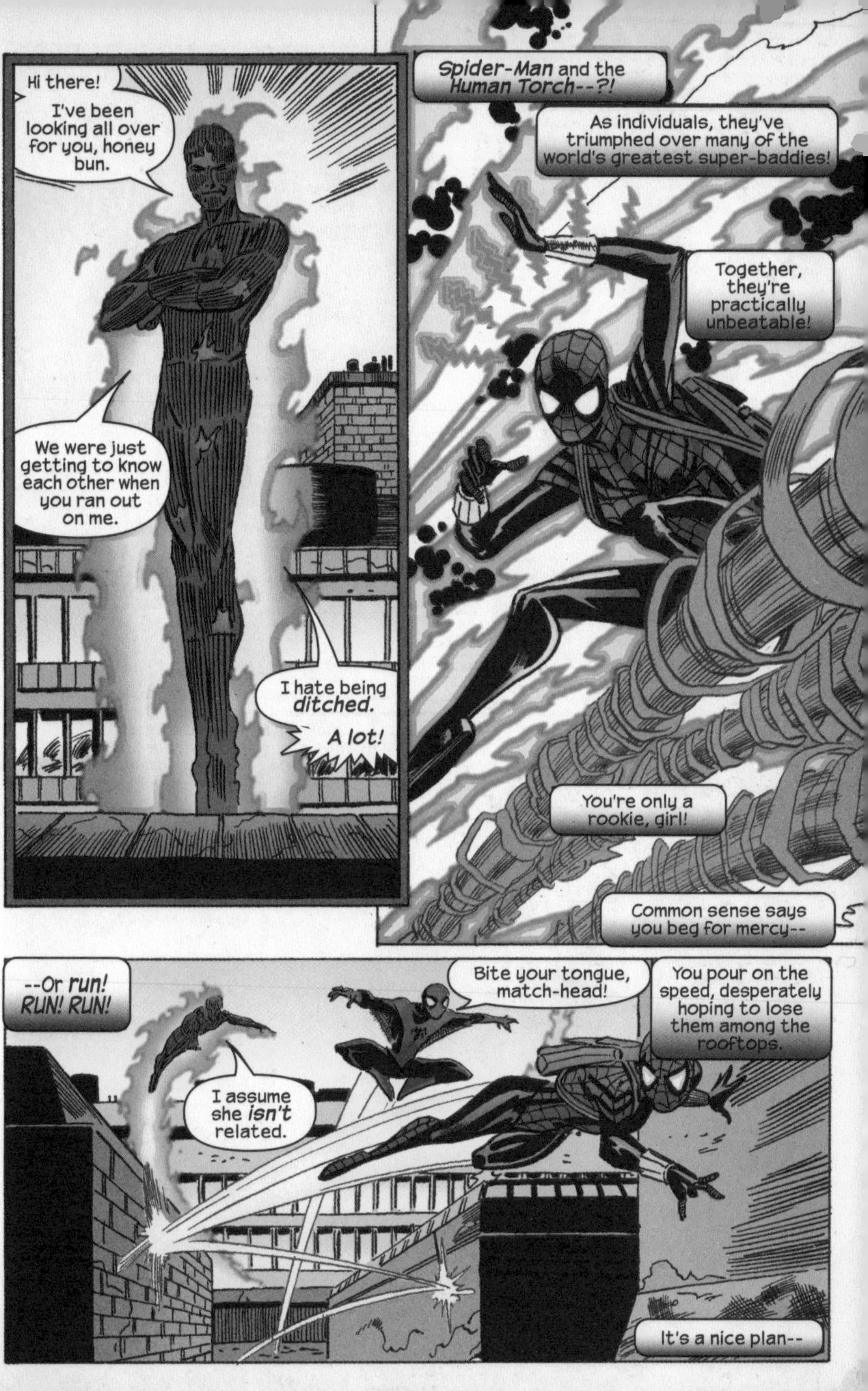
Hi there!
I've been looking all over for you, honey bun.
We were just getting to know each other when you ran out on me.
I hate being *ditched.*
A lot!
Spider-Man and the *Human Torch--?!*
As individuals, they've triumphed over many of the world's greatest super-baddies!
Together, they're practically unbeatable!
You're only a rookie, girl!
Common sense says you beg for mercy--
--Or *run! RUN! RUN!*
I assume she *isn't* related.
Bite your tongue, match-head!
You pour on the speed, desperately hoping to lose them among the rooftops.
It's a nice plan--

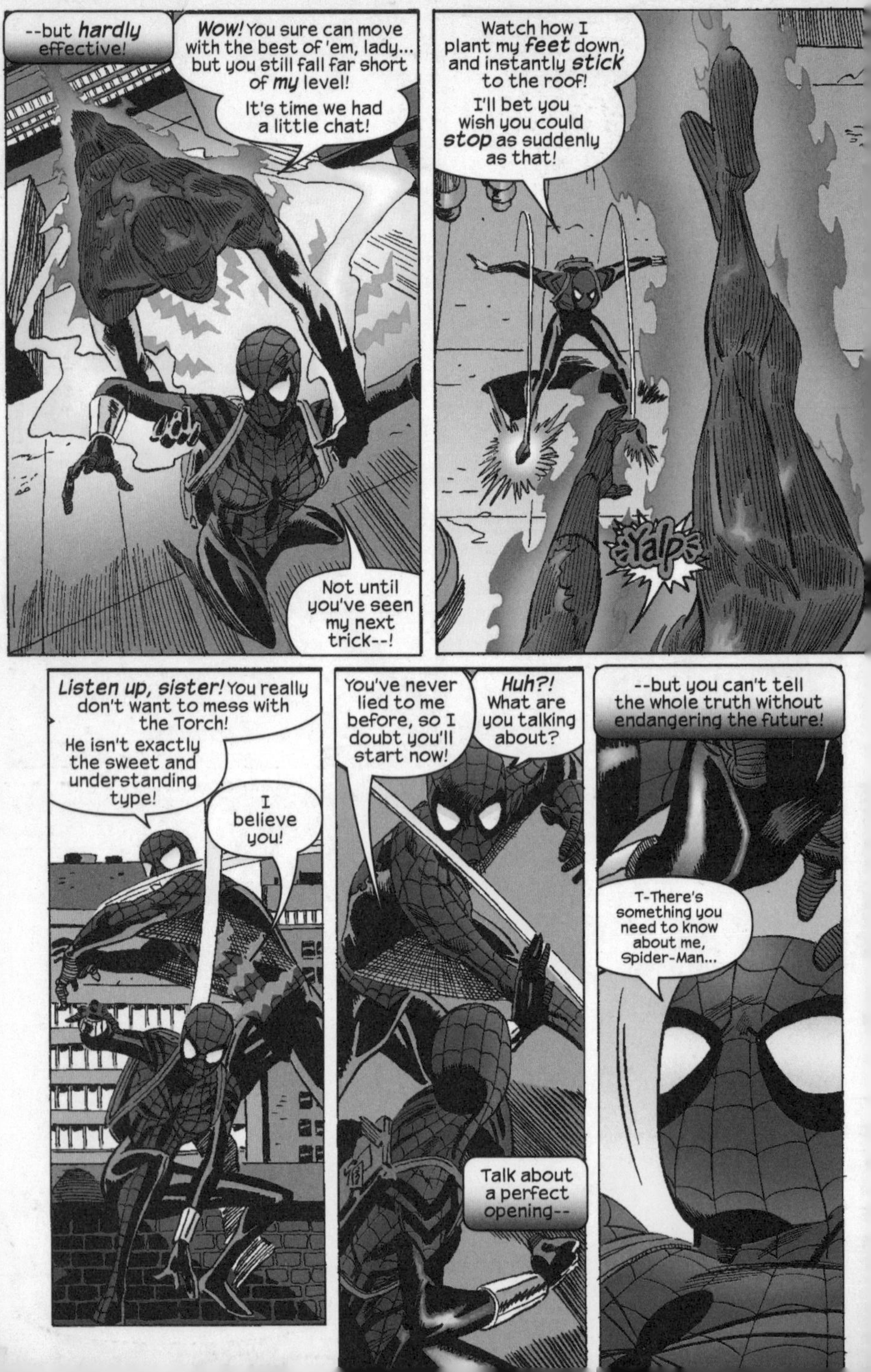

--but hardly effective!
Wow! You sure can move with the best of 'em, lady... but you still fall far short of my level!
It's time we had a little chat!
Not until you've seen my next trick--!
Watch how I plant my feet down, and instantly stick to the roof!
I'll bet you wish you could stop as suddenly as that!
Yalp
Listen up, sister! You really don't want to mess with the Torch!
He isn't exactly the sweet and understanding type!
I believe you!
You've never lied to me before, so I doubt you'll start now!
Huh?! What are you talking about?
Talk about a perfect opening--
--but you can't tell the whole truth without endangering the future!
T-There's something you need to know about me, Spider-Man...

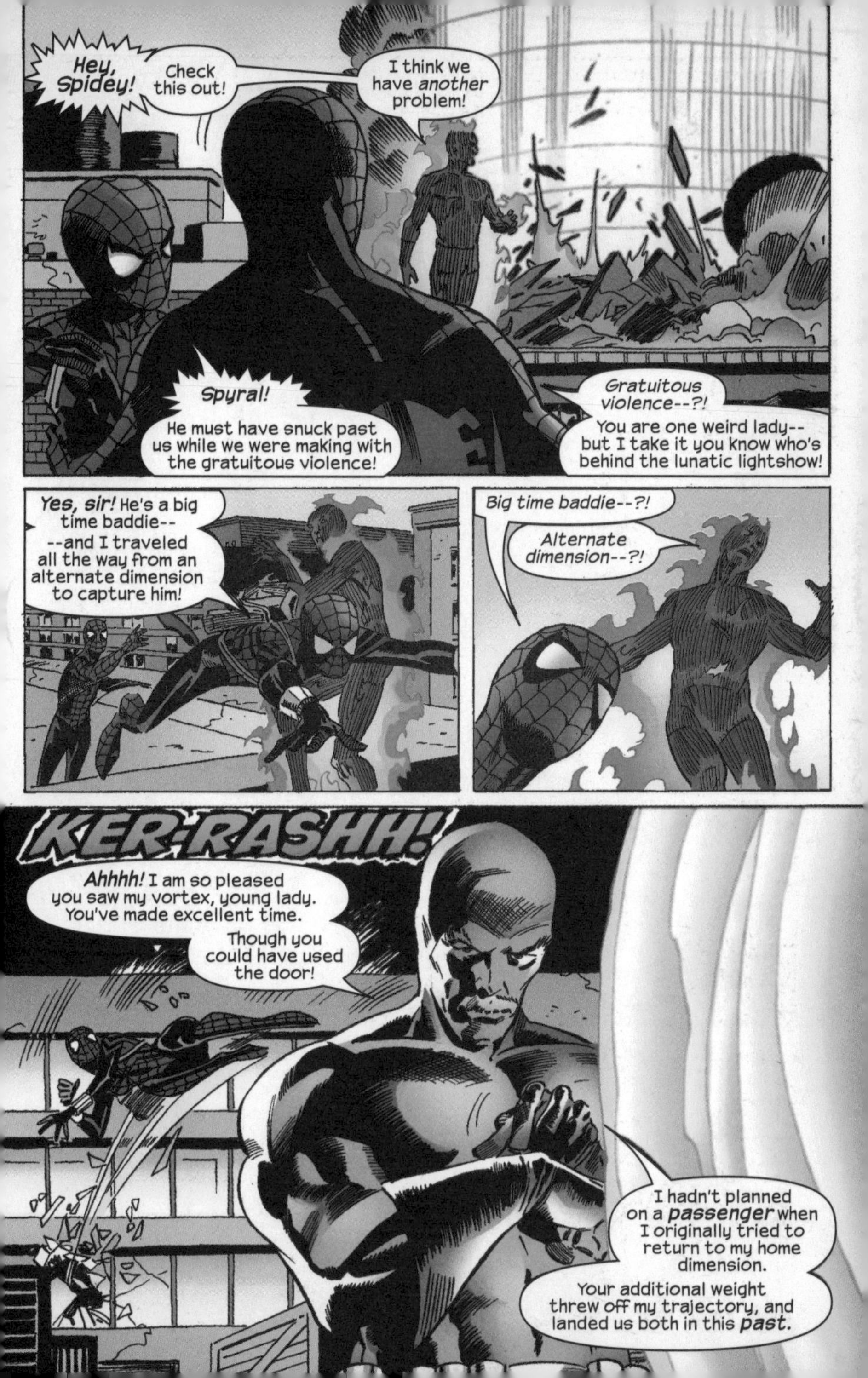

Hey, Spidey!
Check this out!
I think we have another problem!
Spyral!
He must have snuck past us while we were making with the gratuitous violence!
Gratuitous violence--?!
You are one weird lady--but I take it you know who's behind the lunatic lightshow!
Yes, sir! He's a big time baddie--
--and I traveled all the way from an alternate dimension to capture him!
Big time baddie--?!
Alternate dimension--?!
KER-RASHH!
Ahhhh! I am so pleased you saw my vortex, young lady. You've made excellent time.
Though you could have used the door!
I hadn't planned on a passenger when I originally tried to return to my home dimension.
Your additional weight threw off my trajectory, and landed us both in this past.

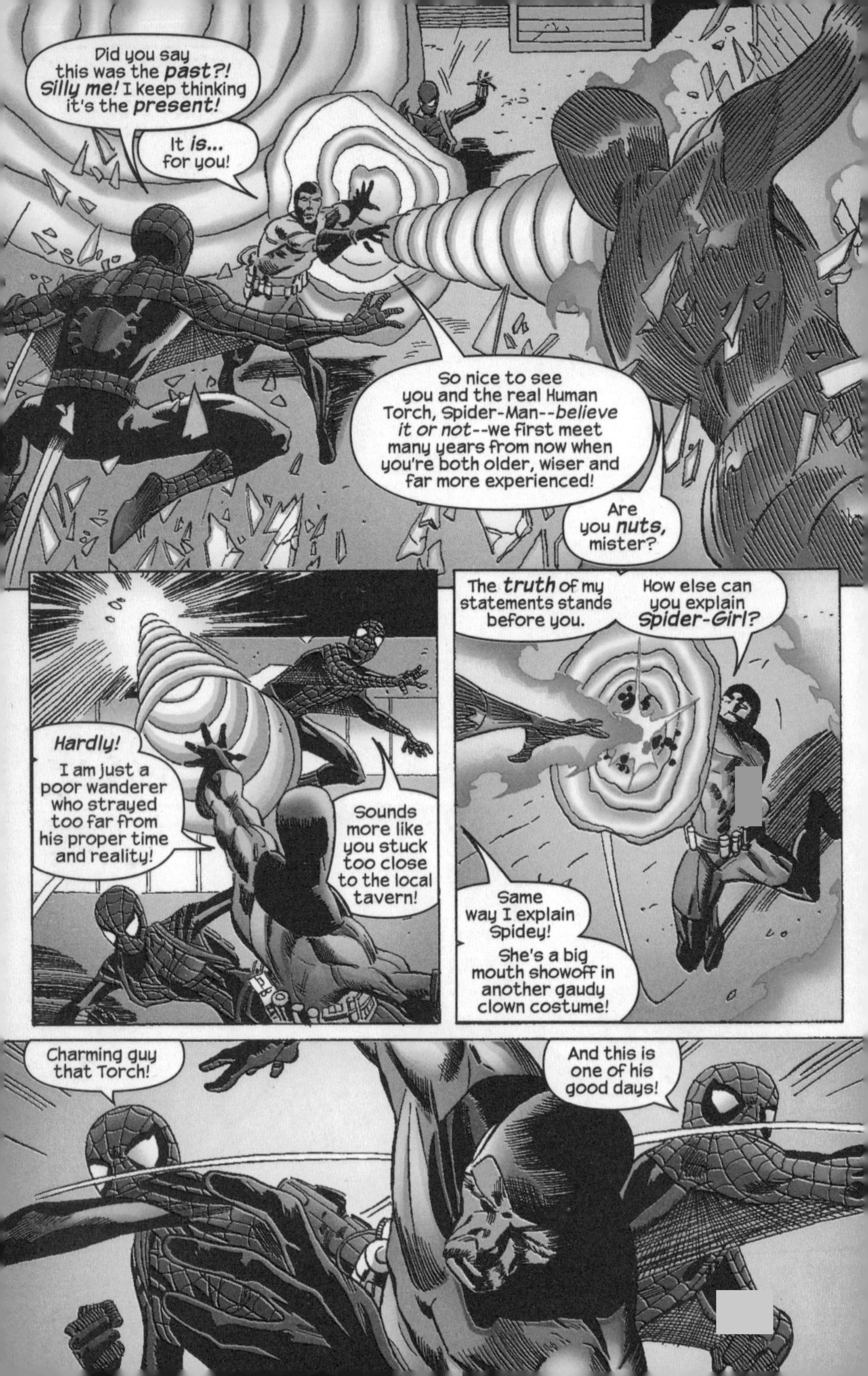
Did you say this was the *past?!* *Silly me!* I keep thinking it's the *present!*
It *is...* for you!
So nice to see you and the real Human Torch, Spider-Man--*believe it or not*--we first meet many years from now when you're both older, wiser and far more experienced!
Are you *nuts,* mister?
Hardly! I am just a poor wanderer who strayed too far from his proper time and reality!
Sounds more like you stuck too close to the local tavern!
The *truth* of my statements stands before you.
How else can you explain *Spider-Girl?*
Same way I explain Spidey!
She's a big mouth showoff in another gaudy clown costume!
Charming guy that Torch!
And this is one of his good days!

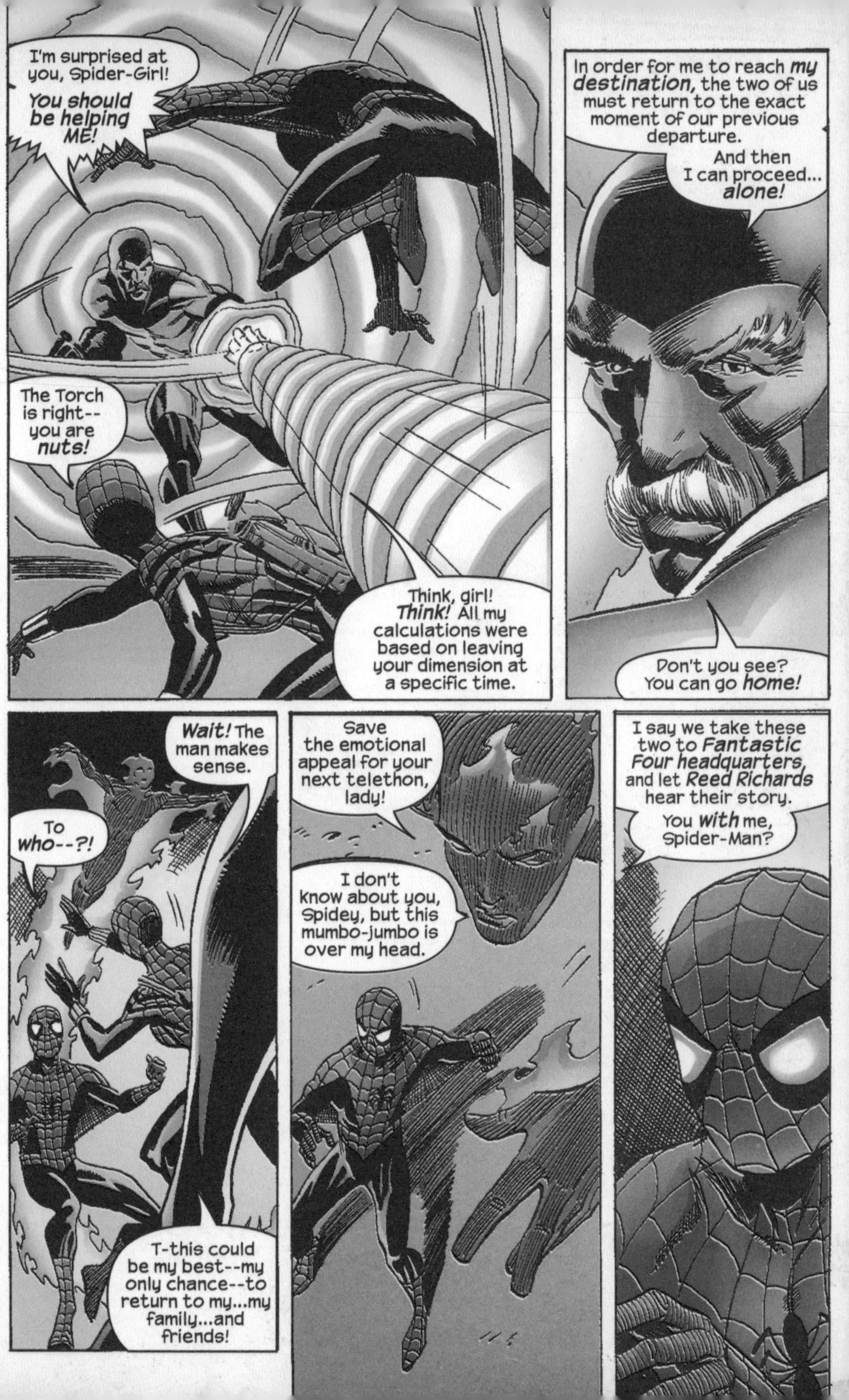

I'm surprised at you, Spider-Girl! *You should be helping ME!*
The Torch is right-- you are *nuts!*
Think, girl! *Think!* All my calculations were based on leaving your dimension at a specific time.
In order for me to reach *my destination,* the two of us must return to the exact moment of our previous departure.
And then I can proceed... *alone!*
Don't you see? You can go *home!*
Wait! The man makes sense.
To *who--?!*
T-this could be my best--my only chance--to return to my...my family...and friends!
Save the emotional appeal for your next telethon, lady!
I don't know about you, Spidey, but this mumbo-jumbo is over my head.
I say we take these two to *Fantastic Four headquarters,* and let *Reed Richards* hear their story.
You *with* me, Spider-Man?

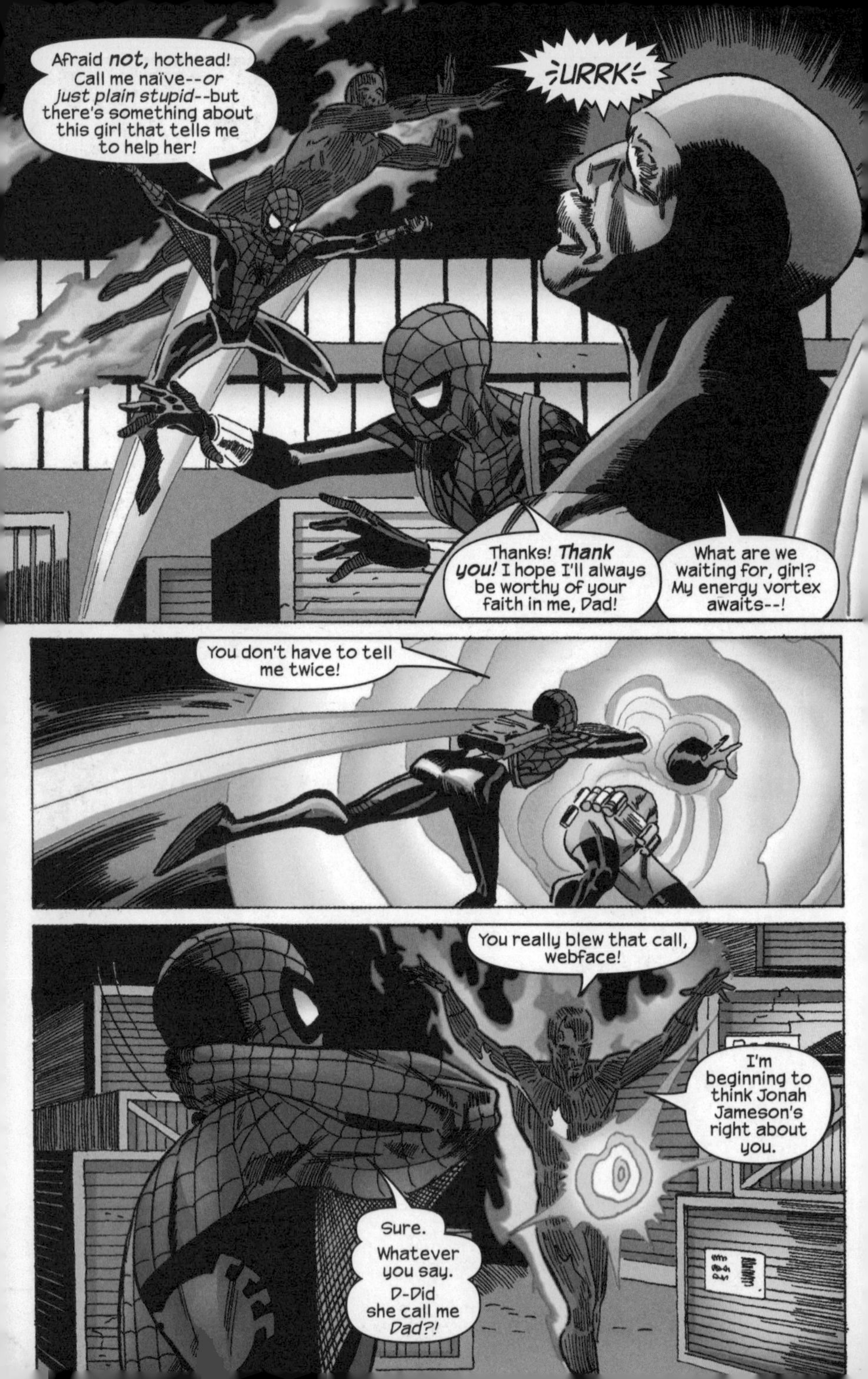
Afraid *not*, hothead! Call me naïve--*or just plain stupid*--but there's something about this girl that tells me to help her!
URRK
Thanks! ***Thank you!*** I hope I'll always be worthy of your faith in me, Dad!
What are we waiting for, girl? My energy vortex awaits--!
You don't have to tell me twice!
You really blew that call, webface!
I'm beginning to think Jonah Jameson's right about you.
Sure.
Whatever you say.
D-Did she call me *Dad?!*

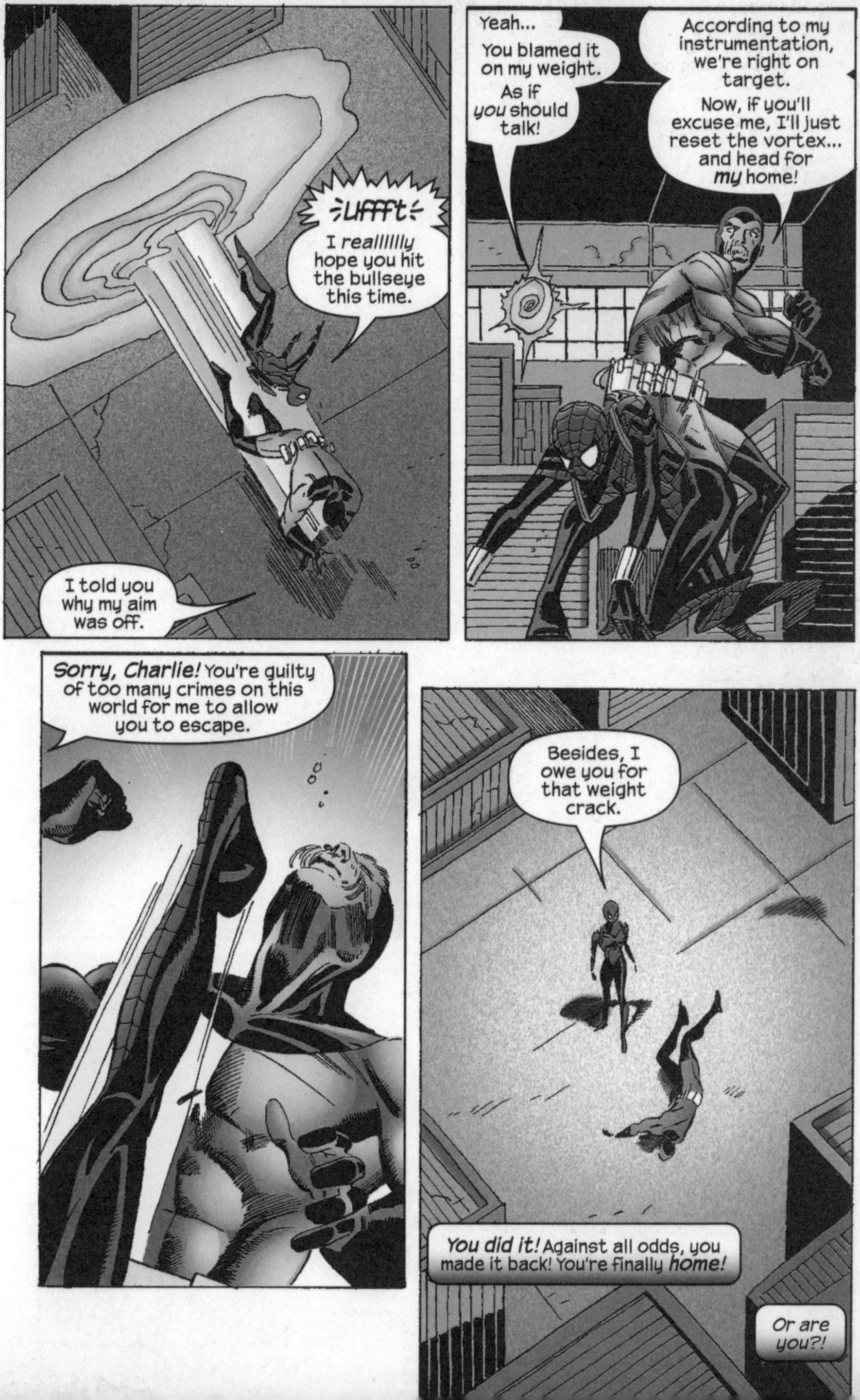

UFFFT
I realllllly hope you hit the bullseye this time.
I told you why my aim was off.
Yeah...
You blamed it on my weight.
As if *you* should talk!
According to my instrumentation, we're right on target.
Now, if you'll excuse me, I'll just reset the vortex... and head for *my* home!
Sorry, Charlie! You're guilty of too many crimes on this world for me to allow you to escape.
Besides, I owe you for that weight crack.
You did it! Against all odds, you made it back! You're finally *home!*
Or are you?!

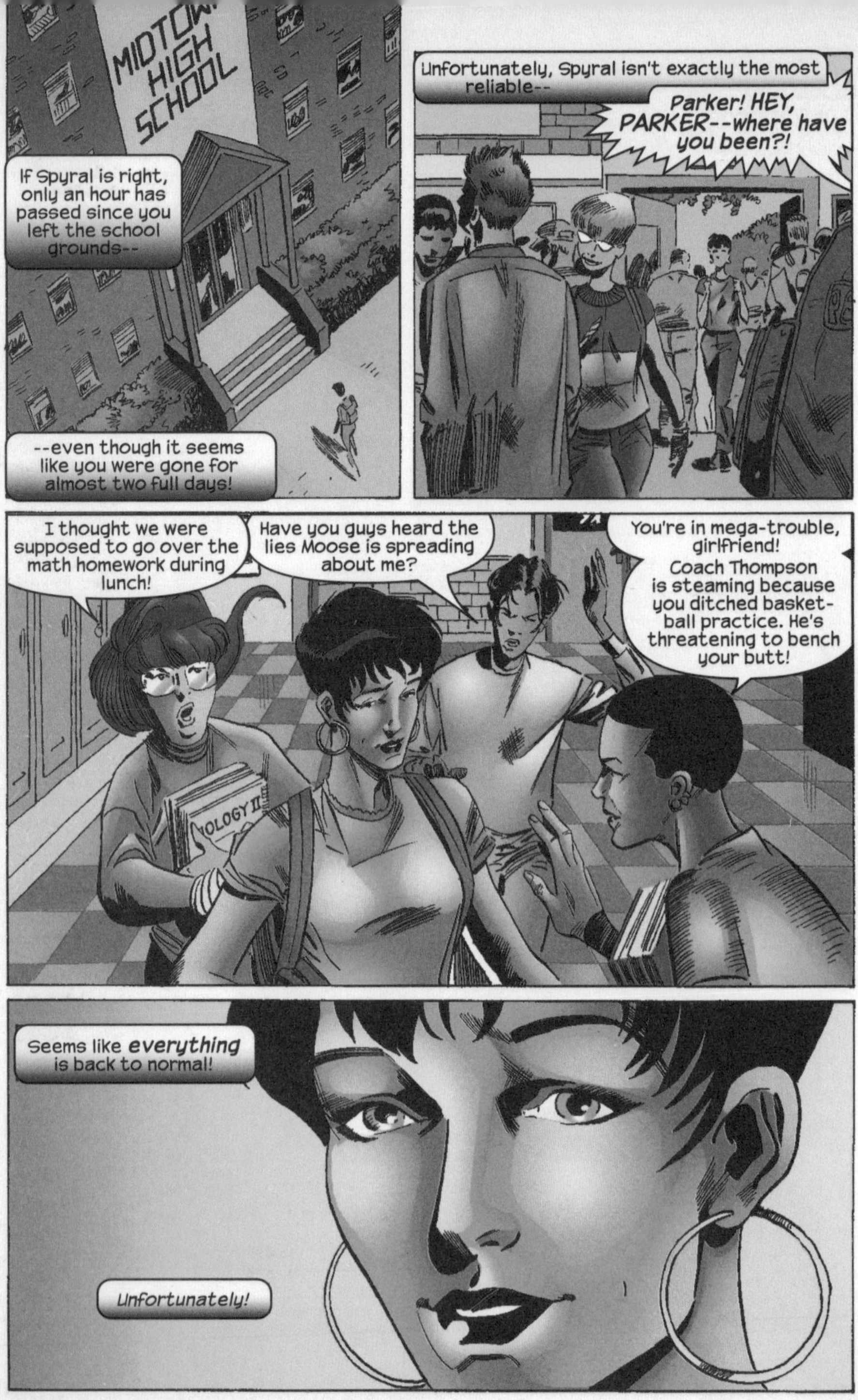
MIDTOWN HIGH SCHOOL
If Spyral is right, only an hour has passed since you left the school grounds--
--even though it seems like you were gone for almost two full days!
Unfortunately, Spyral isn't exactly the most reliable--
Parker! HEY, PARKER--where have you been?!
I thought we were supposed to go over the math homework during lunch!
Have you guys heard the lies Moose is spreading about me?
You're in mega-trouble, girlfriend!
Coach Thompson is steaming because you ditched basket-ball practice. He's threatening to bench your butt!
Seems like *everything* is back to normal!
Unfortunately!

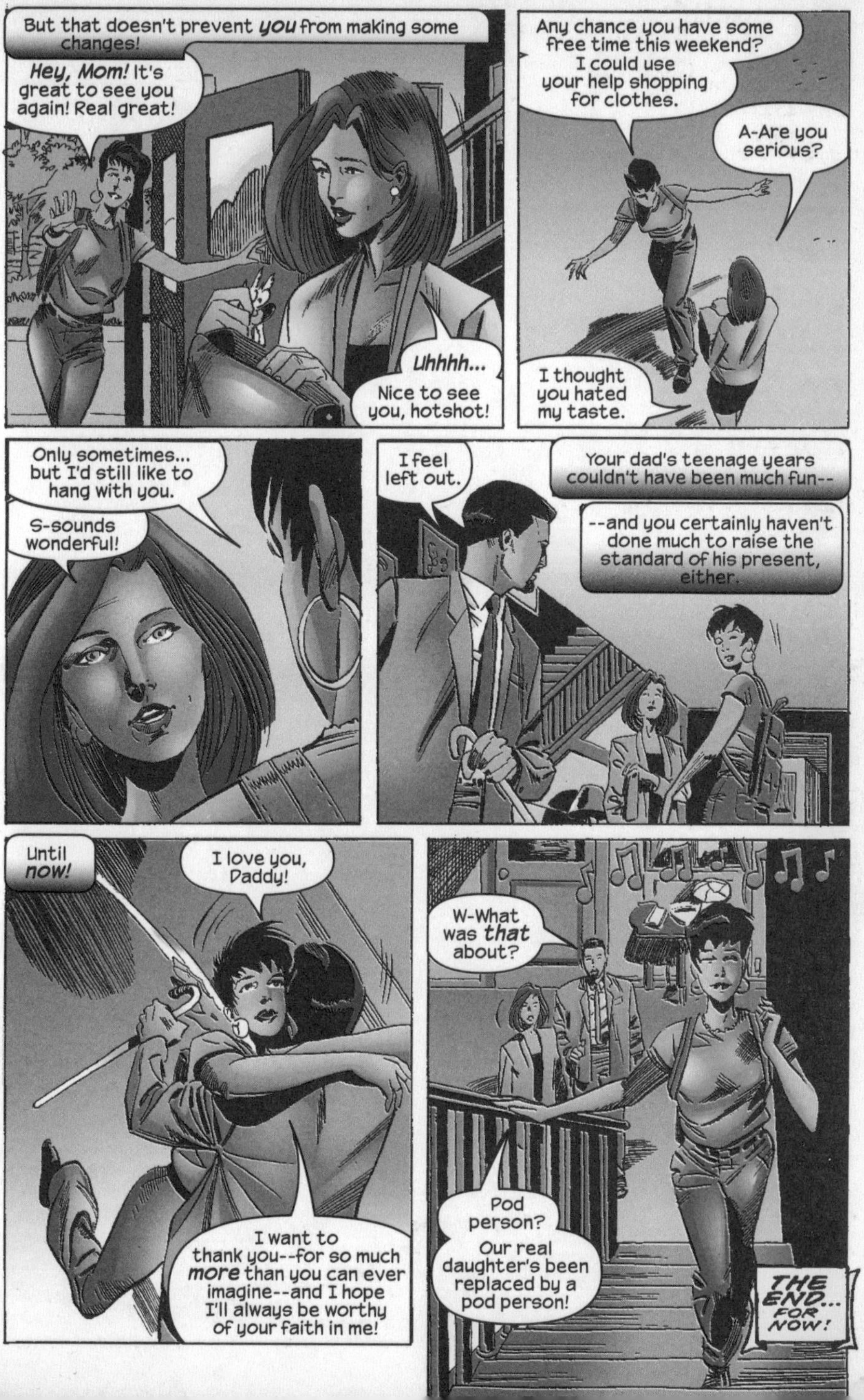
But that doesn't prevent *you* from making some changes!
Hey, Mom! It's great to see you again! Real great!
Uhhhh... Nice to see you, hotshot!
Any chance you have some free time this weekend? I could use your help shopping for clothes.
A-Are you serious?
I thought you hated my taste.
Only sometimes... but I'd still like to hang with you.
S-sounds wonderful!
I feel left out.
Your dad's teenage years couldn't have been much fun--
--and you certainly haven't done much to raise the standard of his present, either.
Until *now!*
I love you, Daddy!
I want to thank you--for so much *more* than you can ever imagine--and I hope I'll always be worthy of your faith in me!
W-What was *that* about?
Pod person? Our real daughter's been replaced by a pod person!
THE END... FOR NOW!

SPIDER-GIRL

pin-up

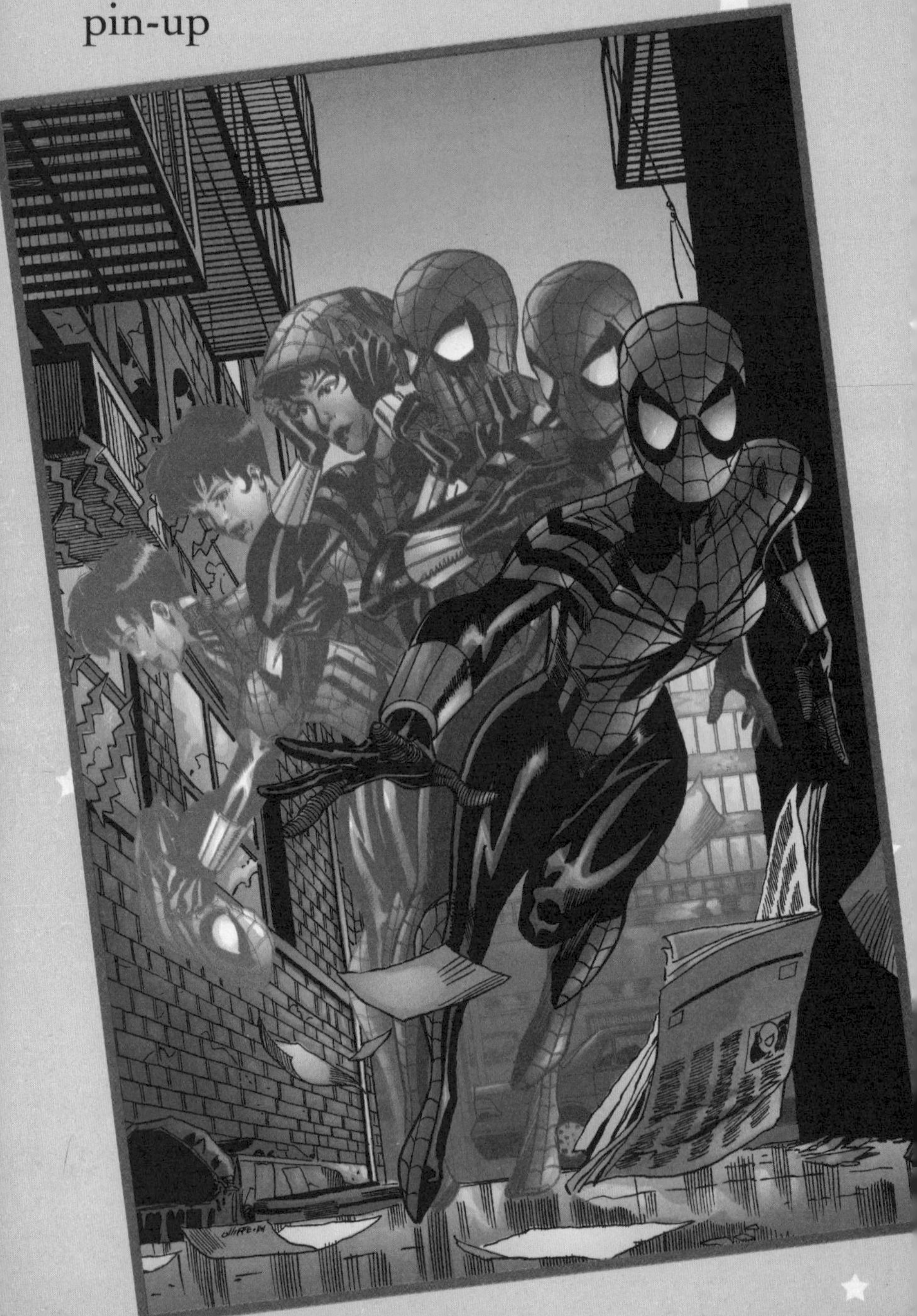

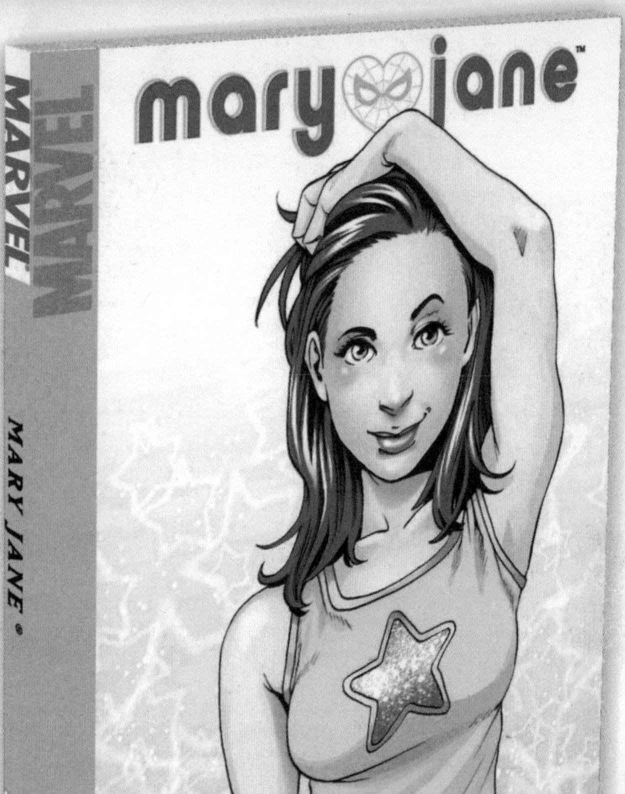
mary jane™
MARVEL
MARY JANE®
circle of friends
VOL. 1
MARVEL AGE

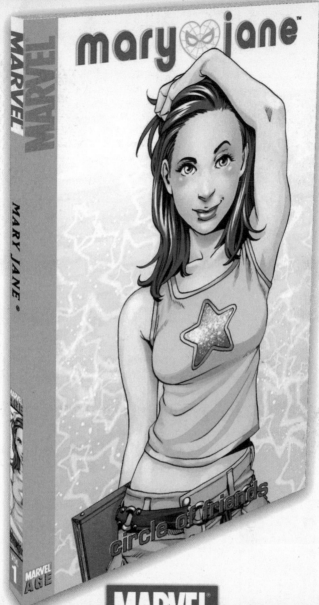

MARVEL AGE BACK PAGE

COLLECT ALL THE MARVEL AGE TITLES!

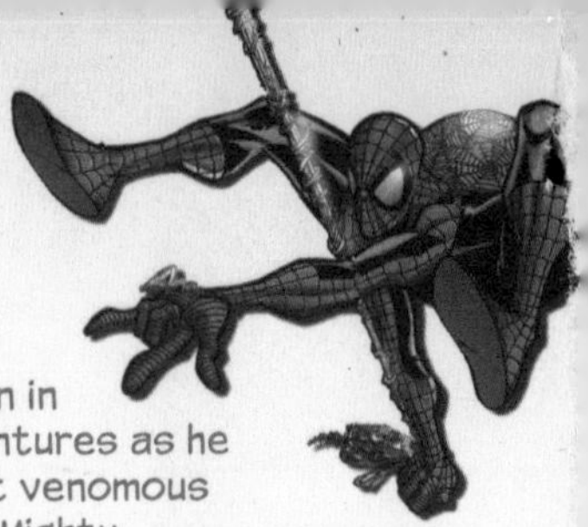

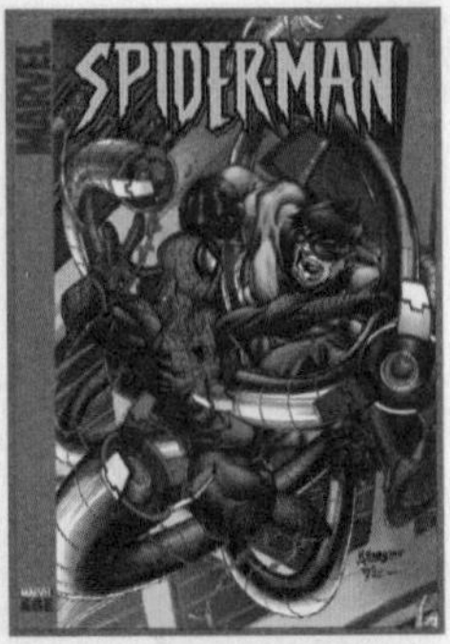
MARVEL
SPIDER-MAN

Catch Spider-Man in his thrilling adventures as he tackles the most venomous villains from the Mighty Marvel Mythos!

- ☐ Marvel Age Spider-Man vol 1 (pictured)
- ☐ Marvel Age Spider-Man vol 2
- ☐ Marvel Age Spider-Man vol 3
- ☐ Marvel Age Spider-Man vol 4

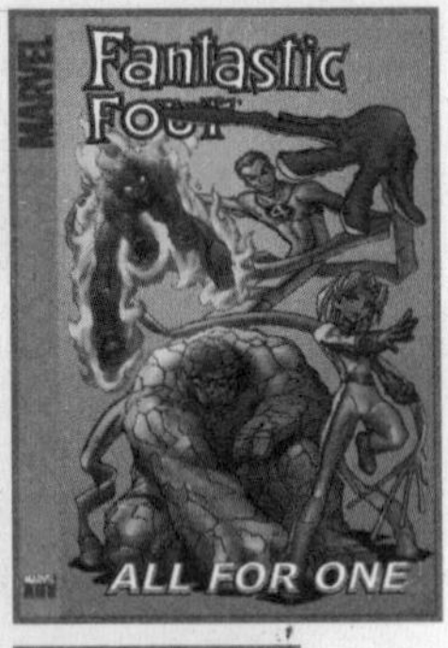
MARVEL
Fantastic Four
ALL FOR ONE

Join Marvel's First Family on their fantastic adventures, from the deepest depths of the ocean to the farthest reaches of outer space!

- ☐ Marvel Age Fantastic Four vol 1 (pictured)
- ☐ Marvel Age Fantastic Four vol 2

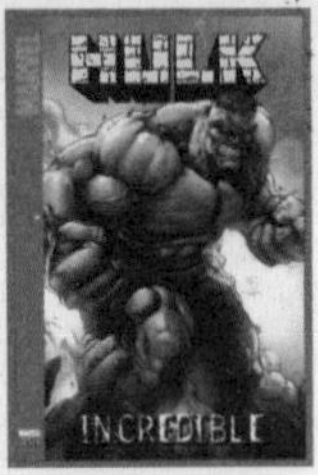
HULK
INCREDIBLE

- ☐ Marvel Age Hulk vol 1: Incredible

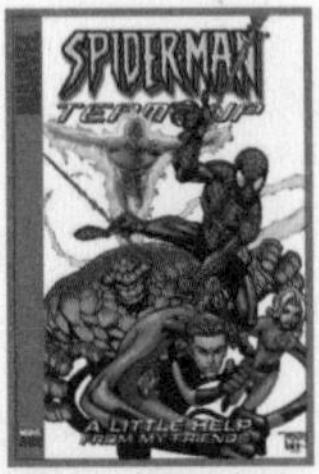
SPIDER-MAN

- ☐ Marvel Age Spider-Man Team-Up vol 1: A Little Help From My Friends

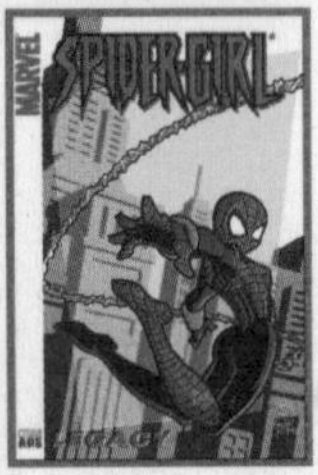
MARVEL
SPIDER-GIRL

- ☐ Marvel Age Spider-Girl vol 1: Legacy (pictured)
- ☐ Marvel Age Spider-Girl vol 2: Like Father Like Daughter

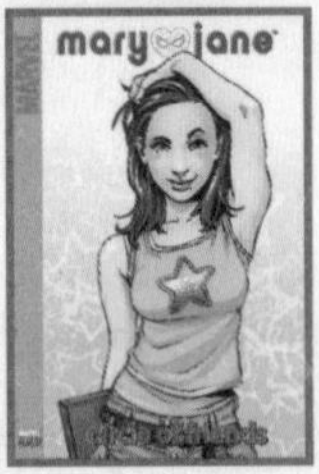
mary jane

- ☐ Marvel Age Mary Jane vol 1: Circle of Friends

Available in bookstores and your local comic shop! Don't miss out!